REIMAGINING DIVERSITY, EQUITY, AND JUSTICE IN EARLY CHILDHOOD

Situated against a backdrop of multiple global pandemics—COVID-19, racial injustice and violence, inequitable resource distribution, political insurrections, and unrest—this timely and critical volume argues for a divestment in white privilege and an investment in anti-racist pedagogies and practice across early childhood contexts of research, policy, and teaching and learning. Featuring established scholar-practitioners alongside emerging voices, chapters explore key issues around equitable and inclusive practices for young children, covering topics such as multilingualism and multicultural practices of immigrant communities, language varieties, and dialects across the Black diaspora, queer pedagogies, and play at the intersection of race, gender, disability, and language. Thoughtfully and compellingly written, each chapter offers an overview of the issue, the theoretical framework and critical context surrounding it, and implications for practice.

Haeny Yoon is an Associate Professor at Teachers College, Columbia University.

A. Lin Goodwin 葛文林 is Thomas More Brennan Chair Professor in Education at Boston College. She served as Dean of the Faculty of Education at the University of Hong Kong from 2017 to 2022.

Celia Genishi is Professor Emeritus at Teachers College, Columbia University.

Changing Images of Early Childhood

Series Editor: Nicola Yelland

Books in this forward-thinking series challenge existing practices in early childhood education and reflect the changing images of the field. The series enables readers to engage with contemporary ideas and practices of alternative perspectives which deviate from those theories traditionally associated with the education of young children and their families. Not only do these books make complex theory accessible, they provide early childhood educators with the tools to ensure their practices are backed by appropriate theoretical frameworks and strong empirical evidence.

Titles in the *Changing Images of Early Childhood* series include:

Found in Translation: Connecting Reconceptualist Thinking with Early Childhood Education Practices
Edited by Nicola Yelland and Dana Frantz Bentley

Educating for Social Justice in Early Childhood
Edited by Shirley A. Kessler and Beth Blue Swadener

Visual Arts with Young Children: Practices, Pedagogies, and Learning
Edited by Hayon Park and Christopher M. Schulte

Reimagining Diversity, Equity, and Justice in Early Childhood
By Haeny Yoon, A. Lin Goodwin, and Celia Genishi

For more information about this series, please visit: https://www.routledge.com

REIMAGINING DIVERSITY, EQUITY, AND JUSTICE IN EARLY CHILDHOOD

*Edited by Haeny Yoon, A. Lin Goodwin,
and Celia Genishi*

Routledge
Taylor & Francis Group

NEW YORK AND LONDON

ISBN: 978-1-032-14001-8 (hbk)
ISBN: 978-1-032-12081-2 (pbk)
ISBN: 978-1-003-39915-5 (ebk)
ISBN: 978-1-003-23188-2 (eBook+)

DOI: 10.4324/9781003399155

Typeset in Bembo
by KnowledgeWorks Global Ltd.

CONTENTS

CONTRIBUTORS

Editors

Haeny Yoon is an Associate Professor of Early Childhood Education in the Department of Curriculum and Teaching. As program director of the early childhood program, she works with both pre- and in-service teachers in designing spaces for children's play and inquiry. She extends conceptions of play to reach beyond curricular design in early childhood settings and argues for more playful, intellectual, and creative approaches to research methodologies and academic production. Her co-hosted podcast "Pop and Play" explores the inter generational connections of play across age, disciplines, and boundaries. Professor Yoon is committed to the merging of public space and academic space, engaging in opportunities where productive conversations converge. She is a former teacher and professional developer and continues to support teachers as public intellectuals.

A. Lin Goodwin (葛文林) is the Thomas More Brennan Endowed Chair in Education at the Lynch School of Education and Human Development at Boston College. She is Honorary Professor at the University of Hong Kong (HKU) and served as Dean of the Faculty (i.e., School) of Education at HKU from 2017 to 2022. Professor Goodwin's research focuses on teacher/teacher educator beliefs, identities, and development; equitable education and powerful teaching for immigrant and minoritized youth; international analyses and comparisons of teacher education practice and policy; and the experiences of Asian/Asian American teachers and students in US schools.

Celia Genishi taught preschool in Berkeley, CA, where she earned a doctorate in Early Childhood Education at the University of California. She then taught at the University of Texas at Austin, Ohio State University, and Teachers College, Columbia University. Because of her longstanding commitment to bilinguals and bilingualism, her articles and books have emphasized the importance of listening to and observing young children as they learn in diverse ways.

Authors

Sherilyn Analla is Akimel O'odham/Pee Posh (from the Gila River Indian Community) and K'waikameh (from the Pueblo of Laguna). She is a mother of two sons. She has been in the early education field for over 20 years as a preschool teacher and program administrator in both tribal and nontribal programs. She is a doctoral student at the University of Arizona majoring in Teaching and Teacher Education with a minor in Linguistics. Her areas of research include Indigenous motherhood, Indigenous early education, and Indigenous language education.

Cassie Brownell is an Assistant Professor of Curriculum, Teaching, and Learning at the Ontario Institute for Studies in Education (OISE) of the University of Toronto. A former grade 1 and 2 teacher, her research takes up issues of educational justice and equity in early childhood.

Ranita Cheruvu is a Senior Lecturer of Early Childhood Education and Director of the Center for Young Children at the University of North Texas. She is a former classroom teacher of young children and has been an early childhood teacher educator for more than 10 years. Her scholarship and teaching focus on issues of equity and justice in early childhood education and teacher education. More specifically, her work focuses on culturally relevant and sustaining teaching practices, racial literacy, and antibias and antiracist practices, and issues related to the preparation and retention of preservice teachers of Color.

Leah Durán is an Associate Professor of Teaching, Learning and Sociocultural Studies at the University of Arizona. Prior to that, she taught second grade in bilingual (Spanish/English) and ESL classrooms in Texas. Her scholarship focuses on the intersection of literacy, bilingualism, and young children. Specifically, she studies (1) emergent biliteracy; (2) the design of curricular and instructional approaches which draw on bilingualism as an asset; and (3) the ways that beliefs about language influence the educational experiences of bilingual students.

Anne Haas Dyson is Professor of Educational Policy, Organization and Leadership at the University of Illinois at Urbana-Champaign. She is a former teacher of young children and a fellow of the American Educational Research Association. Among her previous appointments was as a longtime professor at the University of California, Berkeley, where she received the campus-wide Distinguished Teaching Award. She has spent over 40 years studying the childhood cultures and literacy learning of young schoolchildren, for which she has received numerous awards. Dyson aims, first, to bring respect and intellectual attention to childhood cultures and their relationship to school learning. Second, she aims to document the diversity of resources (languages, popular culture texts, semiotic tools, everyday experiences) our diverse school children bring with them with which to participate intellectually and socially in school, especially through composing. Among her recent publications are ReWRITING the basics: Literacy learning in children's cultures (2013), and Writing the school house blues: literacy, equity, and belonging in a child's early schooling (2021).

Amanda Fellner is a Lecturer in the Curriculum and Teaching Department at Teachers College, Columbia University and Faculty Co-Director at the Rita Gold Center, Teachers College. Her research focuses on expanding understandings of the diverse ways infants and toddlers come to know the world around them. Grounded in spatial Theory and critical childhoods perspectives, she uses multimodal methods to participate in the sensory world of very young children. Amanda has spent most of her career working with, and teaching teachers of, infants and toddlers. Amanda has published in journals such as *The Journal of Early Childhood Research* and *Bank Street Occasional Papers*.

Emmanuelle Fincham is an Assistant Professor of Early Childhood Education at Western Washington University. Building on over 15 years of teaching infants and toddlers, much of her scholarship focuses on toddlers and their teachers. She engages in critical practices of narrative practitioner research incorporating feminist poststructural, and more recently, new materialist methodologies as a way to reconceptualize understandings of practice, play, and young children's development and ways of knowing. Emmanuelle's research also seeks to deconstruct and reimagine interventionist practices related to play-based learning in early childhood, specifically in inclusive spaces with neurodivergent young children.

Brittany L. Frieson is an Assistant Professor of Literacy and Antiracist Education at the University of North Texas. She is a former elementary and middle grades language education and literacy teacher. Her research interests include critical perspectives of bilingual education, Black languages and literacies in dual language bilingual education, anti-racist and critical pedagogical practices in literacy and bilingual education. Her research has appeared in multiple academic outlets including *Race Ethnicity and Education, Annual Review of Applied Linguistics, Bilingual Research Journal, The Reading Teacher, Teaching and Teacher Education, Literacy Research: Theory, Method, and Practice,* among many others.

Muyanwi Lum Fube is currently a doctoral student at Teachers College, Columbia University. Lum's areas of interest include humanizing pedagogy and research, pedagogies of love and care, childhoods/youth studies, teacher preparation and development, popular culture, and multimodal qualitative research. Fube is a former early childhood teacher.

Roberta Price Gardner is an Associate Professor of Reading and Literacy Education in the Department of Early Childhood and Elementary Education at Kennesaw State University. Her research and writing explore African American children's literature, reader-response the social-cultural and political contexts that impact the literacies of Black children and Black childhoods. She is the coeditor of Reading and Teaching with Diverse Nonfiction Children's Books: Representations and Possibilities (2021). Her work can also be found in journals such as Urban Education, Journal of Children's Literature, Language Arts, Children's Literature in Education, and Research in the Teaching of English. Dr. Gardner was a National Council Teachers of English (NCTE) Research Foundation's Cultivating New Voices Fellow, a recipient of the International Literacy Association's Supporting Young Scholars program, and the University of Georgia President's Fulfilling the Dream Award.

María Paula Ghiso is Professor of Literacy Education in the Department of Curriculum and Teaching at Teachers College, Columbia University. Her scholarship investigates literacy in multilingual and transnational contexts and community-based research methodologies. She has published in venues such as *Teachers College Record, Research in the Teaching of English, Language Arts, Harvard Educational Review, Urban Education,* and *Journal of Literacy Research.* María Paula is also coauthor of Partnering with Immigrant Communities: Action through Literacy (Teachers College Press). Her current work is being funded by the Spencer Foundation.

Lindsey Allene Hall is a doctoral student in the Department of Teacher Education at Michigan State University. Her research interests include child voice and participation across diverse primary education spaces, in particular how bi/multilingual children and their families make meaning through and across languages and literacies in both the United States and East African contexts. Having previously worked as a primary school teacher and teacher educator in the United States and in Uganda, East Africa, her scholarship explores how curriculum, instruction, and teacher education may cultivate teacher pedagogies and practices that are linguistically and culturally sustaining, as well as contextually appropriate and meaningful, in collaboration with children, their families, and communities.

Lil Miss Hot Mess is the author of the children's books *If You're a Drag Queen and You Know It* (Running Press Kids, 2022) and *The Hips on the Drag Queen Go Swish, Swish, Swish* (2020) and serves on the board of Drag Queen Story Hour. She has appeared on world-class stages like SFMOMA, Stanford University, and Saturday Night Live, was a founding organizer of the #MyNameIs campaign that challenged Facebook's "real names" policy, and has published in *Curriculum Inquiry* as well as *The Guardian, Wired,* and *Salon.* When not twirling, Lil Miss Hot Mess is a Professor of Public and Applied Humanities at the University of Arizona.

Lee Iskander is an Ontario-certified teacher and doctoral student in the Faculty of Education at the University of British Columbia. Their research has explored LGBTQ youth activism, the experiences of LGBTQ pre-service and in-service teachers, and trans pedagogies. Their writing has been published in the *Journal of LGBT Youth, Teachers College Record,* and *Teaching Education.*

Harper Keenan is an Assistant Professor in the Department of Curriculum and Pedagogy at the University of British Columbia. He currently serves as the inaugural Robert Quartermain Professor of Gender and Sexuality in Education. Dr. Keenan's scholarship examines how adults and children relate to each other within the structures of schooling and other educational contexts. He is particularly interested in what the treatment of social and historical topics as complex and/or difficult in the education of young children might reveal about society more broadly.

Jungmin Kwon is an Assistant Professor of Language and Literacy in the Department of Teacher Education at Michigan State University. Her research centers on immigrant children and families, transnational migration, multilingual learning, and teacher preparation for linguistically and culturally diverse students. To amplify the voices of immigrant children and families, she adopts a community-engaged approach and employs child-centered research methods. She is the author of *Understanding the Transnational Lives and Literacies of Immigrant Children* (Teachers College Press, 2022). She has published in journals such as the *International Journal of Bilingual Education and Bilingualism, Bilingual Research Journal, Language and Education, Language Arts,* and others.

Rebecca Lopez is the Director of Early Childhood Education at the University of Arizona. She earned her Ph.D. in Teaching and Teacher Education with an emphasis in early childhood education from the University of Arizona in

2021. She also has a master's degree in special education from the University of Kansas. Her research interests include providing equitable learning opportunities for young children in early childhood classrooms and examining play-based pedagogy that prioritizes the cultural and community strengths that young children and their families bring into classrooms. In addition, Rebecca has 10 years of teaching experience in classrooms from preschool through second grade.

Carmen Martinez is a Chicana who has recently received her bachelors' degree in bilingual education and is presently and continually working toward multiculturalism and multilingualism in early education spaces. Carmen is committed to racial and social justice for all marginalized people within the education system but especially people of Color. She aims to create a critical curriculum and a healing space for educators and students alike to grow authentically within their intersectional identities.

Joseph D. Nelson is an Associate Professor of Educational Studies at Swarthmore College, and Chair of the Black Studies Program. He is also a Senior Research Fellow with the *School Participatory Action Research Collaborative* at the University of Pennsylvania. His research primarily examines race, boyhood, and education within learning environments that largely serve Black students from neighborhoods with concentrated poverty. His forthcoming book is entitled, *(Re)Imagining Black Boyhood: Portraits of Academic Success during the Middle School Years* (Harvard Education Press). In 2020, he was named Editor of the historic journal *Men and Masculinities*. On the northside of Milwaukee where he grew up, he taught first grade in a single-sex class of Black and Latinx boys.

LeRoi Newbold is a cofounder of Freedom School Toronto, which is a community-based project to teach Black children and youth about Black history and existence in Canada and globally from a queer- and trans-positive lens.

Vivian E. Presiado is an Assistant Professor of Bilingual and Bicultural Education in the School of Teaching and Learning at Illinois State University. She is a former early childhood bilingual education teacher who is deeply passionate about the language and literacy practices of young linguistically diverse children and their families participating in bilingual programs. Her research has appeared in various academic outlets including, *Literacy Research: Theory, Method, and Practice, The Reading Teacher,* and *Journal of Literacy Research.*

Ana Christina da Silva is a Professor of Education at the Peabody College of Vanderbilt University, who specializes in Language, Literacy, and Cultural studies. Her research centers on the teaching and learning of linguistically/culturally/racially diverse students; on understanding family and community resources in diverse urban in- and out-of-school contexts; and on partnerships between family-community-school-university that support the literacy learning of linguistically, culturally, and racially diverse learners and emphasize educational opportunity and equity. She is the author of the edited volume *"Re-Designing Teacher Preparation for Culturally and Linguistically Diverse Young Students: An Ecological Approach."* She has been the Associate Editor for the *Journal of Literacy Research* and is currently the Associate Editor for the *Urban Education Journal.*

Tran Templeton is an Assistant Professor of Early Childhood at Teachers College, Columbia University. Taking up a critical childhood studies framework, Tran's work explores young children's knowledge productions vis-a-vis images, narratives, and play; she situates children as part of larger ecologies of human and more-than-human. Tran is a former early childhood and special education teacher and school director. She is currently the faculty co-director of Rita Gold Early Childhood Center, serving children from 0 to 5 years. She has published in journals such as *Harvard Educational Review, Language Arts,* and *Children's Geographies.*

Jon Wargo is an Associate Professor of Educational Studies at the University of Michigan—Ann Arbor. An educational researcher who attends closely to qualitative and arts-based methodologies, Wargo's scholarship examines how media and technology mediate young children's social and civic education. With a focus on leveraging children's ingenuity and difference as signs and sights for critical literacy learning, his teaching and research focus on understanding and sustaining the literacies and lifeworlds of minoritized communities amid the context of social change.

Axa Khalid Warraich is a doctoral student at The Ohio State University. She is interested in researching children's engagement with culturally relevant children's literature in and out of school, with a focus on social justice and identity development. She is also an editor-in-chief of a children's print magazine with a readership of around 250,000 children across Pakistan. Formerly, she has taught English Language, History, and Sociology to high school students in Pakistan.

Brian L. Wright is an Associate Professor and program coordinator of Early Childhood Education and coordinator of the middle school cohort of the African American Male Academy at the University of Memphis. His research focuses on high-achieving African American boys in urban schools P-12, racial-ethnic identity development of boys and young men of color, African American males as early childhood teachers, and teacher identity development.

He is listed via "RISE for Boys and Men of Color Expert Directory" which is a searchable directory of more than 100 researchers and evaluators who rigorously and routinely study boys and men of color and evaluate programs to serve them (http://www.risebmoc.org/directory). He is the author of the award-winning book, The Brilliance of Black Boys: Cultivating School Success in the Early Grades published by Teachers College Press/Columbia University.

ACKNOWLEDGMENTS

This project has really been a labor of love—and a long one. Like others, COVID-19 has forced us to reorient our priorities, to cling to our relationships, to care for loved ones, and to grieve for time and people lost. We are grateful for family members and friends who remind us that time is precious and never guaranteed. In our "virtual" meetings around this book, we became aware of the significance of three Asian-American women across ethnicities and generations putting together a book about diversities in early childhood education. In the wake of increased anti-Asian violence, we are grateful to be in community with each other. That is, an edited volume gave us space to catch up and laugh and process and grieve because both are legitimate acts of sustenance. When we *see* each other, we are reminded of our own im/migration stories as Japanese-American, Chinese/SouthEast Asian-American, and Korean-American daughters of "foreigners". The hardships and difficulties our parents/mothers encountered to ensure our access and inclusion is not lost on us. We are grateful for their courage, resourcefulness, and endurance. The stories in this book are testimonies to the ingenuity and strength of those pushed towards the margins. For those who came before us and those who follow, this book attempts to bring those on the margins to the center.

Any chance we have to bring together some of our mentors, colleagues, mentees, and friends is an endeavor worth pursuing. An acknowledgments section falls short of the immense gratitude we feel toward those who have been generous with their time, effort, energy, and support. We thank all the authors who contributed their words to bring together an exquisite, dynamic collection. Each of you has stretched our thinking and imagination. In your collective work, there are teachers, caregivers, program directors, community leaders, and young children whose experiences leave imprints on our social imaginations. Although only named as pseudonyms, we thank and honor the invaluable lessons each of them taught us about care, love, and hope in early childhood education.

We thank Nicola Yelland, series editor, who believed in and nurtured this project from the beginning. Your optimism and enthusiasm for this project helped propel it forward, especially when deadlines were missed and motivation was low. Thank you to Nicole Salazar, Olivia Powers, Alexis O'Brien, and others at Routledge who masterfully organized and crafted together this finished volume. We marvel at their patience despite our constant pining for extra time and "we're almost there" promises. Finally, we thank our editorial assistant and doctoral student extraordinaire, Nicole Fox. She was all things to the project—a careful reader, an editor, a taskmaster, a thought partner, a communications liaison, and a steady force throughout the project. Inundated with emails and frantic texts, she was a picture of grace and poise. She encouraged and believed in the work as a thoughtful and committed early childhood educator herself. We were lucky to have someone with such expertise read through and edit these chapters. We are excited for the future of the field that includes Nicole as she, too, works toward liberation, decoloniality, and freedom.

Finally, a big thanks to the children in our lives that consistently inform how we see the world—Finn, Dean, Emmy, Max, Ezra, and Ava. We imagine these new futures for you.

SERIES INTRODUCTION

Changing Images of Early Childhood

Series Editor: *Professor Nicola Yelland*

Melbourne Graduate School of Education, The University of Melbourne

The books in the *Changing images of early childhood* series consider contemporary and alternative theoretical perspectives in the domain of early childhood education. The aim of the book series is to introduce readers to new and alternative theoretical perspectives and to make them accessible, so that their relevance to the everyday practices that are possible in early childhood settings, is highlighted. The topics span the whole range of contexts of centers and classrooms, as well as considering family and community settings to provide readers with *rich* descriptions of everyday lives in global contexts. The books in the series enable us to engage in meaningful conversations around the personal and complex sets of interactions that we experience in the early childhood years (birth to 8 years of age). The topics are wide ranging but our focus is to showcase pedagogies and practices that will enable early childhood educators to design learning ecologies that are underpinned by a respect for all participants, equity and social justice and which encourage deep learning and engagement with ideas.

The *Changing Images of Early Childhood* books challenge and confront educators with a wide range of topics. They reflect the *complex* nature of our lives in a postmodern world where issues around globalism, capitalism, democracy and the multifaceted nature of our contemporary experiences are not easily resolved, yet need to be confronted. The books in the series also bring to the forefront the issues faced by marginalized groups so that they might be interrogated with *respect* and from perspectives that are relevant to the nature and culture of those groups and individuals. Additionally, we want to share the innovate practices of educators who are at the forefront of thinking dynamically about the challenges inherent to living in the 21st century.

The first two books in the series were published in 2004 and entitled; *Unsettling the colonial places and spaces of early childhood education* by Gaile Cannella and Radhika Viruru, and *Rethinking parent and child conflict* by Sue Grieshaber. Reimagining *Diversity, Equity, and Justice in Early Childhood* is the sixteenth book to be published in the collection and it broadens, deepens and compliments the notions and provocations evident in each of the books published to date. It is also the first book to be published after we experience the global pandemic caused by Covid-19. I am not sure any of us can recall what life was like before 2020 which makes it complex to return to a 'new normal' when you never knew what 'normal' meant. An alternative viewing would be to move forward confidently to our collective future with ideas that confirm "collective liberation." Each of the chapters arranged in the four sections are invitations for us to reconceptualise radical possibilities that will lead to a more socially just and equitable society with an education system in place that reflects these possibilities and opportunities for *all* young children and their families. While this is our goal for *all* children the particular focus is on those whose lifeworlds are experiencing the intersecting ramifications and repression of race, gender, citizenship, language, disability.

The collection edited by Haeny Yoon, Lin Goodwin and Celia Genishi, is organised in four parts all of which reflect transformative ideas and practices which call on us as early childhood educators and practitioners to *reconceptualise, reconsider, rethink and re-engage* our experiences with young children, their families and the communities they inhabit. Each of the authors invite us to contemplate new and alternative ways of being and doing early childhood education and viewing young children's lifeworlds. As Yoon writes in the introduction, each of the chapters in the four sections invites us to reflect on what is often missing in contemporary early childhood education; that is, an considered attempt to foreground diversities that should be deliberated in discussions about what are culturally relevant practices, incorporating the resources available and the funds of knowledge found in diverse communities look like, which in turn would lead us to perpetuate equitable opportunities for *all* children.

This edited volume challenges our understandings about big picture contemporary educational issues such as; How we understand the ways in which institutional and societal biases, like racism, may be (re)produced in experienced childhoods. The chapters in the four sections are wide ranging and seek our interrogation of complex issues, so that we may consider them in our own learning ecologies. They call for us to reconceptualise the current debate around literacy, for example, in order to connect becoming multiliterate with identities and making meaning. To also ask us to reconsider our methods of inquiry as early childhood scholars and practitioners, to capture multimodal engagements, to review the complex intersections, crossings and interactions between children and adults and request that we reengage with families and communities in new ways in a post pandemic world.

As Yoon notes in the introduction to the book; the new sociology of childhood reminds us that how we view childhood and children not only depends on how we conceptualise childhood and children, but also the ways in which we use frames of reference to encapsulate and describes their lives. All the authors in this volume view young children as capable and reject deficit framings of their lives. They value the funds of knowledge that all children bring to schooling and suggest that they should be incorporated into how we design our learning ecologies in early childhood education to ensure that schooling enables all children to thrive and reach their potential. This volume shares radical possibilities for the future of early childhood education which we hope will act as a catalyst for action and the foundation for changes in our approach and design of early childhood education.

INTRODUCTION

Reimagining Diversity, Equity, and Justice in Early Childhood Education

Haeny Yoon

> Today, in the midst of the most death-filled summer of our lives, I bought my first two books back from the publisher so I could revise and reissue them. I paid ten times what the publisher initially paid for the books. I'm thinking a lot about debt, reparation, vengeance, residue, and the tendrils of humiliation caused and withstood. I am thankful to have made it to a place where I will never waste my words on anyone … Revision did that … I hope you find radical possibilities and guts galore in this revised piece of art.
> —Kiese Laymon, *How to Slowly Kill Yourself and Others in America, Revised Edition*

We are emerging from a global pandemic—one of the most "death filled" summer(s) of our collective consciousness. In the first summer of lockdown, Laymon (like many of us) took time to contemplate on his own journey as a memoirist, essayist, and social commentator. Spending the summer in Mississippi, he revisited the origin story of his critically acclaimed memoir, *Heavy* (2018), to reflect on the politics of writing and recognition. *Heavy* is a book about home, of belonging, of love. It is also a story about trauma, betrayal, and shame—because all of those things can exist in the same space and at the same time. Many of us can relate to the emotional toll of pandemic life that bubbled up the complicated tensions we stifled to the bottom. Consequently, these long pushed-down feelings began to percolate up. For many years, Laymon felt as if he was not writing *his* stories in the way he envisioned and in ways he wanted to tell them. As a writer in a publishing industry dominated by white people, he contended with self-doubt and the desire to please shrouding much of his

DOI: 10.4324/9781003399155-1

childhood. As a young, naïve writer, he entered the writing world to be in community. However, he quickly came to understand that publishers do not always *love you* back or care for you in ways you expect. These same feelings often surface for many people of Color entering a white-dominated field: disappointment, inferiority, exploitation, and erasure. He writes, "I've been slowly killing myself and others close to me" (2020, p. xiii), in an effort to solidify his place in literary circles. Therefore, he made a bold move to *revise* his earlier work and open himself up to radical possibilities as the "most loving acts I can do for my work, my body, my Mississippi" (p. xv).

Revision

For many writers, revision is a dreadful and all-consuming task—an obstacle to finishing a piece of work. By the time we arrive at "revision," our fervor and passion for our own work is depleted. But, what if we imagine revision as a liberatory act—one that helps us see, ideate, live, and dream differently and more clearly. Writing is not the only space that can use a revision. Our imaginations require a reimagining—an awakening—a *revision* in the simplest sense. Our current social imaginary "gives us borders, gives us superiority, gives us race as an indicator of capability" (Brown, 2017, p. 19), preventing us from engaging and collaborating on "the ideas that will liberate all of us" (p. 19). How can we revise our collective consciousness?

This collection of work from early childhood scholars across disciplines ideates toward collective liberation. The chapters are invitations to revise and reimagine radical possibilities and equitable futures by learning from/with/ alongside young children and their communities. They collectively work toward *revising* a future that is truly equitable and just, particularly for those children whose lives are marked by the intersecting oppressions of race, gender, citizenship, language, and disability. These chapters are written as loving acts of care for the communities encircling children's lives, knowing that we are all part of the stories that inhabit these pages. And of course, all these ideas gesture toward *revision*. As time moves forward, I imagine these ideas will grow, shift, and transform into "something large enough and solid enough that it becomes a tipping point" (Brown, 2017, p. 19). The conversation only starts here— incomplete, unfinished, in-process, and waiting for others (e.g., scholars, educators, policymakers, community leaders, caregivers, general public) to extend the work of justice and equity.

Overarching Frame: Pedagogies of Liberation and Freedom

Early childhood education continues to be a contested field where developmental timelines dominate the discourse around what is "good" for young children. In the spirit of non-linearity, I begin by thinking sideways across the topics of each of these chapters. Situated against a backdrop of these multiple global pandemics—COVID-19, racial injustice and violence, inequitable resource distribution, political insurrections, and unrest—the authors argue that diversity and inclusion must be coupled with a *divestment* from white privilege and an *investment* in anti-racist pedagogies and practices across early childhood contexts of research, policy, and teaching/learning.

The Serious and Intellectual Work of Play

Play in early childhood education has long been a precious and enduring concept. For many decades, Vivian Paley (1981, 1993, 2009) enraptured us with magnificent stories of children processing and theorizing about life at a young age. Likewise, cultural theorist bell hooks (2006) often reminisced about children in her own life—neighborhood children who would walk in and out of her home to comment on art, to inadvertently interrogate social issues, to gossip about adults and their ways. They became a part of her intellectual circle, and she listened to them as children and cultural theorists who had anything and everything to say about their world. As we theorize play here, I want to move away from debates that politicize play. To be clear, play can be obviously political. But to politicize play means that adults use play for their own power and gain. For instance, play (at times) is only recognized when it has curricular value and academic connections. Play is allowed when children need a break from the serious work of school. Play has a timeframe—too little or too much is frowned upon. Re-engaging with these long-standing debates on play is not the goal of the chapters here. Instead, the attention is on what play *does* for children in stoking their social imaginations.

In classrooms, children are challenging us to rethink what constitutes play—who, what, when, where, and how do we decide what forms of play are acceptable and unacceptable (Fincham, this volume). Rather than romanticize versions of play, the authors look to play as a cultural artform to express and assert oneself in landscapes that diminish creativity and encourage conformity. There are children who are demanding to be heard and understood in exclusive spaces, often raced and classed (Dyson, this volume). Some are inviting us to peer into their family and community networks to see with more clarity how language, play events, and relationships work together to form sophisticated language moves (Frieson & Presiado, this volume). Play can also be a social commentary on the disciplinary systems that regulate children's lives (Wargo, this volume) or on how identity markers limit and open up the ways children position themselves in classrooms (Fube & Yoon, this volume). In particular, whose childhoods (and by extension, the right to play) are often cut short at the intersection of race, gender, and class (Nelson & Wright, this volume)?

Lil Miss Hot Mess extends and solidifies the meaning(s) of play through Drag Story Hour,

> I hope that kids and their parents come away with an implicit sense that drag is a practice of play: we're adults who continue to dress up because we know that often transforming how we look on the outside can be an essential part of expressing who we are on the inside, as well as making over the world around us ... I hope that educators of all varieties can borrow some of this spirit in their approaches to teaching and learning. That doesn't necessarily mean putting on a wig or a pair of pumps, but rather finding ways to bring a spirit of play, creativity, and specialness into their work.

In other words, the serious forms of some play defy renderings of play as only frivolous and devoid of purpose. It can be both, and again, it comes down to what it *does* for people (Vasudevan, 2015). Play, then, is also a practice of reimagination—of trying out and trying on ideas that remake the world we live in. Play is a valuable, cultural activity, allowing for innovation and (re)invention in schools, communities, homes, and even our *work*places. Inevitably, it connects adults and children together and offers all of us a space to consider different perspectives, "to abandon one-dimensional viewing, to look from many vantage points and, in doing so, construct meanings scarcely suspected before" (Greene, 2001, p. 187)—imagining possibilities rather than reproducing static ideas. Through play, we *revise* or transform how we express ourselves. To me, that sounds far from frivolous, but special.

The Intergenerational Relationships that Constitute Childhoods

This creativity and specialness are not reserved just for children but tie together the relationships of adults and children. While many of these chapters feature children as central, their lives are intertwined and juxtaposed alongside those of adults who are also navigating systems of their own. Many authors here suggest an intentional shift away from children and adults as always separate, but interdependent (Ghiso, this volume; Kwon, this volume). To illustrate, *Station Eleven* (St. John Mandel, 2015) tells the fictional story of survivors of a global pandemic. Written years before COVID-19, the story illustrates the intergenerational crossings between children and adults. Post-pandemic, the survivors were forced to destabilize existing hierarchies of adult/child. They relied on each other to survive, and children became a symbol of hope in a desolate world in need of reimagination. Like the previous section articulates, creativity and imagination sustained lives. What readers come to realize is *things* were not capable of "saving us," it was play, art, and the intergenerational relationships. When confronted with a new reality, adults and children found generative and altered ways to relate to each other. Therefore, as we decenter traditional hierarchies delineated by things like age, race, gender, and class, we should ideate toward more sustainable futures in teacher education (Cheruvu & Martinez, this volume; Price Gardner, this volume), in methodologies (Brownell, this volume; Fellner & Templeton, this volume; Fube & Yoon, this volume), in classroom communities (Dyson, this volume; Frieson & Presiado, this volume; Wargo, this volume). Like *Station Eleven* illustrates, perhaps this forces us to emerge from the pandemic with different ideas of how to engage communities, particularly those without the same access and resources (Durán et al., this volume; Ghiso, this volume; Warraich & da Silva, this volume).

María Paula Ghiso poses a powerful question eluding to the import of intergenerational relationships. She asks, "How can our pedagogies be affirming of children's legacies while also inviting inquiry into broader sociopolitical histories that shape the complexities and contradictions of (im)migrant identities?" In other words, rather than constructing binaries of the child/adult, we can affirm the *legacies* of how adults and children are situated in this particular time and space. Joseph D. Nelson and Brian L. Wright propose relationships between Black boys and men that center joy and radically shift their future possibilities. Like Harper Keenan, Lil Miss Hot Mess, LeRoi Newbold, and Lee Iskander describe, they envision similar spaces where creative expression is not only encouraged but cultivated. Notably, the most generative spaces of inquiry and expression exist where adults and children learn to play, live, and inquire together. Therefore, understanding lived experiences is a dialogic interchange of many narratives and stories of becoming—they are "stacked" on top of each other (Fube & Yoon, this volume). Ghiso describes "intergenerational exchanges as sites of learning about migration and global justice, and children as active directors of these dialogic moments." Muyanwi Lum Fube and Haeny Yoon are reminded of their own immigrant story in relationship to Lily, a Haitian kindergartner in New York City. While there are many connections that tie the three together, there are dialogic moments that cause their experiences to diverge with Lily and with one another. It is in this dialogic space that children and adults are part of third cultures (Kwon, 2019)—retaining resonances of both identities and constructing new ones. Emmanuelle Fincham draws from her own teaching memories to reflect and reconsider her instruction. Brittany Frieson and Vivian Presiado juxtapose their own language and schooling experiences to deepen their analysis of children's out-of-school literacies. In each of these instances, our *becoming* was actively "directed" by the children we encountered.

Thus, where do children and adults coalesce in shared activity? Jungmin Kwon and Lindsey Hall highlight the spaces where language and culture are preserved in places like supermarkets. They elucidate the literacy resources (in the forms of books and flyers) that act as materials and sites for intergenerational learning in Korean communities. Similarly, Frieson and Presiado highlight the Black church as a similar space for Black language to cultivate and thrive. LeRoi Newbold traces the beginning of Freedom School Toronto, designed to center Black liberatory pedagogy. In collaboration with the Kiki Ballroom Alliance, the community members created their own space with their own standards where both children and adults could express and imagine otherwise possibilities. Across all three chapters, children are positioned as both learners and experts, participants and contributors, cultural brokers and bridges.

Carmen Martinez recalls her own connections to learning Spanish in elementary school. Learning the language was not only a functional skill, but a familial one that allowed her to maintain connections to her Mexican community. She reflects on the dissonances experienced in school (even in higher education) where culturally sustaining pedagogies are overlooked in the education and care of preservice teachers. Rather than applying these ideas to only children, Ranita Cheruvu and Carmen Martinez maintain, "BIPOC preservice teachers have had limited opportunities to critically examine the intersectionalities of their identities and experiences against the historical and sociopolitical contexts that have shaped their lived experiences." In the same way, as societies consider the "loss" that children experienced in the pandemic, Leah Durán, Rebecca Lopez, and Sherilyn Analla highlight the strain placed on caregivers and teachers (particularly of Color) as they navigated the demands of remote schooling. Their insights emphasize how children and adults experience life—the joys and trauma—together. They reframe how we view children and adults, not simply as students or caregivers, but as multi-faceted. In the same way, Axa Warraich and Ana Christina da Silva underscore the collaborative work of non-government organizations, schools, families, and communities in designing a magazine for children's learning during the pandemic. While attending to the "academic" needs of children's development, particularly in rural, low-resourced areas, they emphasize how the magazine brought together adults and children in shared conversations about the tensions and difficulties experienced in their communities.

Many authors in this volume acknowledge the difficulty in truly centering children's perspectives, especially as adults who un/knowingly pursue our agendas (Brownell, this volume; Fellner & Templeton, this volume; Fincham, this volume; Wargo, this volume). We cannot presume to fully understand contemporary children under the guise that we have once been children ourselves. Ghiso, Kwon, Durán et al., Keenan et al., Warraich and da Silva argue for the convergence of adult/child relationships as a vital thread sustaining the family or community unit. Children *and* the adults committed to their wellbeing have a role to play and identities worth understanding. These chapters highlight the possibilities inherent when adults and children are honored and recognized as partners and makers of their space.

Multimodal Communication and Child Voice in Adult-Mediated Contexts

Multimodality is defined as the multiple modes employed to communicate meaning (Kress, 2004). In literacy studies, multimodality is associated with texts (Jewitt, 2008), illustrated by how visual images, gestures, orality, print, and drawing work iteratively to construct meanings (Dyson, this volume). For example, Roberta Price Gardner focuses on children's literature as a space of multimodal and aesthetic representation. Like other scholars also lament (McNair & Edwards, 2021; Toliver, 2018), Rudine Bishop Sim's concept of "mirrors, windows, and sliding glass doors" (1990) has been watered down and taken up in schools to check off diversity initiatives rather than celebrate complexity through visual imagery—on classroom walls, in literature, in digital media, and in classroom artifacts. Instead, while many of us may witness increased representation, we still see a one-dimensional image of the *other* that ignores the beauty and complexity of everydayness. This is what leads to, Price Gardner argues, narrow versions of Black life as dichotomous rather than a spectrum of possibilities. Like Nelson and Wright assert, Black children are socialized to *aspire* for greatness, mobility, and respectability. Told through the lens of trauma (e.g., slavery, Jim Crow) or postracial ideologies, children's literature forefronts Black middle-class life without a nuanced rendering of the Black diaspora. Visibility, then, is reserved for people of Color who support the dominant narrative of meritocracy and proximity to whiteness as desirable. Through an analysis of visual and textual elements elevating both the hardships and joys of Black working class communities, Price Gardner shares the potential and necessity of amplifying diverse representations of Blackness.

Moving from the multimodal compositions of texts, many authors alert us to children's multimodal, entangled relationships with their world. Amanda Fellner and Tran Templeton deploy mapping and tracing to highlight children's sensory engagement with their space, particularly the non-verbal gestures and sounds that epitomize mobility for children from 0 to 5. Therefore, if we accept children's experience of their worlds as embodied, we must confront the discursive control of children's bodies in particular spaces (Dyson, this volume; Fincham, this volume; Nelson & Wright, this volume). Jon Wargo highlights sonic mobilities and the recognition that the more-than-verbal constitute children's experiences. "Noisy" and "willful" children are positioned as troublemakers. These positionings ignore sound as a form of meaning-making—the aural geographies that may help us attune more fully to children's multimodal movements (Brownell, this volume). Cassie Brownell insists that children adhere themselves to these sounds in ways that adults often overlook, from the whir of machines to the muffled sounds from distant corners. Children's attention to sound reframes ideas like noise (Wargo, this volume), ambient sounds (Brownell, this volume), and spinning plates (Fincham, this volume) as meaningful ecological encounters. Together, many of these authors imply that children's entangled relationship to their place insists on new ways of understanding lived experience and resists static representations of children's meaning-making (Fellner & Templeton, this volume). A multi-sensorial, multimodal stance widens what we consider children's lived experiences. Attending to the aural sensations that populate schools (Brownell, this volume), attuning to the mutisensorial experiences of young children (Fellner & Templeton, this volume), and making space for multimodal composing (Dyson, this volume) draws our attention away from the adult gaze and brings us closer to children's perspectives.

Organization of the Book

With these three overarching ideas, I turn now to a more linear rendering of the book. Before this volume came together, headings existed only as guideposts. However, the four parts of this book emerged from critical engagement with each chapter. As Nick Obolensky writes, "emergence is the way complex systems and patterns arise out of a multiplicity of relatively simple interactions" (2010, p. 88). That is, the strands of this work are multiple and complex. While the connections between them are made more salient here, organized in a readable format, I hope they spark new ideas and grow outward.

Reconceptualizing Literacies and Children's Identities in the Current Visual and Linguistic Landscape: Reading, Writing, and Liberation

Part I begins with a reconceptualization of literacies as they intersect with children's identities within and across communities. Anne Haas Dyson begins this section with how children *read* each other through deficit framings. These peer readings exacerbate harmful perceptions of race and class, mediated by institutional discourses that work their way into the children's everyday relationships. She describes the transition of Ta'Von—a Black boy entering kindergarten with mostly white, middle-upper class children. While it may have taken Ta'Von longer to reach the arbitrary ladder of literacy skills valued in school, he was clearly a sophisticated user of language whose written, oral, and reading skills leveraged relationships and community. However, his story *reads* similarly to many Black boys in early childhood who often get dis/placed as "not bright," "low achieving," and in need of support. While we know that schools regulate and discursively identify children along deficit terms (Dudley-Marling, 2019; Nxumalo, 2019; Yoon, 2015), Dyson demonstrates how children take up these measures to inadvertently and superficially label one another. Equally dangerous are the deleterious effects of such labeling in segregating children's friendships by age, ability, race, gender, and class. Furthermore, the "innocuous" everyday classifications of reading groups or even lunch lines continue to reify and solidify how children are read and marked as intellectual beings. In other words, we have trained children to surveil, regulate, and position each other.

In Dyson's prolific body of work (1997, 2013, 2021), she demonstrates young children of Color navigating a language and literacy landscape that consistently diminishes their capacity—Ta'von is no exception. What she shows in Ta'von is "resilience" and a will to fight for his social and intellectual place in a classroom dictated by discursive structures meant to purposefully exclude children like him. But why should young children have to fight for a place to be seen, heard, or understood? Recognition and visibility also thread through the work of Brittany Frieson and Vivian Presiado who further interrogate the language politics in classrooms, even in dual language bilingual education programs. Language hierarchies presuppose certain versions/dialects of language (e.g., Standard English and European Spanish) as dominant and correct. Although multiple languages are used for instruction, dominant language practices undermine the rich vernaculars, dialects, and communicative repertoires of ethnic and racial diasporic communities. Focused on Black language users, Frieson and Presiado elevate Black language as a functional, cultural, and social language form. They demonstrate children fluidly moving across languages from Standard English, Black Language, and various forms of Spanish. Therefore, language "dualities" or bilingual programs still fall short of making space for language varieties, and by extension, cultural communities that remain on the margins. Language diversities are underrecognized (e.g., European Spanish as the norm) and Black language is made invisible in conversations around multilingualism.

Finally, Roberta Price Gardner demonstrates how these perceptions of identity are (re)produced through literature; particularly how visual images, language choice, linguistic turns, and textual elements contribute to deficit framings of Black children. While moves to increase the visibility of Black people have been widely appropriated as a response to inequities around diversity and inclusion, Price Gardner points out that Black working-class identities remain scarce in children's literature and visual material. The overemphasis of the Black middle class alongside the trauma narratives constructed to teach children about "racial progress" centers Black respectability rather than Black diversity. Like Dyson, and Frieson and Presiado, she calls our attention to the subtle discursive and institutional structures that erase the diverse cultures and identities *within* cultures, not simply across. Moreover, she suggests that we deepen our understanding of ideas that claim equity and social justice: "mirrors, windows, and sliding glass doors" (Bishop, 1990) and culturally relevant/ sustaining practices (Ladson-Billings, 2014). Rather than denigrating these revolutionary ideas into tropes, she challenges us to consider whose experiences are still missing or narrowed in calls for diversity, equity, and inclusion.

Thus, we still fail to see the depth and richness of Black communities—the familial and community networks that sustain working-class life. Analyzing picture books that purposefully reveal this depth and sophistication move white teachers away from savior mentalities and reposition them as learners of Black cultural life in its fullness.

By calling into question what "diversity" means and how it falls short in literacy learning, language politics, and visual imagery, the authors imply that the current rhetoric around racial reckoning is still incomplete. Missing from increased representation and antiracist pedagogy are the positionings of Black communities (for example) at the intersection of race, gender, language, ability, and class. As we envision a more just future, we should also interrogate the ways children are dehumanized for their intersecting identity markers, particularly through language and literacy. The authors here argue that communicative competence is socially situated and cultivated through repeated and sustained participation in churches, after-school programs, families, community spaces, etc. By examining how children participate in language activities outside of school, educators might reframe deficit views of children's capacities and experience children's language dexterities.

Reconsidering Methods: Sensory Engagements and the Resounding Traces of Children's Lives

Part II also considers communication, attuning to the multimodal ways children voice their experiences of the world and self. The authors attend to the more-than-human, more-than-verbal expressions of children who may not always enact oral language as their primary modality. Moving beyond "school literacies," they urge us to pay attention to children's ways of communicating with the world, with things, with their environments. Amanda Fellner and Tran Templeton remind us that children's more-than-verbal enactments yield critical insights into how children experience the world. That is, they push us to rethink how we might do research, how we make choices on curriculum (even when we claim it is emergent), and what adults even believe is worth paying attention to. By tracing and mapping as methodological tools, they show the potential of attuning *with* and *alongside* children's experience as they move through their worlds—be it everyday playgrounds or urban streets. They ask us to consider how children place themselves in relation to others, self, materials, and the geophysical world. Centered on movements and relationships networked across space, they animate children's sensory engagements, emphasizing how bodies move in relation to the environment.

With an attention to Autistic children, Emmanuelle Fincham further elucidates the more-than-verbal as a way of reorienting verbo-centric conceptions of play and being. Noting research heavily amplifies verbal interactions, she describes how Leo, an Autistic child, mobilizes materials to facilitate play, different from but not less significant as peer-to-peer interactions. In most early childhood centers, play is recognized as important to children's development. However, Fincham notes that unintelligible and unrecognizable play is censored and surveilled, met with interventions to "normalize" the "abnormal" child. She acutely notes that developmental discourses also dictate children's social and emotional identities. Therefore, children are socialized into certain archetypes of *ideal* children, implying that the ladder of skills previously described by Dyson is not simply applied to basic skills. Predisposed ideals of "normal" and "typically developing" work to regulate play for Autistic children, illustrating how childhood practices are inequitably construed by the intersecting politics of race, gender, class, and disability. In the case of children deemed "not normal," what is not knowable is often feared and placed in the margins, rectified by interventions that view children as a monolith—modeled after white, middle-class, able-bodied, and heteronormative identities. She emphasizes the more-than-human intra-actions—those that don't always involve the kinds of peer play highlighted in research—Autistic children demonstrate in relationship to the material world (i.e., spinning plates) and pushes us to consider the joyful and diverse forms of play entangled with nonhuman networks. By decentering the child, she makes the case that we might (in fact) amplify who children are, beyond their identities and related "deficiencies."

Research has often highlighted the discursive ways children's identities are constructed in school spaces via tests, evaluations, and other benchmarks measuring school competence. Jon Wargo highlights the objects and materials that "stick" to children's bodies, positioning them as noisy or in need of discipline. Spaces and the objects that constitute such spaces mark certain children as not normal. That is, they are often disciplined and regulated by objects (i.e., bike chair, taped squares) which agentively constitute how children are perceived and known by peers and the teacher. Through a stacked stories approach, he articulates the resonances and reverberations that often go unheard in our attempts to subdue the sensory and affective experiences of becoming "willful" children at school. School conditions children to be silent, behaved, and compliant. Wargo considers who or what we silence in the process. Noting that "noise is [an] expressive index that symbolically and materially claims space," he describes the reciprocity between children, objects, and unmediated sounds as a philosophical and rhythmic coproduction. Early childhood classrooms are already set up to facilitate and (re)produce how children's bodies move. Wargo reframes noise and other sounds as vibrant matter in the classroom, (im)mobilizing children's bodies and identities as well. Children are mobilized by their affective encounters with the nonhuman. Like Fellner and Templeton, he highlights the intra-action and agency of the networks and ecologies in which children take part.

Cassie Brownell, like Fincham and Wargo, further extends new ways of knowing how children move and interact in the world. She reminds us that adults are prone to mis/understand and mis/read children, particularly when our intentions and goals are out of sync with children's daily, sensorial experiences. Tuning to the sounds that reverberate at school, she motions toward the aural geographies that are not necessarily inhibitions to learning, but a critical part of how children understand their relationship to one another and the world. To "hear children out" (Yoon & Templeton, 2019), and in this sense, literally, means we attune ourselves to how subtle and overt noises construct how space is experienced by young children. Furthermore, she suggests pedagogies and methods that engage the senses fully—multimodally—so that adults learn from and with the poignant observations of children. Through sound recordings taken by children in school, she reflects on how noise became a taken-for-granted concept in renderings of children's lived experience. Listening to the ambient sounds inaudible or simply ignored by adults, she draws us into children's playful and astute (re)conceptions of school. What adults deem undesirable—chaos, noise, distractions—is significant to children's multisensorial and affective experiences of school.

Together, these authors articulate the *undoing* that must occur for adults to reorient their senses. The material aspects of children's worlds deepen our understanding of the diverse and sophisticated ways children express who they are, want to be, and how they desire to be known in communities. They push us to see, hear, and experience differently—to move through city spaces and parks from the perspective of toddlers who intuitively sense and connect to the world; to take up definitions of play that do not look or feel like the play we are accustomed; to interrupt the discursive and material elements of classrooms that work to construct children as problems, as *willful*; to attune our senses to the multimodal ways that children actively and fluidly communicate lived experience.

Rethinking the Relationships Between Children and Adults: Intergenerational Intersections, Crossings, and Interactions

The first two parts looked at the relationship of adults and children and attempt to destabilize hierarchies that dis/place children in schools and research. Asking us to reframe how we understand children's practices, moves, and capacities, the authors collectively forward an agenda of liberation and flexibility. In spite of preexisting demarcations between adults/children in research and in classrooms, they offer ways to make those relationships more equitable and reciprocal. In Part III, the focus shifts to the interrelationship between adults and children where boundaries intentionally blur. We see children acting as transnational brokers and exemplars of ethnic affiliations. We see adults activating the child within to connect with children in the present. This section makes visible the experiences of teachers, immigrants, mentors, caregivers, and other adults who attempt to create space for children in marginalized communities. All the authors in this section are also immigrants and people of Color themselves, and it is no coincidence that intergenerational threads tie these chapters together. As many of us still grapple with the tensions of childhood/adulthood, multiple cultures, and complicated affiliations, we endear ourselves to children and families who share and relate to our own accumulated struggles. Therefore, this section considers what happens when adults and children coconstruct and seek to unpack these struggles alongside one another rather than apart.

In María Paula Ghiso's work, children interview their parents to better understand the complex and diverse experiences of immigrants and transnationals. When set against the backdrop of trauma, assimilation, and multicultural education, she wonders if we subsume immigrants' personal and familial stories under the politics of immigration, presenting such experiences as a monolith. While acknowledging the horrifying state of detention centers and border policies in the United States, Ghiso repositions immigrants as knowledge holders and contributors to families and communities. She understands them as holding trauma, but not sole bearers of that identity. In conversations between children and adults, she humanizes and narrates stories of complexity and diversity. She describes the intergenerational learning that occurs at the intersection of language, culture, and global citizenship. Reorienting our gaze to the assets and transnational funds of knowledge accumulated as families migrate across nation-states and borders, she offers an ethos of interdependence whereby children and their families construct epistemic knowledge together. Furthermore, she moves beyond American exceptionalism to one that extends binaries of the US and home country to that of ideological, geographic, cultural, and linguistic fluidity.

Like Ghiso, Muyanwi Lum Fube and Haeny Yoon illustrate how children and adults weave together stories to establish and sustain cultural practices. Fube and Yoon ask adults to reengage with childhood memories as more than a reflective exercise, but as a lens for understanding contemporary children. Like Ghiso, they center the immigrant experience as one that constructs particular insight into the ways children participate, contribute, and (at times) contend with the demands placed on them as raced, classed, gendered, etc. Drawing on their own tensions between cultures, the authors unpack how these memories frame their understanding of other children's transitional identities. How do these stories converge and diverge? At times, the strong connections bridge adults and children together around shared experiences. Other times, particular lenses, may inhibit and limit our understanding of children in the world. By acknowledging our own attachments to childhood, we learn from children, thus destabilizing the built-in hierarchical relationships between adults and children. Focused on Lily, a Haitian child of immigrants, the chapter brings together generational stories as pedagogical tools for analyzing children's *multi*cultural identities.

Jungmin Kwon and Lindsey Hall continue to emphasize how transnational families build communities across the United States. They point out that grocery stories, bookstores, restaurants, and heritage schools intentionally serve as spaces of community learning and cultural preservation. In this chapter, Korean language and literacies were represented and cultivated as sites of learning for children embedded in these communities. They discuss the ways writing, reading, and languaging across Korean/English, physical/digital, and home/school provided entry points for fluid linguistic and cultural practice. Furthermore, children served as cultural brokers and contributors to ethnic public spaces, mobilized by text and print. Extending from Ghiso's work, they attend to how epistemic knowledge is coconstructed with and alongside children who navigate between multiple cultures. They portray the resourcefulness of immigrant communities who cultivate vibrant and sustaining communities, even in smaller, sub/urban areas.

Ranita Cheruvu and Carmen Martinez highlight the importance of educators in the lives of children, particularly educators of Color who share the cultural affiliations of children and their families. Yet, they point to the enduring systemic structures that marginalize BIPOC experiences in early childhood to adulthood. They describe the failure of teacher education programs in supporting early childhood teachers of Color, despite calls for antibiased/antiracist practices. Clearly, equitable curriculum and pedagogy in early childhood classrooms that claim inclusion and liberation for all must care for and nurture the BIPOC teachers that serve within these communities. Martinez shares her experiences as a BIPOC preservice teacher— the cultural affiliations that made certain spaces feel safe, the gate-keeping mechanisms excluding BIPOC teachers from entering the workforce, and the enduring systemic obstacles that begin at childhood and continue to adulthood. Choosing to graduate without a teacher certification, Martinez's story is a wake-up call for teacher education programs purporting social justice and equity. What structures and policies keep white supremacy and privilege in place in our institutions of higher education?

Reengaging with Communities and Families in a Post-World

Part IV addresses what spaces could look like when boundaries are opened up. Each of the chapters here addresses how we organize experiences for children, from read-alouds to remote learning to printed text distribution to mentoring programs. Programs designed *for* children, at times, typify adult agendas and goals. Harper Keenan, Lil Miss Hot Mess, LeRoi Newbold, and Lee Iskander argue for pedagogies of liberation that highlight the possibilities of play, rooted in queer and trans pedagogies. Inclusion and tolerance are not enough in desta-bilizing the boundaries that push children toward straight, white, cis-gendered identities as desirable and normal. Critical to their chapter is the community of adults actively committed to creating space for new futures—the possibilities inherent in adults who ran Freedom schools that focus on Black and queer lib-eration; or the play of adults in drag performances, storytelling, and ballroom to invoke new ways of being and existing in the world. They remind us that play is serious, intellectual, and culturally important work. Illustrated by the meticulous preparation of Lil Miss Hot Mess in preparation for her first Drag Queen Story Hour, play stems from a commitment to creativity; and this crea-tivity is cultivated and sustained through time, within a community that cares and honors the well-being of those involved. In a climate where trans lives are deemed unimaginable, they call for a rethinking of pedagogy that truly celebrates how children and adults imagine and position their full selves in the world. Keenan et al. remind us that some children's identities are constantly in peril and futures not always promised, emboldened by political parties, legisla-tion, policies, and special interest groups.

Children across the globe have lived with uncertainty for most of their young lives—demonstrating that "resilience" and flexibility are second nature to chil-dren. That is, children learned to navigate this "new normal," particularly when adults could not. Amidst continuing discourses around what children have lost or how their learning fell behind, Leah Durán, Rebecca Lopez, and Sherilyn Analla turn our gaze to the possibilities that pandemic times revealed. Remote schooling afforded more flexibility for teachers who made a concerted effort to connect with children and families via screens. Technical difficulties, per se, were not always a hinderance, but an opportunity to engage and interact in new ways across peoples' homes. Many educators found themselves entering the spaces in which children live, surrounded by those in the home that cared for and supported their well-being. The teachers in Durán et al.'s chapter re-oriented their pedagogy to include more communicative flexibility across lan-guages, spontaneous engagement with caretakers, and divergent conversations that accessed family funds of knowledge. They underscore the difficulties and labor of teaching during this time, particularly teaching at the border between the United States and Mexico in working-class communities. They highlight the role of caring and loving educators whose reach extended beyond classroom walls [or screens].

Like Durán et al., Axa Khalid Warraich and Ana Christina da Silva highlight the relational connections and networks that were collaboratively facilitated between schools, community organizations, and families in safeguarding the cultural and social well-being of children in times of crisis. Through the exam-ple of Pakistan, the authors relay how the global pandemic disrupted the lives of many young children, making more recognizable the persistent inequities embedded in each of these communities. Moreover, the digital divide, instability of resources, and access to proper health care continue to reproduce uncertain futures. Warraich and da Silva describe these taken-for-granted inequities in rural areas of Pakistan where ideas like remote learning and digital programming further illuminated class divisions. In describing their efforts to create a print magazine for children with unstable electricity and internet in rural areas, they stress that technology is both a tool to expand possibilities as well as shed light on disparities.

These inequities circulating around geographic location, economic means, and ethnicity are endemic of life in the United States as well. Joseph D. Nelson and Brian L. Wright remind us that childhood—a fleeting and precious moment of time—is denied to Black boys despite the intervention and prevention programs aimed at "saving" Black children. While acknowledging the real institutional and societal conditions that render Black boyhood "unimaginable" (Dumas & Nelson, 2016), they argue for programs that amplify joy, play, and creativity for Black boys; that is, a space to simply be children who are afforded opportunities for exploration and experimentation that many of their white counterparts take for granted. Along the lines of race and gender, they urge us to imagine flexible physical and ideological boundaries that allow Black boys to be more than strong men, successful students, and protectors of their community. Instead, what would it feel like for Black boys to try out multiple identities before they are assigned to a future already presumed by criminality, hypersexuality, failure, and danger? Reinforced by these narratives, there is a proliferation of mentorship programs aimed at Black boys focused on their future roles as adults and not their identities as Black boys in the present. In their analysis of mentorship programs, Nelson and Wright imagine adult/child relationships that center community, play, and creativity. In other words, Black boys would find themselves enjoying the present rather than fearing the future.

Conclusion

Allison James writes, "What childhood is and who children are depend not only on where one looks but also on the lens through which that gaze is directed" (2003, p. 25). To illustrate, the *Erased Lynching Series* by Ken Gonazales Day (2022) powerfully redirects and reorients the gaze in America's tainted history of lynching. In his collection of visual images, Gonzales Day erases the victims of lynchings in digital photographs so that one is forced to look at the onlookers instead. What Gonzales Day's (2022) series does for our imagination is shift the focal point to the white audience—their complicity, their ambivalence, and even their delight. With photoshopped selections of visual imagery, he makes a provocative statement of white supremacy in American life. Lynching, and now even other subtle forms of racism, satiate the white gaze. In schools, we are accustomed to learning about the trauma and suffering of Black Americans (e.g., civil rights, slavery), as well as other people of Color to understand the reverberations of racism and the promise of racial progress. We gaze, linger, and immerse ourselves in images of immigration, internment, slavery, border control, war, and so on. For some, the traumatic images gratify a need for superiority and violence. For others, it summons a sense of justice that mobilizes our progressive politics. Either way, it is an exercise in service of white people. In these chapters, the authors aim to reorient the gaze and reframe the lens by which we understand children's experiences. Where do we look? What do we center? What do we miss in the process? What commitments frame how we interpret childhood? How can adults widen the lens and interrogate our gaze? *Who are we actually serving?*

In 2008, A. Lin Goodwin, Ranita Cheruvu, and Celia Genishi introduced an edited collection addressing diversities in education with a compelling and noteworthy history of diversity and equity in the United States. They, too, wrote about liberation, observing "… the purpose of schooling was not to liberate but to sort and classify, not to intellectually expand but to standardize, not to transform but to conform" (Goodwin et al. 2008, p. 4). Since its publication, the discourse around kindergarten readiness (Genishi & Dyson, 2012), the recent resurgence of "reading wars" and debates around the "science" of reading (Worthy et al., 2018; Yaden et al., 2021), and how we understand "high quality" preschool (Park et al., 2021) marginalize and undermine children from diverse communities. Current efforts at "closing the achievement gap" argue for access to early childhood programs, asserting that ability gaps can be reduced through early intervention; hence, increased funding for universal pre-K and Head Start. Perceived ability gaps in the early childhood years are blamed for crime, unemployment, and welfare in urban areas (Pew Center on the States, 2011). Therefore, high achievement on basic skills beginning in the early years (e.g., reading, writing, and numeracy) is a panacea for persistent social ills engulfing communities of Color. Consequently, children are positioned along a binary of success/failure, reified through test scores and developmental benchmarks. College and career readiness goals for children starting at birth continue to replace the joy of experiencing childhood in the moment in favor of a future adulthood that is unpromised. These discursive moves are also racist—blaming communities of Color for failure rather than acknowledging the failure of systems in setting up equitable conditions; circulating meritocratic narratives that elevate hard work and grit without acknowledging how access and opportunities are unequally distributed; and privileging whiteness as the norm in curricular, pedagogical, and policy-oriented conversations on early education. Missing from such arguments is an earnest attempt to forefront culturally relevant practices, sustaining the resources and knowledges of diverse communities while providing access and equitable opportunities for *all* children (King

& Swartz, 2015; Ladson-Billings, 2014). Rather than widen our imagination, adults are battling over curricular ideologies and basic human rights while asserting political authority to uphold status quo thinking under the guise of protecting children. Therefore, more than 10 years since Goodwin et al. published their edited volume, we find ourselves in an educational moment that is still about sorting, benchmarking, standardization, and conformity.

They echo salient arguments made by revolutionary thinkers like James Baldwin (1963) who said, "What societies really, ideally, want is a citizenry which will simply obey the rules of society" (n.p.), not a citizenry that questions, disrupts, or upends the dominant order. No one wants that kind of person around, he argued, because that kind of person is dangerous and a threat, particularly to whiteness. While many of us emerge in and out of the COVID-19 pandemic against the continued racial violence that pervades many of our communities, we are still grappling with the same tensions that Baldwin articulated in 1963, that Goodwin, Cheruvu, and Genishi rearticulated in 2008, and that many education scholars contend with in 2022. When will education be about freedom? When will school act as a space of possibility, hope, and liberation? On the heels of one school shooting after another, shortly after the heartbreaking tragedy at Robb Elementary School in Uvalde, Texas, when will schools be safe—not just from the threat of physical violence but the everyday violence inflicted upon children's intersecting identities?

Jacob Blake, a Black man from Kenosha, Wisconsin, was shot seven times in the back and left paralyzed. Only one of many stories populating the media landscape exemplifying disregard for Black lives, make note that he was shot in front of his children, ages 8, 5, and 3 who were sitting in the back seat of the car. Although our proximity to violence differs, depending on where we live, who we are, what our economic and social circumstances provide us access to, this proximity does not mean children aren't subject to the discourses and practices that racialize, stereotype, marginalize, and even kill many communities of Color in the United States. Children are experiencing and participating in a world fraught with turmoil and tension. They are taking part in conversations, observing (in)action, encountering limitations to their agency and voice, and understanding the threats to their own livelihoods. Writing does not solve these deeply rooted systemic problems. Writing, though, is a form of social action and a written commitment to act. I hope, like Kiese Laymon, that you find "radical possibilities" and "guts galore" in this re/vision.

References

Baldwin, J. (1963). A talk to teachers. *The Saturday Review*.

Bishop, R. S. (1990). Mirrors, windows, and sliding glass doors. *Perspectives: Choosing and Using Books for the Classroom*, 6(3), ix–xi.

Brown, A. M. (2017). *Emergent strategy: Shaping change, changing worlds.* AK Press.

Dudley-Marling, C. (2019). Rejecting deficit views of children in poverty in favor of a philosophy of abundance. In *Disrupting and countering deficits in early childhood education* (pp. 53–66). Routledge.

Dumas, M. J., & Nelson, J. D. (2016). (Re)Imagining Black boyhood: Toward a critical framework for educational research. *Harvard Educational Review, 86*(1), 27–47.

Dyson, A. H. (1997). *Writing superheroes: Contemporary childhood, popular culture, and classroom literacy.* Teachers College Press.

Dyson, A. H. (2013). *Rewriting the basics: Literacy learning in children's cultures.* Teachers College Press.

Dyson, A. H. (2021). *Writing the school house blues: Literacy, equity, and belonging in a child's early schooling.* Teachers College Press.

Genishi, C., & Dyson, A. H. (2012). Racing to the top: Who's accounting for the children? *Occasional Paper Series, 2012*(27), 18–20.

Gonzales Day, K. (2022). *Erased lynchings series.* Retrieved from https://kengonzalesday.com/projects/erased-lynchings/

Goodwin, A. L., Cheruvu, R., & Genishi, C. (2008). Responding to multiple diversities in early childhood education: How far have we come?. In *Diversities in early childhood education* (pp. 3–10). Routledge.

Greene, M. (2001). *Variations on a blue guitar: The Lincoln Center Institute lectures on aesthetic education.* Teachers College Press.

hooks, b. (2006). Introduction: The heartbeat of a cultural revolution. In *Outlaw culture: Resisting representations* (pp. 1–8). Routledge.

James, A. (2003). Understanding childhood from an interdisciplinary perspective. In *Rethinking childhood* (pp. 25–37). Rutgers University Press.

Jewitt, C. (2008). Multimodality and literacy in school classrooms. *Review of Research in Education, 32*(1), 241–267.

King, J. E., & Swartz, E. E. (2015). *The Afrocentric praxis of teaching for freedom: Connecting culture to learning.* Routledge.

Kress, G. (2004). Reading Images: Multimodality, representation and new media. *Information Design Journal, 12*(2), 110–119.

Kwon, J. (2019). Third culture kids: Growing up with mobility and cross-cultural transitions. *Diaspora, Indigenous, and Minority Education, 13*(2), 113–122.

Ladson-Billings, G. (2014). Culturally relevant pedagogy 2.0: Aka the remix. *Harvard Educational Review, 84*(1), 74–84.

Laymon, K. (2018). *Heavy: An American memoir.* Simon and Schuster.

Laymon, K. (2020). *How to slowly kill yourself and others in America: Essays (Revised Edition).* Simon and Schuster.

McNair, J. C., & Edwards, P. A. (2021). The lasting legacy of Rudine Sims Bishop: Mirrors, windows, sliding glass doors, and more. *Literacy Research: Theory, Method, and Practice, 70*(1), 202–212.

Nxumalo, F. (2019). Disrupting racial capitalist formations in early childhood education. In *Disrupting and countering deficits in early childhood education* (pp. 164–178). Routledge.

Obolensky, N. (2010). *Complex adaptive leadership: Embracing paradox and uncertainty.* Routledge.

Paley, V. G. (1981). *Wally's stories.* Harvard University Press.

Paley, V. G. (1993). *You can't say you can't play.* Harvard University Press.

Paley, V. G. (2009). *A child's work: The importance of fantasy play.* University of Chicago Press.

Park, S., Lee, S., Alonzo, M., & Adair, J. K. (2021). Reconceptualizing assistance for young children of color with disabilities in an inclusion classroom. *Topics in Early Childhood Special Education, 41*(1), 57–68.

Pew Center on the States. (2011). *Transforming public education: Pathway to a pre-k-12 future.* Retrieved from http://www.pewtrusts.org/en/research-and-analysis/reports/0001/01/01/transforming-public-education

St. John Mandel, E. (2015). *Station eleven.* Penguin Random House.

Toliver, S. R. (2018). Imagining new hopescapes: Expanding Black girls' windows and mirrors. *Research on Diversity in Youth Literature, 1*(1), 3.

Vasudevan, L. (2015). Multimodal play and adolescents: Notes on noticing laughter. *Journal of Language and Literacy Education, 11*(1), 1–12.

Worthy, J., Lammert, C., Long, S. L., Salmerón, C., & Godfrey, V. (2018). "What if we were committed to giving every individual the services and opportunities they need?" Teacher educators' understandings, perspectives, and practices surrounding dyslexia. *Research in the Teaching of English, 53*(2), 125–148.

Yaden, D. B. Jr, Reinking, D., & Smagorinsky, P. (2021). The trouble with binaries: A perspective on the science of reading. *Reading Research Quarterly, 56*, S119–S129.

Yoon, H. S. (2015). Assessing children in kindergarten: The narrowing of language, culture and identity in the testing era. *Journal of Early Childhood Literacy, 15*(3), 364–393.

Yoon, H. S., & Templeton, T. N. (2019). The practice of listening to children: The challenges of hearing children out in an adult-regulated world. *Harvard Educational Review, 89*(1), 55–84.

PART I

Reconceptualizing Literacies and Children's Identities in the Current Visual and Linguistic Landscape: Reading and Writing for Liberation

1

"YOU'RE HOT LUNCH, AREN'T YOU?"

(Re)Producing Inequity in Children's Worlds

Anne Haas Dyson

> Milo is a little boy who takes a long subway ride with his big sister every
> month on a Sunday. As the train moves along, Milo, a Black child, feels like
> a "shook up soda," a mix of bubbling emotions (de la Pena, 2021, n.p.). To
> distract himself, he draws the faces of the people on the subway and, based
> on their looks, imagines their lives. But when he arrives at the prison to visit
> his beloved mom, he is surprised to see a little White boy from the subway
> train; he had imagined that child living a royal existence in a castle … but
> here he is, same place as Milo. And Milo thinks about how a person can't
> know anyone just by looking at them at one time in one space, and he won-
> ders how people imagine his own story when they look at him.
>
> (based on the picture book *Milo Imagines the World* [de la Pena, 2021])

In this chapter, I consider the complexity of reading others, especially children's reading of each other. What do children assume about those they classify
as "the other"? The question gains urgency when considered against the backdrop of deficit ideology; given that discursive ideology, mainstream adults may
read minoritized and low-income children as academic "problems," as children
on the wrong side of the "achievement gap" (e.g., Barbarin & Crawford, 2006;
Garcia & Otheguy, 2017; Kendi, 2019). How, then, might this pervasive discourse, this superficial reading, figure into children's lives together in particular demographic contexts?

My wondering was prompted by a small Black child named Ta'Von. In my
ethnographic case study, I accompanied him for 4 years during his journey
through early schooling, beginning in his much-loved preschool and continuing through second grade (Dyson, 2021). In so accompanying Ta'Von, I was

DOI: 10.4324/9781003399155-3

originally interested in changes in children's composing experiences as they transitioned from a child-centered preschool to a literacy and basics-focused kindergarten (which is the new "first grade" [Bassok, Latham, & Rorem, 2016]) and on through the early grades. However, ethnographic research is never static; as Marcus (2015) explains, new perspectives emerge collaboratively, including as one learns from and with one's participants. And so it was with me and Ta'Von and, indeed, so it is with any educator who learns from and with their students. As I witnessed how racialized peer encounters emerged as Ta'Von moved from the interracial preschool serving primarily children from low-income families to the mainstream-dominated elementary school, my major research focus became how Ta'Von experienced and negotiated racial relations in childhood worlds. The nature of institutional discourse, policies, and practices became integral to this inquiry since they provided dynamic contexts for Ta'Von's peer negotiations. The variable nature of Ta'Von's multimodal composing (involving peer talk, drawing, and writing) became a key mediator of his negotiated relations.

As his story illustrates, in Ta'Von's movement from preschool to elementary school, he transformed from "one of the gang" of preschoolers to a "different" child among grade schoolers; in so doing, the "gap" discourse, with its deficit ideology, became part of his childhood relations with other children. In this chapter, I follow the thematic thread of neighborhood "bright" children's superficial reading of Ta'Von and their assumption that he would need academic help; I link their assumptions to institutional policies and practices that reinforced such assumptions. I begin with an introduction to Ta'Von's journey, emphasizing the critical transformation entailed in the movement from preschool to kindergarten.

Introducing Ta'Von's Journey into School: A Sharp Relational Turn in the Road

At the very beginning of his school journey, preschooler Ta'Von was in a very inclusive place. His preschool served mainly low-income 3- to 5-year-olds, categorized by the school as African American, like Ta'Von, Asian, Hispanic, white, and "mixed." The children themselves embodied their diversity—some spoke multiple languages; others had culturally marked hairstyles (like Ta'Von's braids) or ways of referring to kin folk ("tia"), and on and on. Classroom media, including books, were culturally and racially inclusive. Most relevant for this chapter, whether they were building with Legos, storytelling, or writing their name, the children were varied in their resources, but all participated in school activities however they could. If one had trouble, then one practiced and eventually one could (and would) say "I did it!," and others could say, "You did it!" Learning was a part of living, and play, which dominated the day, was a means of learning.

But then came the time when Ta'Von started kindergarten in an elementary school. The school's city had a segregated history, in which Black and white folks dominated in different city sections which historically had different degrees of city support. To try to overcome the city's and, thus, the schools' de facto segregation, the school district developed a plan for constrained parental choice of five, rank-ordered desirable or preferred schools. There was a great reluctance of white folks to send their children to predominantly Black schools; still, despite substantial white flight from public to private schools, there were certain neighborhood schools serving mainly white students. Ta'Von was assigned to one of these schools, situated in a relatively affluent neighborhood. He was usually one of two Black boys in a class. Alas, racial divides cannot be resolved by just moving kids around, especially not by making minoritized kids a numerical minority (Benner & Crosnoe, 2011; Clements, cited in McCarty & Castagno, 2018; Wilson & Rodkin, 2011).

Ta'Von's new school was part of the neoliberal accountability movement that has dominated the country's schools (Au, 2016). Thus, the district's policies mandated periodic testing (every quarter in the kindergarten), which located children on a ladder of designated common core or fundamental skills; learning was not so much a process but a product—a displayed (and scoreable) matter of possessed knowledge. There was a singular way to progress—to move up the skills ladder—and dates by which a step should be made. Unlike in preschool, where there was a sense of a curricular jungle gym that children could enter in varied ways, now there was just that ladder and its inevitable result, an academic hierarchy of children.

The teacher was loving and supportive of all her children. But given the district's, and the school's, push toward accountability, that benchmark ladder was important; the fact that young children have diverse resources and learning pathways, in addition to varied timetables, was not important. This curricular ladder took place against that pervasive "achievement gap" discourse, which assumed a homogenized group of low-performing children of color, especially Black children. Certain neighborhood children seemed to have heard this talk, particularly those the school labeled "bright"; they assumed, from Day 1, that Ta'Von would need help—he wasn't an equal.

Thus, from Ta'Von's very first days as a kindergartener, he faced his peers' superficial reading of him, and I, a researcher but also, as he said, "my friend from preschool," had to pay attention. To illustrate these peers' early enacted assumptions, and, also, how this inquiry arose, I take you now into Ta'Von's first days in kindergarten.

As you enter, you may notice right away how Ta'Von searches for connections to his new classmates. He smiles at everyone and makes friendly overtures like "How old are you? [pause for the response] I'm five too!" Still, the stiffness of his body as he sits and his perpetual smile raises the possibility that Ta'Von, like the fictional Milo, is all shook up. Another indicator is his pleasure at seeing me—the recipient of a tight hug and a whispered "I knew you'd come." I seemed of no great interest in preschool; but a familiar face in this new space is welcomed. At this time of unease but social optimism, you witness the following event:

The kindergarteners have gone to a second-grade classroom to meet their "buddies." (Ta'Von soon figures out that "buddies" no longer has its pre-school meaning of "friends to play with"; it means "older student to help.") Ta'Von's buddy, Wyatt, a white child from the surrounding neighborhood, looks at Ta'Von and asks, "Are you hot lunch?" (He is.) Wyatt says he is "cold lunch."

Back from the kindergarten now, having just witnessed this event, you may wonder what was behind Wyatt's question, as I did at the time. Indeed, I sensed a relational border steeped in institutional history. With the passage of time, I noted how this relational border was strengthened by recurrent school prac-tices. Ta'Von's kindergarten teacher used the distinction as an opportunity for groups of children to stand and be counted (the many bring-your-own "cold lunch" kids vs. the handful of eat-the-school's-food [government-subsidized] "hot lunch" kids). Except for one white child, the hot lunch kids comprised the minoritized children who rode a bus to this out-of-neighborhood school. Moreover, in the lunchroom, the cold lunch kids quickly sat down, taking the seats at the front of each long table, and opening their decorated lunch boxes; the hot lunch kids waited in line, moved a plain tan tray down the cafeteria counter as the lunch ladies made sure each child got the often-cold food on of-fer, and then sat down near the back of the table. Thus, the hot lunch kids were the last to go out for the short lunch recess.

As institutional routines and structures became familiar, I could read that "lunch" episode as a child contributing to a racialized peer border. Wyatt read Ta'Von's appearance—he had nothing else to go on. As schooling evolved, related peer readings occurred and re-occurred over the course of the project; these were mediated not only by lunch category but by, for example, hairstyle (Ta'Von's braids), peer-valued possessions (e.g., Ta'Von's use of the school bub-bler vs. neighborhood children's private [and decorated] water bottles), and, most significantly, peer-judged academic competence, that is, the assumption that Ta'Von would need help.

Related experiences within childhoods have been told by varied Black writ-ers, among them, Langston Hughes and W.E.B. Du Bois (see Tolson, 2008 for references and excerpts). Nancy Tolson (2008, p. 4) refers to these recounts as "racial awakening" stories or, more bluntly, "racial reality slap[s]." They demonstrate how race matters in childhood worlds. This seems particularly so in classrooms like Ta'Von's—ones in which minoritized children are indeed a numerical minority (Benner & Crosnoe, 2011; Tatum, 2017; Wilson & Rodkin, 2011).

In the sections ahead, I first explain the theoretical tools that guided my construction of Ta'Von's case. Then, after describing the data set, I highlight selected institutional policies and practices, illustrating how they played themselves out in Ta'Von's schooling, drawing from his kindergarten and second-grade experiences. As I will illustrate, literacy and testing practices, and their underlying learning ideology, contributed to racialized peer borders and, also, to the infusion of the so-called achievement gap into the peer worlds children constructed.

Conceptual Tools

To understand the complexity of children's racial relations with others, I called on the conceptual tools of three distinct but compatible perspectives to inform my query: Childhood Studies, Deficit Discourse, and Sociocultural Learning. In the following, I discuss these perspectives, linking them to each other and to studying Ta'Von's experience.

Childhood Studies

Paying close attention to peer relations implicitly acknowledges the agency of children as social beings. Dominant research perspectives on school children have considered them, not as full human beings, but as current or future products of the socializing (including the pedagogic) methods of adults. The interdisciplinary field of Childhood Studies (Corsaro, 2017; James & James, 2008; Thorne, 1993) is fundamentally about the relationship between societies' social construction of childhood, including assumptions about a "normal" and a "good" child, and children's own active interpretation of their experienced worlds. Corsaro (2017) argues that, in community gatherings like schools, children's interpretations happen in the communal activity of a peer culture. This view highlights how children appropriate, reinvent, and recontextualize in peer worlds discourses and structures from the adult world, including discourse about the so-called achievement gap. Children, adults may forget, are listening.

Deficit Discourse

Discourse has to do with the use of language, or, more broadly, communication in the enactment of a social practice (Street, 2001). The medium might be some combination of oral or written language, visual image, auditory signs, or bodily movement. Language and other semiotic choices represent and, at the same time, produce an interpreted world (Blommaert, 2005; Hall, Evans, & Nixon, 2013; Mauter, 2008). In this way, power and inequalities are constructed through dominant discourses, in which social roles and positions are enacted and their underlying values and beliefs indexed.

In this chapter, the discourse of interest has to do with the longstanding and structurally embedded ideology assuming the language and learning deficiencies of minoritized children (Garcia & Otheguy, 2017). In Ta'Von's district, the discourse of the so-called achievement gap between white and Black children was pervasive. Its underlying ideology of learning and knowledge was behavioristic, its rationale resting on test scores: knowledge is having the correct answer; "bright" children have more right answers (especially, in the kindergarten, about letters and sounds).

In Ta'Von's school journey, children's challenges in literacy learning could be observed across racial categories, but the district's "gap" discourse singled out Black vs. white children. The discourse is deficit-oriented, privileging children who are primed to climb up a narrow skills ladder, as mediated by literacy tests, which, in Ta'Von's district, began right before or at the very start of kindergarten. The test-identified "bright" children were all from the surrounding neighborhood, no doubt aided, said Ta'Von's teacher, by the networking of neighborhood parents who prepared their children for the tests they knew were to come.

From the beginning of school, then, the groundwork for the expected "gap" was laid. Its roots were deep in the city's long history of racial segregation and its continuation was in the schools themselves. In Ta'Von's school, the neighborhood children deemed "bright," as a result of test performance, could themselves act toward Black children in accord with the discourse of the "gap," as will be illustrated. This occurred during the very opening days of school, when the children had only Ta'Von's physical features as semiotic material for reading him. Raciolinguistic scholars Rosa and Flores (2017) emphasize the reality-producing power of white listeners to non-white communicators, and this was visible and audible in Ta'Von's journey. His case thus materializes the raciolinguistic conception of language and race as co-constructed; undergirding the social concept of "race" was an ideological concept of language deficiency, whether oral or written.

Sociocultural Learning

In preschool, the reigning ideology of learning was notably different. In that institution, children were viewed as learning by engaging in playful and/or creative activity over time, getting guidance through reciprocal interaction with teacher and peers. Learning is what human beings do, at different paces, in different ways. We are all learners. In its essence, this is a sociocultural view of learning (Miller & Goodnow, 1995; Rogoff, 2003; Vygotsky, 1978). In schools, along with learning whatever is entailed in accomplishing an activity, children also learn about social roles and social status, expected actions, and the kinds of knowledge and, indeed, human beings most valued (Miller & Goodnow, 1995).

So, if a child is read by certain peers as not bright, then that child may be denied respectful peer inclusion in an event's interaction—that is, in reciprocal involvement; in essence, that child is being denied opportunities to learn. The dynamic relationship among institutional policies and practices, peer respect (i.e., reciprocity), and opportunity to learn was evident in Ta'Von's full case history. Also evident, though, was his resistance to being disrespected, his own responsiveness to others, along with his strong sense of racial identity.

In the following, I elaborate on the source of the illustrative vignettes to come, and then, using those vignettes, I demonstrate the superficial peer reading of Ta'Von. Next, I turn directly to exemplifying the major research finding presented herein: the dynamic link between institutional policies and practices, peer inclusion, and opportunities to learn. I'll concentrate on the concept of "help": Who is seen as needing help? Who offers help to whom? What is the nature of "help"?

Ta'Von, the Journey, and the Data Set

Accompanying Ta'Von on his journey over the years yielded multiple notebooks for each of his classrooms. Notebooks were compiled of my fieldnotes (based on observational jottings) integrated with transcribed audiotapes of Ta'Von's interactions with others and coordinated with his written products and other relevant materials. The main notebooks were for preschool, kindergarten, and second grade. (Ta'Von's first-grade teacher had a serious accident; I did not observe the classroom substitutes, but I kept visiting Ta'Von for lunch and recess.) In all, I had 22 hours of audiotaped interactions over a 4-month period in the preschool, 50 hours during 5 months in the kindergarten, and 56 hours over a 5-month period in the second grade.

For each grade-level fieldwork notebook (or notebooks), I compiled a thematic notebook, after studying the data inductively. In this way, I constructed the interplay between key themes of opportunity to learn, peer interaction, and societal and institutional discourse, policies, and practices. It is the sense of that interplay that I aim to capture below. (A more thorough discussion of methodology is found in Dyson, 2021.)

In the sections to follow, I first consider how Ta'Von was initially read by certain neighborhood children in the kindergarten and his response to that reading. His peers responded to varied aspects of his being (e.g., his physical features, his possessions, and his direct way of reaching out to connect with others). For this chapter's purpose, I emphasize assumptions of certain children about Ta'Von's academic smarts (or their lack). Then, I turn to the relational consequences of three dominant institutional practices. My intention is to illustrate the human consequences of a superficial reading of, and by, children, focusing on the concept of peer help.

I begin in the kindergarten. Ta'Von came to dislike kindergarten (although he quite liked composing). As he explained to me, in preschool, "you can play inside and out," but in kindergarten, one does not play. You "do literacy centers and math centers." And "you have to learn. We do." That strong sense of obligation to learn school-valued "basics" is reflected in the vignettes below.

"If You Need Help, Just Ask": Reading Ta'Von's Cover

It is the first day of school. Everyone has by now found their name tag, which marks their place in a set of five rectangular tables. Soon they will be assigned partners with whom to visit the day's preschool-like centers (before those dominant literacy and math centers take over). Ta'Von's partner is a neighborhood boy, Craig. "How old are you?" asks Ta'Von. And when Craig says that he is 5, "We're the same age!" says the delighted Ta'Von.

The "we" in Ta'Von's response is important. Me and Craig, he was saying, "we" are both 5-year-old kindergarteners. This search for connections characterized Ta'Von's response to others. Soon, though, the relationship between Craig and Ta'Von was repositioned as Craig seemed to assume a position as Ta'Von's monitor and helper. For example, in the puzzle center, Ta'Von quickly chose a familiar alphabet puzzle. Craig, however, did not choose a puzzle but sat and watched Ta'Von. After a while, Craig began anticipating what piece Ta'Von would need and providing it.

"I can help," said Craig.

"I don't want you to help," responded Ta'Von.

When Craig left, Ta'Von expressed his exasperation to me. "Why did he try to help me?"

Craig was not the only one who offered to "help" Ta'Von. Other soon-to-be-identified "bright" children did as well. For example, the first time Ta'Von was to use a classroom computer (which he had also used in preschool), his peer Seth told him, "Ask me if you need help." Craig and Seth might well have seen themselves as kind and helpful, just as they should be. The question is, why was Ta'Von the object of this assumption of needed help?

The offering of help to, or the ignoring of, Ta'Von persisted throughout the project. From the first day of kindergarten on, Ta'Von was situated as lower on the academic ladder by children who assumed their own greater competence, even before testing began. Consider Bridget, sitting beside Ta'Von, who saw the teacher Ms. O. help Ta'Von with forming the letters of his name (as this left-handed child had been using his right hand). She asked what Ta'Von was doing in kindergarten since he didn't even know how to write his name. Ms. O. responded that he *could* write his name; he was just learning a new way to write it, just like she was, and Ms. O. moved over to help Bridget. (Ms. O.'s response did not keep Bridget from telling others that Ta'Von couldn't write his name.)

Since this negative view of Ta'Von's competence began on the first day of school, there is a strong sense that the "achievement gap" discourse pervading the district was known by at least some neighborhood children; whiteness and economic privilege were the ideological norm of the "bright" children. Nonetheless, before highlighting the three institutional practices and their consequences, I offer a thought-provoking counter-example of an affirmed Ta'Von in peer relations.

The example is drawn from Ta'Von's relations with a small group of children of color; included in this group was his friend Vida, a recent immigrant from Iran, whom he assumed was Black, and Nia, who was categorized as "mixed." None of these children were members of the designated "bright" students. The illustrative vignette reveals these children's reciprocity as communicators; moreover, as the activity unfolds, the children's composing becomes embedded in their talk and responsive play. In this way, the children's writing is stretched and their intentional action—their agency—is made relevant to the newly emphasized writing medium. It is as if, in this classroom context, situated resegregation is necessary for reciprocal learning and, moreover, for inducing a playful context for extended story-making. I'll move out of the way so you, dear readers, can listen.

> It is late fall when Ta'Von, Vida, and Nia, sitting side-by-side that day, begin their assigned composing task—to describe a holiday celebration in their family. The three begin by drawing as they talk about their holidays. The children's reciprocity is clear, as they respond to each other, help each other, but single out no one as the academic leader. Nia, for example, asks Ta'Von to explain their task again, and, later, Nia tells Ta'Von to put spaces between written words. Ta'Von helps both children spell by sounding a word out with them, something he himself was just beginning to do.
>
> When Ms. O. tells the children to turn to their *writing*, each composes straightforward sentences referencing the drawing (and talking) they have just done. Ta'Von's are:
>
> *I Me SeuBatnig Brdan* [I am celebrating my birthday (he reads *am* for *me*.)]
> *... And I me seubatnig Kimis.* [And I am celebrating Christmas.]
> (Spaces added for ease of reading)

When the children return to drawing and talking, they become quite playful. And that playful talk and drawing stretches Ta'Von's brief sentence
about his birthday into a dramatic (and funny) story:

Ta'Von is drawing his present on a large table with a birthday cake. Nia
and Vida each have a large table with food too, and each is drawing people dancing—Nia's people are dancing for Christmas, Vida's for Nowruz (a
traditional Iranian holiday). Now, in response to Ta'Von's teasing, Nia and
Vida align themselves in social space:

Nia:	These two [people in my picture] are dancing.
Ta'Von:	These two are dancing and kissing!
Nia:	I said they're dancing.
Ta'Von:	They're kissing too.
Nia:	[No they're not.
Vida:	//Uh uh. (indicating "No")
Ta'Von:	That's my present [drawn box on edge of depicted table]. It's falling down. (with urgency) So I'm gonna catch it. Oh no! My present!! …
	It came down here on my head … hard, and it hurted bad, and I had to
	[go to the hospital!
Nia:	//go to the hospital!
	Oo::!
Ta'Von:	Yeah. And then I got some bones squished out of me. And then I got my bones back in because they grew back in. And then when I didn't have a lot of bones in me? I was flat.
Nia:	Bones don't grow back in.
Ta'Von:	Then I'm still going to be flat then….
Nia:	(drawing dancing at Christmas) Ta'Von, you always dance with me.
Vida:	Then we all dance and eat.

(event reported in full in Dyson, 2021)

Ta'Von and his tablemates improvised on their celebratory "reports," which
became present-day play on paper. Their detailed stories needed responsive
peers, and other semiotic tools—drawing, talk, and play, to become more detailed. If the teacher had felt free to listen and talk with the children beyond her
task of helping them with the encoding of words, there might have been more
story to retell and to play out with composing, say, about "The Flat Birthday
Boy." Nonetheless, in interacting together, the children gained experience telling and semiotically representing their stories.

In the extended vignette, reciprocal relations and playfulness contextualized an official assignment and, thereby, infused it with social and cultural

meaning. Those relations existed among these children, all outside the official "bright" label. Given the racialized borders among children, I wondered about their consequences for opportunities to learn. The institutional practices that informed these consequences involved: (a) testing, including the nature and timing of tests and their impact on curricular goals; this provides the basis for the official labeling of children; (b) the designated seating or configuration of children, particularly, distributing the "bright" children among the class and its ramifications for "helping"; and (c) the official assignment of collaborative projects that inadvertently encouraged unofficial, uncollaborative interactions.

Confirming Helpers and Helpees: Persistent Testing of Academic Benchmarks

As illustrated earlier, the reading of Ta'Von as not "bright" began when kindergarten began and persisted through the project. The district required literacy testing before or at the very start of school; these confirmed the expected "achievement gap" before anyone had officially taught anyone anything (at least in terms of the expected literacy skills). Based on these tests, Ta'Von, the successful preschool learner, was ranked near the bottom of the class. This early testing and ranking makes little sense. First, as Leafgren (2015, p. 95) notes, the notion that children begin school behind "does not seem even *chronologically* [sic] possible (how do you *start* behind?), much less possible in practice."

Second, literacy is a complex social activity, inclusive of multidimensional, sociocultural practices, but the tests have an adult-centric view of a single ladder of skills. Children's steps up that narrow ladder are laid out in a series of expected benchmarks—where children should be when. Yet, within literacy practices, children will learn different skills on different timelines, following different pathways, building on culturally familiar practices and personally available resources and inclinations, recognized or not by the institution (Bussis, Chittenden, Amarel, & Klausner, 1985; Clay, 2014; Genishi & Dyson, 2009). In fact, the local state guidelines for preschools stressed that every child was a distinct "wayfarer" in preschool literacy practices (Ingold, 2007; for a description of preschool, see Dyson, 2021). Preschoolers progressed on a jungle-gym-like structure with many possible routes, unlike the primary grade children (K-2) marching up that narrow ladder of skills.

Finally, tested skills were focused on exactly that—aspects of literacy use that converted easily to testable items (e.g., letter names and sounds). These graphic items were presented without a meaningful context (i.e., children named isolated letters, rather than, for example, naming the letters of names they knew). Moreover, such items narrowed teachers' attention to perceived deficiencies in children (Au, 2016; Solomon et al., 2005). Thus, teachers could easily miss child resources upon which to build.

Ta'Von had many skills irrelevant to the testing regime: his thorough enjoyment of hearing and talking about books and even of reading them himself in his own way; his preschool-based skill of remembering and comparing characters, actions, even themes across shared books; and his interest in exploring letters and their links to peer names and beloved objects referenced in books. (He loved reading the railroad sign in a big book on trains.) Indeed, kindergartener Ta'Von learned to write with relative ease, following his own pathway, using multiple media, attending to letter patterns in displayed words, and initially selectively writing words in a planned, orally recited message. His orthographic knowledge, so dominant in those initial literacy tests, began to emerge in the second month of school.

Ta'Von was appropriating knowledge from others to guide his own exploration of how this writing worked; all the while, though, he was engaging in meaning-making. In fact, by midyear, his teacher noted that he wrote more and more inventively than the "bright" children, which implies that he himself was not bright. The "bright" children were confirmed early on by those mandated tests, which testing would only increase as Ta'Von continued his journey.

The judgment that Ta'Von was not "bright" did not change among his "bright" peers either. In schools like Ta'Von's, the "bright" children may be learning that "we" are not all learners, that "we" do not all have knowledge and talent to contribute. After all, it was they who were asked to read when, for example, classroom and hall posters appeared; it was they who could be distributed among literacy centers, which might become, for example, "Caitlin's group"; and it was they who were expected to write most fluently, not Ta'Von. Moreover, there was no sharing time in which children could learn of, and appreciate, others' composing.

Consider "bright" Benji, a child friendly to Ta'Von during lunch and recess, but one who assumed he himself was the smart one, not Ta'Von. Listen:

Benji and Ta'Von are sitting with a few girls at a round table during literacy center time. The children are to draw pictures whose names begin with letters chosen from a deck of alphabet cards. Benji selects X, and he immediately rejects the logic of the letter's inclusion:

Benji: Nothing starts with an X.
Ta'Von: X starts *x-ray*.

Benji firmly rejects this:

Benji: ...It doesn't start with an X.

Since Benji stops listening to him, Ta'Von turns to me, explaining that he learned about X on "Cookie Monster show," which he watches at his grandma's place.

(event first reported in Dyson, 2021)

Such interactions continued as Ta'Von himself continued in school. He remained generally confident in his own competence, his "smartness."

Distributing the "Bright" among the "Others": Who's Helping Whom?

"I know I'm smart," Ta'Von told me one day in the second grade, "'cause I don't copy." That comment speaks volumes about the elementary school's ideology of learning, which focused on a correct product and thus differed strikingly from that of his preschool. In that first school place, as earlier noted, learning was focused on process—on a child's participation in practice amid interaction with the teacher sometimes and almost always with peers. Even in kindergarten, Ta'Von's means of providing needed help to his reciprocating peers, his friends, was still process-focused, as when he guided the process of sounding out words with and for others. But, throughout elementary school, the "bright" children seemed to view Ta'Von as strictly a helpee. And so it was in the second grade; the by-now old pattern persisted, even as the cast of "bright" children changed.

Second-grade "bright children" were "top reading group" children. And, as was also now the pattern, they were seated strategically next to a child not so categorized. As for Ta'Von, he was seated next to Dirk, who seemed to value that "top group" label. He once said to Ta'Von, as the latter child looked through his box of books, "the books are to your ability level [and so not like mine]." Such rhetoric seems consistent with Dweck's (2013) notions of a perceived "fixed" intelligence as opposed to a "malleable" one. A notion of a genetic "fixed" intelligence was used by white elites after southern reconstruction to justify continuing to severely limit the rights and liberty of Blacks (see Gould's *The Mismeasure of Man* [1996]); this is still an operating ideology that echoes in school discourse about low-income children and those of color (Hatt, 2012; Nieto & Bode, 2018; O'Connor, 2006).

In this cultural climate, the peer "helping" practice now became consistent with a school culture tightly linked to testing, that is, to having the right answer. Indeed, in second grade, language arts units, highlighting concepts like antonyms, synonyms, and genre definitions, were the subject of unit tests, whose results were reported to the district; the evaluation of principals was linked to those test scores. How then would children "help" each other? Logically, by giving their products with the right answers, usually gifts from one child to a nearby peer perceived as less smart. Help was a gift, a power play that put the recipient in a needy position.

Ta'Von understood this way of helping as "cheating," and he never asked for "help." And he never stopped responding to others in a reciprocal way, even on academic matters. He tended to be dismissed when he did so with the "bright." Consider the following example:

> On this day, all children have a worksheet task in which they are to cut out each of the boxed contractions in one list (e.g., [can't]) and each of the boxed two-word phrases in a second list (e.g., [will not]); each list seemed to be randomly ordered. On a separate paper, they are to match contraction and word phrase. Dirk is thrilled because he has thought up a "short cut." One can just cut out each list as is and paste the two lists as they were on another paper!
>
> Dirk shows Ta'Von his short cut and expects him to follow his lead. But Ta'Von does not. He tells his seatmate that they are supposed to cut out all the little boxes and then "sort them and match them" on the new sheet.
>
> "No," says Dirk, "Just cut the paper in half."
>
> "No, you have to match them—"
>
> "Just do it like I'm doing it," Dirk firmly reiterates and goes to put his paper in the "done" pile, and Ta'Von goes back to his cutting.

Ta'Von's belief in himself, displayed from the beginning of the project, proved useful when his teacher assigned groups for collaborative projects, and it's to an example of such a project we now turn.

Promoting Official Collaboration (?): Unofficial Assumptions of Power

Ta'Von told me that he loved working with others, and observations confirmed this ... when he was able to actively participate. Dirk and Benji, like others, were not prone to giving Ta'Von maneuverable space, but, as it happened, one day his classmate Sonya did, to some extent. A neighborhood white child, she seemed to take her "smartness" for granted, like Dirk, but she was also conscious of letting others "do something," to quote her.

On the day in question, Ms. G., the second-grade teacher, had organized collaborative groups, whose assignment was a follow-up to a non-fiction piece in their language arts textbook. The groups were to use Chrome books— Chrome books! Ta'Von had *longed* to use a Chrome book (an inexpensive kind of laptop, useful primarily for internet connection); using those books, the groups were to look up information on what could be recycled and then make posters displaying their findings. Ta'Von's assigned collaborators, so to speak, were Sonya and his reading group peer, Jon—an officially "mixed" child (with a "Hispanic" father). In the following description compiled from field notes and audiotape transcriptions of that "collaboration," Sonya's assumed position and Ta'Von's persistent bids for participation are clear, as is Jon's discomfort;

he spent his time walking around the other two children, occasionally making equalitarian comments on the group's shared competence:

Sonya assumes control from the beginning of the group's work. She is the one who retrieves a Chrome book from its cart on the way to the assigned table and immediately begins to search for information. As she studies the listed possible sites, Ta'Von pulls his chair close to hers and listens carefully as she reads the website information aloud. (Jon, meanwhile, is circling their seating area offering constant critiques, e.g., "You don't need to read; we can all read.")

Ta'Von wants a turn with the Chrome book. Sonya obliges, and he scrolls down the "recycling" list for a few minutes. Then Sonya takes the laptop back. She continues reading website names, but an excited Ta'Von interrupts her. His voice is louder and higher than I have heard him in ages. Sonya had just read the name of a nearby city's recycling website:

Ta'Von: MY GRANDMA LIVES IN [that city]. *Fin*ally, we get somewhere.

Note that "we," indexing his collective sense of the group. Sonya clicks on the site, locates the recyclable items, and starts reading the paper items.

Ta'Von: Wait! I found something. No, go down. It's about aluminum cans. (He is actively participating, as he begins reading the list of aluminum items.)

Jon is still circling, repeating that "We can read."

Ta'Von: We can list the items, the recycling items. (said with eager intent)

Sonya returns to reading the paper items. but Ta'Von repeats his idea with enthusiasm:

Ta'Von: We could write this down on a poster!
Jon: We don't have a poster.
Ta'Von: We could get one.

With that comment, Ta'Von springs up and retrieves a poster paper from the pile at the back of the room. On his way back to his group, he starts moving to an inaudible rhythm.

Ta'Von: I'M CELEBRATING!! (His voice and movement exude joy.)

Ta'Von writes "Recycling" on the top of the poster. Then Sonya takes the marker and makes 3 columns: paper, cans, and bottles. Ms. G. announces that time is up for now, which Sonya reiterates to the group.

On the way back to his regular seat, Ta'Von is dancing again. "I loved that," he tells me. And that is clear.

(event first reported in Dyson, 2021)

Ta'Von had sought to participate, just as he had with others ranked above him. Unlike Jon, he was not defending his academic honor, potentially a response to Sonya's assumption of control. Ta'Von sat close to Sonya, listening and looking, seeking participation. As educational scholars would predict, finding a personally meaningful connection to the task boosted his energy level immediately. The curricular task inadvertently became "permeable" (Dyson, 1993) to his own interests and experiences. The website was for his grandma's city! He himself lived with his grandma a great deal of the time. In that city, residents were required to separate recyclable and unrecyclable trash—he would have experienced that. Wow! Not only did he get to use the Chrome Book for a little bit at least, the website connected this school task to his beloved grandma's city. He was part of the "we" of this small working group, and it was connected to a place he knew well. He spoke up with great energy. He wasn't "helping" in the second-grade sense; he was assuming his own reciprocal engagement. He mattered. That's worth dancing about.

It's also worth noting that it didn't come about for Ta'Von without persistence and confidence in his own competence, which had survived the schooling experience and the "bright" kids' "help." Other children, like Jon, seemed to be having a much harder time of it.

Toward Inclusive Classrooms Where "We" Belong

This chapter began with the fictional but very real Milo, the small child on the subway train, who, in the end, reimagined the pictures he had drawn of his fellow humans on the bus. He realized that he did not know what their lives were like, and they did not know what his was. Milo thus introduced the limits of superficial observation as a way of getting to know others. We have long known that teachers, like other adults in this society, may have deficit views of low-income and minoritized children (Barbarin & Crawford, 2006; Ladson-Billings, 2021; Rist, 1970). In this chapter, I aimed to examine Ta'Von's journey into schooling from his perspective. That journey illustrates how inequality can be constructed within childhoods themselves, as those childhoods unfold within school discourses like "the achievement gap," policies like testing based on linear ladders of skills, and practices like those that display the designated "bright" children, whose academic status may be linked to tests undergirded by anemic ideologies of literacy and of learning itself.

The "bright" children figuring into Ta'Von's experiences were not mean; they were socialized in a school system that privileges the privileged at a remarkably tender age and, at the same time, homogenizes and problematizes the so-called at-risk minoritized and low-income children. Since learning in and out of school happens within social relations, children's opportunities to be seen as competent by peers is related to their opportunities to participate in learning activities and, thereby, stretch their competence in new ways. In other words, learning is entangled with belonging—with having respectful, reciprocal relations with others as a part of the classroom community, the "we."

The dominant events where Ta'Von found such reciprocal learning were with other children of color; in this school, they needed to resegregate themselves into a lively community of learners. We all negotiate close relations with those with whom we share experiences, challenges, and personal and societal history. But if our institutions work against inclusive classroom communities, then we help construct the gap. Children appropriate and recontextualize in their own world what they observe in the adult world, and, in school, they learn what and who is valued.

Inspired by teachers I have known over the years, including Ta'Von's preschool teacher, I offer these summarizing implications for educators aiming to work toward inclusive classroom communities:

1 Classrooms, whatever their demographics, should reflect the normalcy of variation in racial and ethnic identity and in socioeconomic circumstances; this may happen through classroom talk, texts, and displayed images. Classroom meetings as open forums for child-initiated talk could provide an avenue for addressing personal and societal misperceptions.
2 Classroom talk should also reflect the normalcy of differences in interests, experiences, and the ease or difficulty one finds in varied kinds of learning. There should be no anointing of the chosen ones, so to speak, that is, the "bright." (For examples of such talk, see Ms. Sylvia in Dyson (2021), and Ms. Rita in Dyson (2003), who explicitly talked to her children about her own struggles with using different kinds of intelligences in her life.)

As for composing itself:

3 Since individuals have differing experiences and resources upon which to build, there will be variations in what is learned when. Thus, knowing students' ways of approaching composing tasks—their intentions, favored symbolic modes and compelling topics, preferred composing companions—is useful for observant teachers.
4 Composing, particularly for the very young, is multimodal in nature; children talk, draw, sing, play, and, within this symbolic activity, they write. Thus, the availability of varied resources, including semiotic modes and media, matters.

5 Among the greatest of children's resources are talk and play; playful talk among children may be channeled but should not be silenced.
6 Children as authors need an audience, so that they may enjoy, and learn from, each other. As teachers, we might model specific, appreciative feedback during classroom sharing times. To be inclusive, a classroom community should support all members. Every child has some unique experience or resource to offer and deserves respect from companions and, indeed, an opportunity to share themselves with others.

Like Milo, I found paying attention to another's life experience contributed to my own understanding of the complexities of human relations, including those of teachers and children, and how those complexities are embedded in institutions. I hope Ta'Von's story contributes to our collective reflections on how and why we might collectively work toward social and institutional change in and out of the classroom. In that way, we, following Milo, may help reimagine a more equitable and welcoming world for all.

References

Au, W. (2016). Meritocracy 2.0: High-stakes, standardized testing as a racial project of neoliberal multiculturalism. *Educational Policy, 3*(1), 39–62. https://doi.org/10.1177/0895904815614916.

Barbarin, O., & Crawford, G. M. (2006). Acknowledging and reducing stigmatization of African American boys. *Young Children, 61*(6), 79–86. https://jstor.org/stable/42729509

Bassok, D., Latham, S., & Rorem, A. (2016). Is kindergarten the new first grade? *AERA Open, 2*, 1–31. https://doi.org/10.1177/2332858415616358.

Benner, A. D., & Crosnoe, R. (2011). The racial/ethnic composition of elementary schools and young children's academic and socioemotional functioning. *American Educational Research Journal, 48*, 621–646.

Blommaert, J. (2005). *Discourse: A critical introduction.* Cambridge University Press.

Bussis, A. M., Chittenden, E. A., Amarel, M., & Klausner, E. (1985). *Inquiry into meaning: An investigation of learning to read.* Erlbaum.

Clay, M. (2014). *By different paths to common outcomes* (illustrated edition). Heinemann.

Corsaro, W. (2017). *The sociology of childhood* (5th ed.). Sage.

de la Pena, M. (2021). *Milo imagines the world* (C. Robinson, Illus.). G. P. Putnam's Sons.

Dweck, C. (2013). *Mindset: The new psychology of success.* Ballantine Books.

Dyson, A. H. (1993). *Social worlds of children learning to write in an urban primary school.* Teachers College Press.

Dyson, A. H. (2003). *The brothers and sisters learn to write: Popular literacies in childhood and school cultures.* Teachers College Press.

Dyson, A. H. (2021). *Writing the schoolhouse blues: Literacy, equity, and belonging in a child's early schooling.* Teachers College Press.

Garcia, O., & Otheguy, R. (2017). Interrogating the language gap of young bilingual and bidialectal students. *International Multilingual Research Journal, 11*(1), 52–65. https://doi.org/10.1080/19313152.2016.1258190.

Genishi, C., & Dyson, A. H. (2009). *Children, language, and literacy: Diverse learners in diverse times*. Teachers College Press and the National Association for the Education of Young Children.

Gould, S. (1996). *The mismeasure of man*. W.W. Norton & Company.

Hall, S., Evans, J., & Nixon, S. (Eds.). (2013). *Representation: Cultural representations and signifying practices* (2nd ed). Sage.

Hatt, B. (2012). Smartness as a cultural practice in schools. *American Educational Research Journal, 49*, 438–460. https://doi.org/10.3102/0002831211415661.

Ingold, T. (2007). *Lines: A brief history*. Routledge.

James, A., & James, A. (2008). *Key concepts in childhood studies*. Sage.

Kendi, I. X. (2019). *How to be an antiracist*. Penguin Random House; One World.

Ladson-Billings, G. (2021). *Culturally relevant pedagogy: Asking a different question*. Teachers College Press.

Leafgren, S. (2015). "Are you my dawg?": Socially and politically marginalized children desiring to be seen and valued by their teachers. In J. M. Iorio & W. Parnell (Eds.), *Rethinking readiness in early childhood education: Implications for policy and practice* (pp. 93–107). Palgrave Macmillan.

Marcus, G. (2015). The legacies of *writing culture* and the near future of the ethnographic form. In O. Starn (Ed.), *Writing culture and the life of anthropology* (pp. 31–51). Duke University Press.

Mauter, G. (2008). Analyzing newspapers, magazines, and other print media. In R. Wodak & R. Krzyanowski (Eds.), *Qualitative discourse analysis in the social sciences* (pp. 30–53). Palgrave Macmillan.

McCarty, T. L., & Castagno, A. E. (2018). Finding the practice in educational policy: A disciplinary genealogy. In T. L. McCarty & A. E. Castagno (Eds.), *The anthropology of educational policy* (pp. 3–22). Routledge.

Miller, P. J., & Goodnow, J. J. (1995). Cultural practices: Toward an integration of culture and development. In J. J. Goodnow, P. J. Miller, & F. Kessel (Eds.), *Cultural practices as contexts for development, no. 67, new directions in child development* (pp. 5–16). Jossey Bass.

Nieto, S., & Bode, P. (2018). *Affirming diversity: The sociopolitical context of multicultural education* (7th ed.). Pearson.

O'Connor, C. (2006). The premise of Black inferiority: An enduring obstacle fifty years post-Brown. *Yearbook of the National Society for the Study of Education, 105*(2), 316–336. https://doi.org/10.1111/j.1744-7984.2006.00088.x.

Rist, R. (1970). Student social class and teacher expectations: The self-fulfilling prophecy in ghetto education. *Harvard Educational Review, 40*, 411–451.

Rogoff, B. (2003). *The cultural nature of human development*. Oxford University Press.

Rosa, J., & Flores, N. (2017). Unsettling race and language: Toward a raciolinguistic perspective. *Language in Society, 46*(5), 621–647. https://doi.org/10.1017/S0047404517000562.

Solomon, R., Portelli, J., Daniel, B., & Campbell, A. (2005). The discourse of denial: How white teacher candidates construct race, racism, and "white privilege." *Race Ethnicity and Education, 8*(2), 147–169.

Street, B. (2001). Literacy events and literacy practices. In M. Martin-Jones & K. Jones (Eds.), *Multilingual literacies: Comparative perspectives on research and practice* (pp. 17–29). John Benjamin.

Tatum, B. (2017). *Why are all the Black kids sitting together in the cafeteria? And other conversations about race* (20th anniversary ed.). Basic Books.

Thorne, B. (1993). *Gender play: Girls and boys in school.* Rutgers University Press.

Tolson, N. D. (2008). *Black children's literature got de Blues: The creativity of Black writers and illustrators.* Peter Lang.

Vygotsky, L. S. (1978). *Mind in society.* Harvard University Press.

Wilson, T., & Rodkin, P. C. (2011). African-American and European American children in diverse elementary classrooms: Social integration, social status, and social behavior. *Child Development, 82,* 1454–1469.

2

BLACK LANGUAGE AS A LIBERATORY PRACTICE

Young Multilingual Black Children Exploring Their Cultural and Linguistic Identities

Brittany L. Frieson and Vivian E. Presiado

Classrooms in the United States have historically been sites of racial and linguistic violence as young children are socialized into white, hegemonic language practices at the cost of their communal and familial communicative repertoires (Baker-Bell, 2020; Boutte & Bryan, 2021; Johnson et al., 2017). Particularly as elementary dual-language bilingual education (DLBE) classrooms in US contexts have been perceived as an "additive space" with bilingualism, biliteracy, and cultural competence as goals (García & Kleifgen, 2018), they can be an extension of the linguistic oppression that young Black children experience in mainstream classrooms (Presiado & Frieson, 2021). The first US-based dual-language program was started in Florida in the 1960s (Flores & Garcia, 2017), influenced by Canadian immersion models that taught two languages *separately* instead of teaching them *bilingually*, paving the way for the dichotomous framing of languages that are found in US DLBE programs (Soltero, 2016). When languages are taught separately in DLBE programs, typically only standardized versions of languages are utilized for instruction, which neglects the richness of language varieties like Black Language (BL).

In a cautionary note to the field, Valdés (2018) interrogated issues of power and privilege as DLBE programs function with an Anglo/Latinx dualism, neglecting the curricular needs of Black children. For example, dominant ways of speaking undergird the linguistic categorization of speakers in DLBE programs as students are grouped as "English speakers" or "English learners," contributing to dominant narratives and anti-Black linguistic racism that seeks to erase BL and literacy practices. Recognizing the linguistic oppression present in these spaces, the purpose of this chapter is to highlight how young Black

DOI: 10.4324/9781003399155-4

American children continue to use BLs and literacies as forms of resistance toward structural anti–Black linguistic racism in multilingual spaces.

Utilizing Lyiscott's (2017) liberation literacies as a theoretical orientation, we show how young Black children draw from their cultural and linguistic identities to advocate for linguistic justice in early childhood DLBE spaces and multilingual environments. In this chapter, we also elevate and amplify the rich linguistic resources that Black children bring to multilingual spaces. Through vignettes, we feature children as teachers who offer practical implications for supporting BL as a liberatory practice, in theory and practice. Although outside of the scope of this chapter, we recognize and critique how DLBE programs structurally erase Black children's language practices. As noted, through ideologies privileging mainstream English to dichotomous instructional and curricular strategies, young Black children are being underserved and their linguistic brilliance unrecognized. Baker-Bell's (2020) description of anti–Black linguistic racism highlights the sociopolitics of curriculum, instruction, and policies Black children across PK-12 endure in schools and their daily lives. This chapter interrogates classroom spaces as sites of anti–Black linguistic racism, advocating for early childhood education that humanizes and builds on Black children's multilayered cultural and linguistic identities. In the sections that follow, we share the theoretical frameworks that guide our work, explicate our research findings through vignettes, and discuss our implications for practice.

Theoretical Orientations

Anti-Black Linguistic Racism

Historically, many educational policies have been designed and carried out to further systemically neglect the rich linguistic practices of Black children (Martínez, Martinez, & Morales, 2022). Black children have been denied the rights to their own language in schools for years, including the policing of their language practices to the omission of their linguistic repertoires throughout the curriculum (Conference on College Composition and Communication, 1974). Language policies that seek to silence the language and literacy practices of BL speakers such as those in DLBE programs reinforce whiteness and cultivate *anti-Black linguistic racism* in educational institutions as the norm. Anti-Black linguistic racism, extended by April Baker-Bell (2020, p. 2), refers to the "linguistic violence, persecution, dehumanization, and marginalization that BL speakers endure when using their language in schools and in everyday life." Despite the framing of DLBE programs as being additive spaces for communities of Color, BLs and literacies are often not centered in these spaces (Frieson, 2021), adding to the surfeit of injustice that have historically underscored the educational experiences of Black children in the United States.

DLBE programs are not an anomaly when it comes to perpetuating anti-Black linguistic racism and excluding BL speakers from its programmatic vision. Language allocation policies that specifically designate "Spanish times" and "English times" without regard for the multiplicity of Englishes and Spanishes spoken by multilingual students is problematic. The dichotomous framing of colonized ways of speaking (and this colonization is across the globe) that maintain underlying assumptions of "discourses of appropriateness" (Flores & Rosa, 2015, p. 150) seek to silence and label Black dialogic expression as illegitimate. Not only is this an extension of the historical anti-Black linguistic racism that we see constructed in many US classrooms, but this is a complete rejection of Black lives, expression, and thought (Baker-Bell, 2020).

Black Language as a Liberatory Practice

Although some Black students do internalize anti-Black linguistic racism and anti-Black messages about their languages (Baker-Bell, 2020), some students resist white supremacist values and utilize their language as a liberatory practice. As mentioned by Lyiscott (2017, p. 52), a Liberation Literacies pedagogy "asserts that as we center Black textual expressions … we center Black cultures, histories, and identities." Instead of conforming to white, colonized ways of knowing in DLBE programs, some Black students use the entirety of their linguistic repertoires as a political and ethical act to center their Blackness (Presiado & Frieson, 2021). For example, Lyiscott (2017) utilized lyrics from Lauryn Hill and Tupac Shakur in a secondary literacy unit on literary devices and critical social analysis. One of Lyiscott's students connected these lyrics to Black victims in the Black Lives Matter movement and penned a piece of poetry about himself and Trayvon Martin (p. 52). In this example, Lyiscott (2017) centered Black textual expressions as cultural artifacts that provided space for Black students to deeply connect with ongoing issues that affected their identities and everyday lives. Similarly in the early childhood classroom, liberation literacies can be achieved with young children too. For example, Presiado and Frieson (2021) illustrate how a first grader took the opportunity to share her fears about her older sister's transition to middle school. This provided her with the opportunity to reflect on her identities as a Black girl and a little sister. During this exchange, she used a wider repertoire of language using features from BL, Spanish, and white Mainstream English, to express where she felt her safe spaces were, which shifted depending on if her sister's presence was there. Although different from how Lysicott's students employed Black textual expressions, the first grader used her own "expressive vernacular arts" to protect herself and her loved ones during a pivotal moment in their lives (Richardson, 2003, p. 329). Like other scholarly literature on Black girls' critical literacies of liberation (Brown, 2009; Winn, 2011), the first grader used her own cultural discourse as a textual expression to explore the relevant social issue of Black girls feeling safe in school (Lyiscott, 2017). In this case, the student centered her identities as a liberatory practice to highlight an important issue about safe spaces in schools for Black children, particularly Black girls.

As Blackness is intertwined with Black lives and identities, utilizing Black dialogic expressions, emphasizes the importance of going beyond supposed linguistic boundaries in DLBE programs to advocate for Black children's linguistic rights and liberation. In addition, employing BL as a liberatory practice enacts Black-centric practices that defend Black lives, identities, and thought; therefore, it is a necessary lens to understand how young Black children intentionally mobilize their linguistic practices and identities to experience linguistic justice in DLBE spaces. In the subsequent section, we will share the research context and introduce the young children who sought to take up space and reclaim their various identities in multilingual spaces.

Building the Research Context

Although the vignettes in this chapter are hypothetically co-constructed, the data are informed by two qualitative studies that used vignettes to address the rich language and literacy practices of young multilingual children who participated in an elementary Spanish/English DLBE program at Parks Elementary. The constructed vignettes are juxtaposed by video and audio-recorded observations, field notes, and artifacts across our research sites. However, these vignettes are also incorporated with our own childhood memories and reflections as multilinguals. Therefore, while we draw on Jewell and Jamaal (children involved in the DLBE program at Parks Elementary), we interlace their stories with our own to create a narrative illustrative of who we know and understand them to be across multiple linguistic spaces.

Parks Elementary was located in a Midwestern, multi-ethnic, and multilingual community where the majority of the children attending the school identified as Black and Latinx. However, within their classrooms in the Spanish/English DLBE program, about half of the students were homogeneously grouped as "Spanish speakers" and the other half were designated as "English speakers." This linguistic designation overlooked the rich linguistic practices of Black/African American Language, Q'anjob'al, other indigenous Guatemalan languages, Puerto Rican Spanish, and Costa Rican Spanish speakers. The young children featured in this chapter, Jewell and Jamaal, were both in kindergarten during the study.

Jewell, a 6-year-old Black American girl, was a BL architect who often created rules to utilize her linguistic repertoire in creative ways that did not compromise her cultural and linguistic identities. Although there were times that were designated as "Spanish time" or "English time," she always employed her linguistic features in ways that surpassed the simplistic nature of DLBE classroom language policies. At any given moment, Jewell could be observed assuming the role of librarian in the biblioteca centro [library center], either telling high-energy oral stories with multiple characters or narrating her own stories from the bilingual books to her peers. As a social butterfly, she could also be seen imitating a vibrant "store manager" on the playground who told her "customers" that they needed to hurry up and make up their minds so she could go back to her casa with her family. Her bright personality continued to show at church, where she and other classmates attended, such as Jamaal, on the weekends.

Jamaal, a 6-year-old Black American boy, was a critically conscious BL artist who too resisted the hegemonic norms of the DLBE program at school and in his community. He always sought to draw from his multilayered identities to center his multiple ways of being, knowing, and doing in various contexts of his daily life. Jamaal was also keenly aware of the sociopolitical and sociocultural contexts, and often made intentional choices about how he employed various features of his linguistic repertoire. Jamaal quickly learned the formulaic phrases offered to learn Spanish features like "Como se dice" and "Yo quiero." As an animated 6-year-old, Jamaal could be seen assuming the role of a teacher who employed BL features of call and response to get the attention of his peers in his imaginative classroom during recess and children's bible study at church.

For this chapter, we heavily relied on qualitative methods of data collection utilized in previous studies to construct a hypothetical case study. Although the setting, participants, and vignettes are informed by memories, they are conceptualized from qualitative case studies that included observations, semistructured interviews, and field notes. We are also informed by our own recollection of childhood memories as a Black girl and a Latina who were enrolled in language education programs from early ages, our experiences as former elementary teachers of multilingual children, and our current roles as teacher educators. Our collaborative research undertaking of this book chapter encompasses insights from case study methodologies and counterstories (Solórzano & Yosso, 2002; Martinez, 2020).

Rooted in Critical Race Theory, counterstorytelling is a methodological tool that utilizes narrative to "theorize racialized experiences" of communities of Color, as the lives of multilingual Black American children are frequently not prioritized or omitted from narratives and critiques on DLBE programs (Martínez, 2020, p. 17). It is our hope that our counterstory serves the pedagogical functions of resisting the dominant discourse about whose linguistic repertoires are highlighted in bilingual education scholarship, encouraging community among educators of multilingual Black American children in DLBE programs, and demonstrating how we can learn about so much from young Black multilingual children in how they mobilize their language practices as a source of liberation in multilingual contexts.

Black Liberation Literacies

In subsequent sections, we illustrate how young Black children engage with Black liberation literacies in various ways. In the first example, we demonstrate how young Black and Latinx children engage with their entire linguistic repertoires to explore their identities as liberatory practices. Following, we show how liberation literacies are displayed to teachers through professional learning as political acts. Lastly, we exemplify how Black children experience liberation literacies at church where they are positioned as teachers and critical thinkers.

Playing with Multiple Identities at "Granny's Diner"

Every morning in Jewell's kindergarten classroom, students rotated biliteracy centros [centers] during the Spanish literacy block. For 20 minutes Jewell and her friends would spend time in various centros such as the biblioteca, escribir cuentos, leer solo, buddy reading, or working on biliteracy skills with their teacher, Maestra Santos, at the table. Unless students were working on targeted biliteracy skills with Maestra Santos, she provided space for them to flexibly access their entire linguistic repertoires. However, Jewell's favorite centro was imaginative play because she got the opportunity to access multiple identities. She didn't feel pressured to utilize certain linguistic features as she often slipped in and out of various characters who employed varied language practices.

In the vignette below, Jewell and her friends were elated to see that they were assigned the imaginative play centro during the last rotation of the morning. She really enjoyed ending the morning with that station, so that her friends could continue their imaginative play during recess which was directly after their Spanish literacy block. During the last few rotations, Jewell had come up with the idea to "play restaurant" (affectionately named Granny's Diner after Jewell's grandmother) and they had been working ever since toward "opening day." In the imaginative play centro, Jewell and her friends negotiated which menu items to include in their new restaurant.

Jewell: So what we gone put up here? It prolly need to be stuff our granny's cook since our restaurant name is Granny's Diner.

Rosalyn: Si, that's a good idea. Well my abuela makes a lot of comida … she make tamales, pescado, arroz con camarones, pero her casados are my favorites (rubbing her tummy to show how yummy she thinks it is).

Jewell: Ok. What kind of casados she make? Like what's in that?

Rosalyn: It depends … arroz, frijoles, salad, plátano, y carne. Es muy rico!

Jewell: Dang, that does sound good. Ok, put that up there on the menú. What else? Let's put some of my granny's stuff up there too since we both the jefés (pointing to their "jefé" nametags that they made out of construction paper during indoor recess).

Rosalyn: Ok.

Jewell: For my granny … let me think about this 'cause she can throw down (tapping the side of her forehead while laughing)! We need some chicken pastry, collards, potato salad, ribs, hot dogs on the grill … but only the burnt ones, and 'nana pudding.

Rosalyn: 'Nana pudding?

Jewell: Yeah, you know … it got cookies, bananas, pudding and whipped cream.

Rosalyn: Mmmm … I like those. Should we put other stuff on the menú?

Jewell: Yeah, but I like this 'cause our diner is different. It ain't the same boring burger and fries like other diners. We got soul food and your abuela's food. I betchu we gone have A LOT of customers 'cause this different!

In this vignette, we can see how Jewell and Rosalyn leveraged their linguistic tools through centering their identities with play. Both girls made flexible use of their linguistic repertoires by employing features of BL, Costa Rican Spanish, and white Mainstream English. For example, Jewell uses multiple features of BL (Baker-Bell, 2020) such as zero copula, regularized agreement ("It prolly need to be…"), and popular BL semantics like "throwin' down." In addition, she also employed multiple features of Costa Rican Spanish that Rosalyn used such as casados and jefés. By utilizing features of BL, Jewell rejected the dominant language ideologies of the DLBE program that ignored Black dialogic expression (Presiado & Frieson, 2021). Additionally, this vignette is also evidence of how language is closely interconnected to families and communities, further demonstrating that rejecting language is also ignoring students' identities and their families.

Further, Jewell's dialogic expression served as Black liberation in the classroom. The dishes that Jewell decided to include in the restaurant menu are grounded in the histories of Black families and Black lives, serving as a linguistic protest to what is normalized in American diners (Lyiscott, 2017). These choices serve "greater than a mere literate act" as they bring a "lens to the self," essentially exploring and writing their world of what it means "to be," and in Jewell's case, what it means to be Black in the United States (Lyiscott, 2017, p. 51).

"We the Teachers Now!": Black Liberation through Professional Learning

In addition to experiencing liberation in the classroom, Jewell's teacher also had the idea to collaborate with her students to engage in professional learning with other teachers. During a staff meeting, one of the administrators mentioned how they would like to have the teachers discuss what had been going on in the DLBE program during the next professional learning session. However, Maestra Santos mentioned that it would be an even better idea to have the students be the experts and show their work during the next professional learning session. The administrator agreed and told them to let them know how they can support them.

During the next professional learning session, Maestra Santos' students were placed in the hallway with tables where they held mini-conference sessions with teachers. Jewell shared a table with her friend Rosalyn. They decided to share a few writing samples and the menu that they made for their restaurant mentioned in the previous vignette. When the teachers came by and asked how they agreed on items from the menu, the girls stated that the menu items were their granny and abuela's favorite dishes, hence the name of the restaurant, Granny's Diner. Another teacher stopped by and asked why burgers nor chicken sandwiches were featured on the menu, all things you would find at a "typical American diner." Jewell stood taller and asserted that the diner was typical for their families and what they ate in their homes. In this moment where Jewell asserted her intentions and demonstrated that her identities as a Black American mattered, she displayed resistance toward the teacher's attempt to erase her literacies in favor of Eurocentric notions of an "American diner," which is an essential component of liberation literacies (Lyiscott, 2017). Rosalyn echoed this sentiment and said that the dishes were special to her abuela and they agreed that the diner should reflect them and not anyone else. Through this sentiment, both Rosalyn and Jewell clarified that their liberation was not intended to coddle whiteness or other tired tropes that reproduce white standards (Kynard, 2018). Their liberation literacies were a *political act*, solely for their communities and no one else. Maestra Santos overheard a lot of these conversations and beamed with pride. Not only were her students showing the brilliance of how they centered their literacies in her classroom, but also advocated for themselves and refused to compromise their multiple identities in the process.

"This Is the Ground of Miracles!": Liberation Literacies at Church

Jewell and Jamaal walked with various forms of literacies, ways of being and existing, sprinkled with voices of their ancestors shaping their language and literacy practices in school, home, and community spaces. Black textual expression and socialization of "what it meant to be Black in the United States" was often explored at Jewell and Jamaal's church (Lyiscott, 2017, p. 47). Jewell and Jamaal attended the same Black church in their community, as their intersecting identities as DLBE students spilled into their home and community spaces. Jewell and Jamaal attended service every week and were active members of their church as kindergarteners. Children at their church were often seen at the front of the congregation holding microphones or assisting with the routines, serving as ushers, musicians, or teachers to other children and the congregation, which is common among Black American religious spaces. A typical church day for the children included an early 7 am arrival to church for breakfast and conversation among church members, followed by service. The first part of service was attended by the entire congregation, and after the initial sermon, the children left to continue the weekly conversation at children's bible study. At the end of service, they reunited with friends and family.

In the following event, Jewell and Jamaal listened and danced to gospel music as the pastor and church members took their places around the room. Jamaal walked to the front of the church with choir members and was handed a microphone, while the other children played their tambourines. Jewell received fans to pass out to church members as the gospel music picked up its pace and members began to dance and sing. The church members took their seats, and the pastor began his sermon.

Pastor: Look at someone and say, "This is the ground of miracles."
Adults and children turn to someone and say: "This is the ground of miracles."
Jewell: (turns to me, Vivian, and we say to each other) "This is the ground of miracles!" Pastor: Your shout makes you triumphant against the enemy. Errbody not goin' to understand you! I am about to introduce Kairos, TIME, the time is now (Pastor looking at the clock. Jamaal and Jewell also look at the clock) …. Learn to be an advocate for God, learn how to invite your haters to church.

At their church, Jewell and Jamaal participated in body movements, gestures, visual and Black dialogic expression. The preacher often incorporated artifacts and gestures, in addition to BL features like call-and-response and testifyin', to emphasize his message during sermons (Smitherman, 1977). Artifacts, words, and movements became meaning-making tools that held stories, messages, and connections for Jewell and Jamaal to participate and create their own narratives as multilingual Black children (Lyiscott, 2017).

Liberation literacies pedagogy asserts that Black textual expressions are recognized with Black cultures, histories, and identities centered (Lyiscott, 2017).

The church space acted as an area where children were socialized and built their knowledge around their racial identity. The church was also a public platform for student participation and voice. This was evident with the way that Jewell and Jamaal were active members. They were literally handed a microphone during services to lead the congregation in song and reflection, as Jewell sometimes did when asked to report to the congregation what the children learned in bible study.

The roles of critical thinkers, teachers, and advocates continued in children's bible study. The children's bible study group had an adult leader that gradually shifted power to the children during reflection and conversation as seen in the following excerpt:

Jewell and Jamaal:	Maestra, sit here! (Vivian sit between Jewell and Jamaal at the rectangular table where about ten children sit with the adult teacher).
Bible Study Teacher:	Today we are going to have Jewell lead us in prayer and reflection (Jewell leads with the Lord's Prayer). Today we are talking about miracles and being advocates for God. Jewell why don't you take over?
Jewell:	Ok! Who wanna tell me what's a miracle?
Children:	Me!
Jamaal:	What you say? (to those that responded)
Children:	Me! (more children respond)
Jamaal:	Errbody say Miracle!
Children:	Miracle! (some children giggle)
Jamaal:	(Turns to me) Come se dice "miracle?"
Me (Vivian):	Milagro
Jamaal:	Errbody say "Milagro!"
Boy next to me:	What that mean?
Jamaal:	It mean miracle in Spanish.
Boy:	But you not Spanish.
Jewell:	We be learning Spanish at school.

This vignette highlights a multilingual space that centers Black expression while positioning children as teachers and critical thinkers. Jewell and Jamaal shifted this context by bringing in another part of their identity as multilinguals. Within this space, they were challenged by a child in the study group because they spoke Spanish, although they were not "Spanish." Their linguistic choices were used as a means to push against dominant mainstream messages about Blackness (Lyiscott, 2017). Additionally, Jewell and Jamaal's use of BL could be seen as survival literacies, or vernacular resistance toward the mainstream perpetuation of negative ideologies toward African American discourses (Richardson, 2003). Jewell and Jamaal used their language and literacy practices to explore their complex worlds, identities, and as tools for linguistic justice and liberation (Baker-Bell, 2020). The formation Jewell and Jamaal received in church was that they were "human and worthy of intellectual thought" no matter how old they were. or how they manifested their thoughts in multimodal ways or multiple languages (Lyiscott, 2017, p. 50). They were "on a ground of miracles."

Conclusion

This chapter highlighted how young Black American children used BL and literacies as forms of resistance toward anti-Black linguistic racism as they drew from their cultural and linguistic identities to advocate for linguistic justice in early childhood DLBE multilingual spaces. We can learn so much from the ways Jewell and Jamaal mobilized their languages to engage in building knowledge, and negotiating existing and new racial identities in school and community contexts (Lyiscott, 2017). As kindergarteners, they showed us that they were engaging with literacies in sophisticated ways. Drawing from the lessons that they have taught us, we have identified three practical applications for bilingual teachers in how they can best support BL as a liberatory practice in their theoretical stances and pedagogical practices.

First, we draw attention to the unique opportunities that arise in DLBE spaces that serve multilingual and multicultural children. Transformative opportunities to create liberating spaces that go beyond supposed linguistic boundaries in DLBE programs to advocate for Black children's linguistic rights and Black liberation are present. In Jewell and Jamaal's case, they blurred boundaries between their worlds. Jewell and her classmates leveraged their linguistic tools through centering their identities with play both in and outside the classroom. Jewell played diner at school and teacher at church, while Jamaal assumed the role of a pastor and a musician. We see how their teachers, both in school and the community, embraced Jewell and Jamaal's role as pedagogues and advocates. Their kindergarten teacher, Maestra Santos, went beyond "respecting the language" as many teachers often pride themselves in doing, as if respect is the end goal. Respect is not enough. What would further enhance these liberatory spaces is infusing them, intertwining school, home, and community practices. An initial, and vital step, would be for classroom teachers to engage and learn with and from the community. For too long, DLBE programs have participated in eradicating language varieties through pedagogies that replace BL with white Mainstream English as the target of instruction (Baker-Bell, 2020a). Rather, witness to the power of BL literacy practices in the community, such as the Black church, and cultivating these same practices in classrooms can be revolutionary.

Second, bilingual educators can benefit from centering Blackness. Specifically drawing from Black cultures, histories, and identities from an early childhood age calls for a new educational system where "Black students, their language, their literacies, their culture, their creativity, their joy, their imagination, their brilliance, their freedom, their existence, their resistance MATTERS" (Baker-Bell, 2020b, p. 3). Jewell and Jamaal's classroom experience could have been further enhanced if the teacher was aware of their home and community lives through personal experiences or conversations with them and their family members. To further strengthen what she had already done, their teacher could have asked the grandmas to visit the classroom, in-person or virtually, to share about their dishes. Books on family cooking, meals, and community could have been added to the classroom library. In learning about the role that Jewell and Jamaal played at church and the opportunity given to the children to serve as pedagogues could generate new knowledges and ways of engaging with literacy in multimodal ways.

Lastly, it is never too early to engage in critical conversations with children. Another common misconception among educators is that teaching children standardized forms of languages and being will "help children be successful." As Baker-Bell stated, "If y'all actually believe that using "standard English" will dismantle white supremacy, then you not paying attention" (2020b, p. 5). The same goes for other standardized forms of language, such as Spanish. Educators would benefit from critical linguistic awareness of BL and windows into broader conversations about anti-Blackness, language, identity, history, and white linguistic and cultural hegemony (Baker-Bell, 2020b). Children receive messages about what is "proper" and "improper" or "good" or "bad" from an early age, hence the importance of engaging in critical literacy in early childhood spaces (Vasquez, Janks, & Comber, 2019). Inviting students to address messages they see and hear in the school and community can help make sense of sociopolitical systems as they are questioned. Directly interrogating negative messages can contribute to changing inequitable ways of being and problematic social practices. For example, Jamaal experienced a message when a church friend questioned his use of Spanish if he was not "Spanish." A comment like that can create a "teachable moment" by addressing the relationships between language and identity.

Jewell and Jamaal provided a window into the brilliance Black children demonstrate when both in and outside of schools, perhaps away from the parameters set by pedagogical gazes and standardization. Like many classrooms, Jewell and Jaamal's teacher was also tied to "end products." Beyond these academic products, there are several opportunities and spaces where children demonstrate linguistic competence. They mobilize their language practices (e.g. call and response; semantics; multimodal and vocal communication) as a source of participation, contribution, and liberation. Jewell and Jaamal, like other multilingual and multiracial children possess multilayered cultural and linguistic identities. We witness these practices in and out of schools where many community and familial spaces are the "grounds of miracles."

References

Baker-Bell, A. (2020a). Dismantling anti-Black linguistic racism in English language arts classrooms: Toward an anti-racist Black Language pedagogy. *Theory into Practice, 59*(1), 8–21. https://doi.org/10.1080/00405841.2019.1665415.

Baker-Bell, A. (2020b). *Linguistic justice: Black Language, literacy, identity, and pedagogy.* Routledge.

Boutte, G., & Bryan, N. (2021). When will Black children be well? Interrupting anti-Black violence in early childhood classrooms and schools. *Contemporary Issues in Early Childhood, 22*(3), 232–243.

Brown, R. N. (2009). *Black girlhood celebration: Toward a hip-hop feminist pedagogy.* Peter Lang.

Conference on College Composition and Communication. (1974). *Students' right to their own language position statement.* Retrieved from https://cdn.ncte.org/nctefiles/groups/cccc/newsrtol.pdf

Flores, N., & Garcia, O. (2017). A critical review of bilingual education in the United States: From basements and pride to boutiques and profit. *Annual Review of Applied Linguistics, 37*, 14–29.

Flores, N., & Rosa, J. (2015). Undoing appropriateness: Raciolinguistic ideologies and language diversity in education. *Harvard Educational Review, 85*(2), 149–171.

Frieson, B. L. (2021). Remixin and flowin in centros: Exploring the biliteracy practices of Black Language speakers in an elementary two-way immersion bilingual program. *Race Ethnicity and Education, 25*(4), 585–605. https://doi.org/10.1080/13613324.2021.1890568.

García, O., & Kleifgen, J. A. (2018). *Educating emergent bilinguals: Policies, programs, and practices for English learners.* Teachers College Press.

Johnson, L. L., Jackson, J., Stovall, D. O., & Baszile, D. T. (2017). "Loving Blackness to death": (Re)imagining ELA classrooms in a time of racial chaos. *The English Journal, 106*(4), 60–66.

Kynard, C. (2018). Stayin woke: Race-radical literacies in the makings of a higher education. *College Composition and Communication, 69*(3), 519–529.

Lyiscott, J. (2017). Racial identity and liberation literacies in the classroom. *The English Journal, 106*(4), 47–53.

Martinez, A. Y. (2020). *Counterstory: The rhetoric and writing of critical race theory.* Champaign, IL: Conference on College Composition and Communication/National Council of Teachers of English.

Martínez, R. A., Martinez, D. C., & Morales, P. Z. (2022). Black lives matter versus *Castañeda v. Pickard*: A utopian vision of who counts as bilingual (and who matters in bilingual education). *Language Policy, 21*(3) 1–23.

Presiado, V. E., & Frieson, B. L. (2021). "Make sure you see this": Counternarratives of multilingual Black girls' language and literacy practices. *Literacy Research: Theory, Method, and Practice, 70*, 1–20.

Richardson, E. B. (2003). *African American Literacies.* Psychology Press.

Smitherman, G. (1977). *Talkin and testifyin: The language of Black America* (Vol. 51). Wayne State University Press.

Solórzano, D. G., & Yosso, T. J. (2002). A critical race counterstory of race, racism, and affirmative action. *Equity & Excellence in Education, 35*(2), 155–168. https://doi.org/10.1080/713845284.

Soltero, S. W. (2016). *Dual language education: Program design and implementation.* Heinemann.

Valdés, G. (2018). Analyzing the curricularization of language in two-way immersion education: Restating two cautionary notes. *Bilingual Research Journal, 41*(4), 388–412. https://doi.org/10.1080/15235882.2018.1539886.

Vasquez, V. M., Janks, H., & Comber, B. (2019). Critical literacy as a way of being and doing. *Language Arts, 96*(5), 300–311.

Winn, M. T. (2011). *Girl time: Literacy, justice, and the school-to-prison pipeline.* Teachers College Press.

3

EXAMINING THE AESTHETICS OF BLACK WORKING-CLASS CHILDHOODS IN LITERATURE FOR CHILDREN

Roberta Price Gardner

In teacher education, the movement for diverse children's literature is increasingly being embraced, as preservice and in-service teachers acknowledge the importance of all children seeing themselves and their experiences represented in literature. Sims Bishop's (1990) seminal essay, which describes her often used but uncited metaphor that children's literature should serve as mirrors, windows, and sliding glass doors, has become foundational knowledge educators use to select literature for classroom libraries to implement culturally relevant and responsive pedagogies. However, Bishop's metaphor is also becoming too easily absorbed and simplified, particularly in an anti-Black capitalistic society. The visibility of the Black Lives Matter Movement has influenced many institutional sectors, including helping to amplify decades-long movements to counter white supremacy in children's literature. As a result, children's literature featuring Black representations is more visible and accessible in the mainstream marketplace. According to the Cooperative Children's Book Center (CCBC), in 2020, 441 books (11.9%) of all books published featured primary characters who were Black (Cooperative Children's Book Center, 2018). Despite the increased visibility of Black representation, a hyperinvisibility of working-class representations simultaneously exists. For example, although award-winning books, such as *Last Stop on Market Street* (De la Peña et al., 2015) and *Saturday* (Mora, 2019), vibrantly reflect Black working-class childhood experiences, these books are exceptions in the field of contemporary children's literature that continues to cater to the aspirational and ideological value systems of a shrinking middle class.

DOI: 10.4324/9781003399155-5

Racialized Class Discourse in Children's Literature

Socioeconomic status is variously defined and ascribed; however, it is never race or gender neutral. For example, this chapter is written in US history when far too many Black and Brown families were experiencing a significant retraction in attaining and maintaining middle-class status (Nopper & Pattillo, 2021). Moreover, conscious and unconscious mental images, biases, and character traits associated with people, geographies, communities, and institutions are associated with race and social-economic categories (Lei & Bodenhausen, 2017). These ideologies are intertwined with reader response and the social, historical, and political contexts of lived experiences (Brooks & Browne, 2012).

Notwithstanding whisper cultures and Title I designations, social class remains a significant silence in education, including in children's literature. Like the larger educational structure, a middle-class default is suffused through every child's literature dimension, structure, and process. One reason is that picture books are market-based commodities and cost-prohibitive for many working-class teachers, teacher educators, and families. Therefore, authors and publishers inevitably appeal to the market economy. Many themes, values, ideologies, material culture, and plot structures subscribe to a middle-class default (Forest et al., 2015; Jones, 2008). As such, despite significant growth overall in publishing diverse books, contemporary children's literature remains oriented toward whiteness and middle-classness.

Throughout this chapter, social class is referenced concerning traditional indicators like income and occupation (Blau & Duncan, 1967) and opportunities for leisure and play, language, dress, and material objects (Bourdieu, 1986). Emphasis is placed on how racialized class and gender are visualized and storied through visual and verbal rhetoric. Racialized class and gendered semiotics are noted through the absence and presence of visual objects and material culture within homes, neighborhood spaces, and cultural and racialized iconography. They are also reflected through the values, actions, and language of characters, racial composition of settings and geographic landscapes, and the naming conventions of geographic locales. Therefore, when Sims Bishop's metaphor is cited, it is rarely applied with an intersectional understanding (Crenshaw, 1991) of representation and identity.

I assert that a substantive use of Sims' metaphor as a methodology and selection tool in literacy teacher education includes engaging in close reflective readings of culturally conscious books and asking guiding questions to expand racialized, class, and gendered consciousness. As McNair and Edwards (2021) assert,

> Bishop has given the field of literacy at least two important gifts: an accessible analogy that articulates the value of all children seeing themselves and

others in their literature and the need to look closely at the literature for consideration of issues related to authenticity and the cultural details that make bodies of work such as African American children's literature distinct.

(p. 210)

Throughout this chapter, educators are invited to embrace Bishop's provocation to "look closely," at the visual semiotics of a Black working-class childhood experience in the award-winning picture book *Saturday* (Mora, 2019). In highlighting the racialized semiotics in this book, teachers are encouraged to explore the following question: how is this Black working-class childhood experience made visible, voiced, and thus validated?

Theoretical Framework

African American children's literature is a critical genre of Black visuality and an effective method historically and contemporarily for countering anti-Blackness in society and school curricula. This visual analysis of class centers on Black Critical Theory (BlackCrit) (Dumas & Ross, 2016) because it is a theory that explicitly addresses anti-Blackness in a racist society. As Dumas and Ross explain,

> BlackCrit, confronts the specificity of antiblackness as a social construction, as an embodied lived experience of social suffering and resistance, and perhaps most importantly, as an antagonism, in which the Black is a despised thing-in-itself (but not a person for herself or himself) in opposition to all that is pure, human(e), and white.

(p. 416–417)

As Dumas and Ross note, BlackCrit acknowledges anti-Blackness as a structural and ideological force and its role in shaping and influencing lived experiences. Anti-Blackness, therefore, is not simply having racist sentiments about Black people; it includes the ways anti-Blackness is rooted in institutions, policies, and geographies. It is important to note that while most educators are unlikely to encounter the overt deprecating images of anti-Black racism that existed in children's literature of the early nineteenth-century literature, teachers should be aware of how the residue of anti-Blackness continually manifests, circulates, and is revised in literature for children through an anti-Black selective tradition. The anti-Black selective tradition in literature is defined as "the historical and continued practice of omitting, limiting, tokenizing, and disregarding Blackness, including Black voices, visualities, subjectivities, and, by extension, Black people's ways of knowing, being in, and narrating the world" (Gardner, 2020, p. 9). Educators must, therefore, ask which Black childhood experiences are reflected in their curriculum and think deeply about what kind of anti-Black cultural work they hope for Black representations in children's literature to do.

The past is instructive for understanding historical practices and the continuity of knowledge and care that should be considered part of the ideological framing of representations of Black people and their experiences in literature for children. In 1920, W.E.B. Dubois, the preeminent Black sociologist, philosopher, and educator, cocreated *The Brownies' Book* (1920–1921). This periodical was one of the earliest and most important contributions to African American children's literature. *The Brownies' Book* featured stories, photographs, and imagery depicting Black childhood in all its complexities and veracity, e.g., participating in silent racial protest, playing instruments, performing in plays, playing games, etc. It provided Black families and Black child readers with access to respectful representations to counter Black face minstrelsy and grotesque representations and caricatures that dehumanized Black children and Black people.

These visualities of sophistication and racial uplift were central and necessary. Many images featured Black people in fine clothing with access to wealth and middle-class status. The representations explicitly disrupted the visual caste of enslavement and Blacks as cheap labor. Representations of middle-class childhoods reflect the reality and range of Black childhood experiences; at the same time, however, any over-emphasis of representations of middle-classness can usher in notions of Black respectability. Maintaining such visualities is a form of stigma management (Crockett, 2017). Stigma management and the erasure and exclusion of diverse Black experiences and voices place boundaries around Black humanity, e.g., which Black experiences and which Black people are worthy of narration and who and what experiences and realities should be validated and respected.

However, the methods, messages, and modes for articulating Black perspectives and narratives of liberation shifted during The Black Arts Movement (BAM). The BAM was started in 1965 by Amiri Baraka after the assassination of Malcolm X. Artistic expression through music, literature, theatre, and visual art were cultural nationalist pursuits created in response to anti-Black violence. Ideologies of Black pride, cultural sovereignty, and artistic expression were central literary themes explored during this era. Some of the prominent intellectual artists who developed literature during the BAM include Maya Angelou, Nikki Giovanni, and James Baldwin. African American children's literature was a key medium for these expressions. Black children, particularly children representing working-class communities, served as critical symbolic and political subjects for articulating ideas of cultural sovereignty. Aesthetic choices in hairstyles, clothing, and settings were visual and literary forms of Black consciousness featured in photographic and picture books. Raised fists, a prominent symbol of Black pride and solidarity, and African artifacts were also iconographic symbols featured in African American children's books like *Black Means* (1970). This imagery largely resisted conservative middle-class representations of assimilation and Black respectability. Authors and illustrators such as John Steptoe, Nikki Giovanni, and June Jordan created literature that included working-class visual landscapes and characters whose sentiments were enlivened and flourished using the authentic syntax and cadence of Black language. *My Brother Fine with Me* (Clifton & Barnett, 1975), and *Uptown* (Steptoe, 1970), are books that reflect the nuanced everydayness of Black working-class childhoods. Black children are featured within their communities dreaming, playing, solving problems, living, and simply being in unremarkable universal class contexts that are simultaneously Black.

Many non-Black authors have attempted to create culturally relevant books, to resist anti-Blackness. However, Sims found that many "well-meaning" white authors also created overt or subliminal narratives that, more than anything else, perpetuated anti-Blackness and helped perpetuate stereotypically biased characterizations of Black childhoods. For example, the shadow narrative (Dávila, 2011) in *Ben's Trumpet* (Isadora, 1979) featured a Black boy living in a low-income community. Ben, the central character, plays an imaginary trumpet throughout most of the story. Unfortunately, as Moore (1985) asserts, Ben remains largely invisible to a cast of neighborhood "friends" and various family members who are uninterested in Ben or each other. For example, Ben's sibling is a baby who is unclothed and unattended, and each family member Ben plays for is ambivalent to his "playing." They are unvoiced, and neither interact with Ben or each other. These overt and subtle moves potentially propagate static images of Black families. Rachel Isadora, the author, sadly reinscribes stereotypes that render Black childhood in low-income communities as sites of deprivation and victimization caused by noncaring communities and fostered by parental and familial neglect.

The continued presence of white authors writing about the Black experience within and outside of class difference (no matter how universal the story) reifies structural marginalization and economic inequality in children's publishing. Philosophically, it also diminishes the Black gaze (Campt, 2021), emphasizing the importance of what Blackness brings to a story as a way of knowing, being, and narrating. Black authors and illustrators who have working-class lived experiences and the accompanying Black consciousness are best suited to create uncompromised narratives that are authentic and respectful since they "circulate their own culturally specific modes of literacy learning and values" (Richardson & Ragland, 2008, p. 31). These authors know "what is going on" and often reveal cultural nuances that sound, look, and feel like they should.

Therefore, teachers must understand racial logics and (il)literacies that students socially and culturally possess to decipher any biases and assets and engage with the range of reading and responses evoked when reading culturally conscious books (Gardner, 2017). For example, dual address which is the ability to read and engage children in book discussions that include topics and plot lines that have both universal childhood experiences and complex issues associated with social identities and critical consciousness related to race, class, gender, ability, and more, is an important skill for teachers (Reay, 2020). Having the dexterity and knowledge to engage in dual address helps teachers resist simplistic or superficial approaches to Sims' call for mirrors and windows. Such knowledge and dispositions also support teachers' ability to respond to literary encounters associated with children's emerging understandings of social hierarchies associated with race, class, gender, sexuality, and other identities. Additionally, it respects their social realities and cultural assets. As Tiffany Nyachae (2021) suggests, culturally relevant literature reading engagements have more depth when teachers plan for and guide critical dialogue, particularly discussions that connect literature to communal, school, neighborhood contexts, and current events.

In what follows, I analyze the award-winning picture book *Saturday* (Mora, 2019) to highlight specific visual rhetoric and literacies of Black working-class childhoods embedded within the book. I highlight how these images help make racialized class and gender elements legible in what, on the surface, appears to be a melting pot book. I begin with a short synopsis of the book. Next, I discuss representational characteristics and the aesthetic and cultural features within the book. I conclude with implications and guiding questions for using visuals to expand critical conversations related to anti-Blackness and social class.

Picturing Black Working-Class Childhoods

Saturday (Mora, 2019) is a vibrant picture book that explores a day in the life of Ava and her mother on their favorite day of the week, Saturday. The day begins with Ava and her mother anticipating the line-up of activities they typically pack into their one day of leisure and family time. Today was a special Saturday because they would end the day with a "bus ride across town for a one-night-only puppet show" (n.p.). Ava's mother's work schedule and the temporal demands of labor and family time are an underlying theme within the book since Ava's mother worked Sunday, Monday, Tuesday, Wednesday, Thursday, and Friday. Saturday was, therefore, "the day they cherished." The book's narrative structure highlights the itinerate retreats Ava, and her mother fit into their limited leisure time, e.g., going to the hairdresser, the library, and the park are activities they engage. As they traverse from place to place, they rely on walking and public transportation.

The endpapers, which are pages that may include art, and or words, that are glued to the inside cover and back of a picture book, are essential tools and peritextual features for pedagogical expansion (McNair, 2021). They provide additional insight into the nature of their activities on other Saturdays. The endpapers also provide additional social and cultural insight into Ava's family structure. For example, details about familial support networks are included on the endpapers that spotlight the family calendar created and maintained by Ava. Although it is not explicitly addressed in the storyline, by all accounts, Ava's mother is a hard-working single mother. No other parental figure is mentioned anywhere in the book. They feature a weekly calendar indicating that Ava will be "w/Gma" on one Wednesday because her mother will be at a "P.T. conf." On another day, the calendar notes that her "auntie" will be picking Ava up "@ 2:00" (n.p.).

Ava's unnamed mother represents a composite of many Black working-class single mothers who create family structures and kinship networks that are not aligned with traditional middle-class ideas of the so-called nuclear family. Her mothering disposition is dutiful, cheerful, and doting. Her mother is actively involved in Ava's well-being and education, e.g., attending school conferences and using her only day off to curate, encourage, and cultivate creative and intellectually stimulating activities with her daughter. The social and political hierarchies related to the institution of motherhood and parenting writ large are freighted with gendered forms of racialization and social class. These ideas continue to stigmatize Black single mothers by constructing them as inherently unfit, negligent, uncaring, and irresponsible, among other negating biases (Roberts, 2002). Therefore, this depiction of Ava's mother is an affirming characterization that counters the controlling images and anti-Black tropes of single Black mothers cultivated in the social-political and public imagination of the past (see, e.g., Moynihan, 1965).

Racialized Class Aesthetic Characteristics

At the beginning of the book, as Ava and her mother envision their plans for the day, her momma is barefoot, wearing a headwrap, a jersey, and sweatpants. Mora's representation of Ava's mother in a headwrap with t-shirt and sweatpants resists the visualities of respectability that were previously necessary to counter the pejorative images of Black people in the nineteenth and early twentieth centuries children's literature. It is not inconsequential that Oge Mora is a Black illustrator and a cultural insider with working-class roots. For example, Mora's artwork is influenced by the late art activist Aminah Robinson whose colorful murals she saw in her youth growing up in Columbus, Ohio. Mora's whimsical misshaped illustrations reflect community sentiment and mimic the aesthetic vibrations she witnessed in her childhood neighborhood. Such joyful visualities and points of reference are not typically attributed to Black working-class communities.

While the park proved to be too noisy, it was a space that affirmatively reflected Black placemaking and creativity (Hunter et al., 2016). Although structural racism is not explicitly problematized within the storyline, as it is in other working-class picture books like *Tar Beach* (Ringgold, 1991), it is present and evidenced within the geographies of the majority of Black neighborhood landscapes that Ava and her mother traverse on their Saturday escapade. For example, subtle but well-known racialized geographies and Black cultural markers like the distinct naming convention of the public library (MLK Library) and the Black colloquial communal reference, "Sisters," hangs on the wall in the hair salon. "Sisters" or "Sistas" is a term of endearment and a marker of gendered racialized solidarity that Black women use to counter misogynoir. This term is what Moya Bailey (Bailey & Bailey, 2018) describes as a specific disdain against Black women. The semiotics of Black hair, including Ava's new hairstyle (Bantu knots), and the hairstyli of stylists in the salon depict Black-gendered pride in wearing natural hairstyles which resist middle-class conservative aesthetics and assimilated beauty standards.

A close reading of the images on the page in which Ava and her mother ZOOM across the city attempting to get to the MLK Library for storytime (which gets canceled) includes a collaged clipping of a news article about a Black architect and North Lawndale, a predominately ethnic and Black enclave in Chicago. This inclusion is easy to miss and is primarily intended for adult readers who can appreciate the symbolic value and substance (Reay, 2020) of imprinting the historical legacy of Blackness onto the pages of this picture book. This nuanced visual recognizes the legacies of racial geographies with Black working-class childhoods and the power of the Black gaze in the authorial and illustrative process.

Ava's subject position and racialized characterization as a Black child are also essential factors for which readers shouldn't be ambivalent. The images of Ava's writing in colored pencil or crayon, located on the endpapers, include a "Saturday Wish List" highlighting previous excursions (marked with an x) and possibilities for future Saturday activities, e.g., "museum! tea party! gallery! movies!" Ava's emphasis, (n.p.). Her list reflects the desire for simple childhood pleasures, e.g., ice cream and skating. However, listing, thinking, and articulating what she'd like to do with her mother on Saturdays reflect agency, creativity, and maturity.

Regardless of race, these are characteristics of working-class childhoods that are often diminished, criticized, and under-utilized in school contexts. These traits ultimately serve as a satisfying ending to the narrative as Ava comforts and reassures her mother that Saturdays are special merely because they are together despite the appearance of their spoiled pursuits. Ava's tired and dedicated mother is so upset after the various failed pursuits that "her mother crumpled" (n.p.), after she realizes that she left the puppet show tickets on the kitchen table. Ava's impervious nature and comfort is agentive and uniquely mature because she helps her mother see the fullness of their imperfect day.

Implications

During our first reading of *Saturday*, many preservice teachers engage in an essentially race and class evasive reading. They summarize *Saturday* as "such a cute book." They appreciate the portion of the storyline that highlights the gender camaraderie of a mother and daughter spending a Saturday together. Students also identify several possibilities for using *Saturday* for ELA curricular expansions, e.g., read aloud to frontload conversations about onomatopoeia or determine the main idea and supporting details of the story. They point out the accessible writing style, precisely repetition, which invites students to engage in a choral reading each time Ava and her mother "ZoooooM" to and from various locales. Unfortunately, many students (including some Black students) also circumscribe Ava's racial identity as incidental, and the working-class elements are not mentioned. In other words, students were unaware of the textual praxis Oge Mora visually embedded within the book, which made conversations about race, class, gender, and time legible.

After our close reading using guiding questions centered on visual and rhetorical elements of racialized class and gender, students rightfully don't change their initial impression of using *Saturday* to elicit pure book joy for children. Nor do they shift their perspective about its utility for broad curricular purposes. Students needed a set of guiding questions to prompt a critical and expansive reading to identify the kind of culturally conscious details and visual layers of authenticity that provide the deep cultural resonance that Bishop championed. For example, although the book is beset by temporal demands fused to race, gender, and class, e.g., throughout the book, Sunday is looming. Thus, they must zoom around to fit in beautification, self-care, rest, and leisure activities, and students miss the critical dimension and demand on time as essentially universal. Unfortunately, to get students to notice the racialized class and gendered elements, I had to prompt students with questions such as, how does work control the narrative? Why do you think Ava's mother works every day? Which students would have connections and disconnections with this narrative? What are some of the ways Ava and her mother get from place to place? Why do they have to zoom everywhere? My embodied reading response as a Black woman, mother, and grandmother prompted me to guide students to read the book cover to cover to consider questions such as: how are Black women, mothers, and Black families and their communities affirmed in the pictures and words? After these prompts, teachers had many "but of course" moments. Some discussions included general references about "everyone and all parents being pressed for time." However, all students acknowledged the importance of looking beyond the surface of culturally relevant books to question, locate, and discuss visual rhetoric to expand critical discourses, comprehension, and student potential for making meaning or articulating disconnections.

There is a spectrum of working classness. Much of it is unwritten, unpictured, or out of print (see Gardner, 2022). Books such as *Uncle Jed's Barbershop* (Mitchell & Ransome, 1993) narrate aspects of Black refusal and resistance to anti-Black racism while reflecting Black working-class values, agency, and self-determination, including how Black businesses help preserve the social, political, and economic needs of Black communities. Black authors like Angela Johnson, John and Javaka Steptoe, Lucille Clifton, Mari Evans, and Jan Spivey Gilchrist have written broadly about Black childhoods, including narratives reflecting working-class aesthetics and experiences. Contemporary fiction and nonfiction narratives that reflect authentically segregated and multi-ethnic Black geographies within schools and neighborhoods (which tend to be working-class and working-poor) remain scarce. There is much diversity within the Black experience. Publishers, authors, and illustrators need to widen the subject matter and visual and linguistic representations of Black experiences in children's literature. Doing so can provide teachers with literature that authentically reflects the needs, relational connections, interests, content, social, and geographic locations that honor the assets, cultural wealth, and knowledge of Black working-class childhoods and experiences. As Sims Bishop asserted,

> Literature transforms human experience and reflects it back to us, and in that reflection, we can see our own lives and experiences as part of the larger human experience. Reading, then, becomes a means of self-affirmation, and readers often seek their mirrors in books.
>
> *(Bishop, 1990, p. ix)*

Deepening Sims Bishop's metaphor requires a full elucidation of culturally conscious literature to affirm and expand readers' ability to see Black working-class lives as part of the larger human experience. To read culturally conscious books critically and expansively, I urge educators to consider some of the following questions:

1 What racial, class, and gender elements of visual culture, including characters, are absent or present (including in the peritextual features)?
2 How is work and or social-economic diversity represented/described/storied verbally and or visually?
3 What are the temporal demands placed on characters and their lives?
4 What are the subject positions available to the characters, and who has agency in the story? How is the agency of the central figure represented?
5 How are neighborhoods, communities, and schools represented?

6 What kind of assets, attributes, and resources are pictured within homes and communities?

7 How does the book intersect with the social location and embodied reading identities of students in the classroom?

References

Bailey, M., & Bailey, T. (2018). On misogynoir: Citation, erasure, and plagiarism. *Feminist Media Studies, 18*(4), 762–768.

Bishop, R. S. (1990). Mirrors, windows, and sliding glass doors. *Perspectives, 6*(3), ix–xi.

Blau, P. M., & Duncan, O. D. (1967). *The American occupational structure*. John Wiley & Sons Inc.

Bourdieu, P. (1986). The forms of capital. In J. Richardson (Ed.), *Handbook of theory of research for the sociology of education* (pp. 46–58). ABC-CLIO.

Brooks, W., & Browne, S. (2012). Towards a culturally situated reader-response theory. *Children's Literature in Education, 43*(1), 74–85.

Campt, T. M. (2021). *A Black gaze: Artists changing how we see*. MIT Press.

Cooperative Children's Book Center. (2018). *Publishing statistics on children's books about people of color and First/Native nations and by people of color and First/Native nations authors and illustrators*. Cooperative Children's Book Center, School of Education, University of Wisconsin – Madison. Retrieved from https://ccbc.education.wisc.edu/books/pcstats.asp

Crenshaw, K. (1991). Mapping the margins: Intersectionality, identity politics, and violence against women of color. *Stanford Law Review, 43*(6), 1241–1299. https://doi.org/10.2307/1229039.

Crockett, D. (2017). Paths to respectability: Consumption and stigma management in the contemporary Black middle class. *Journal of Consumer Research, 44*(3), 554–581. https://doi.org/10.1093/jcr/ucx049.

Dávila, D. (2011). "White people don't work at McDonald's" and other shadow stories from the field: Analyzing pre-service teachers' use of Obama's race speech to teach for social justice. *English Education, 44*(1), 13–50.

Dumas, M. J., & Ross, K.M. (2016). "Be real Black for me": Imagining BlackCrit in education. *Urban Education, 51*(4), 415–442.

Forest, D. E., Garrison, K., & Kimmel, S. C. (2015). "The university for the poor": Portrayals of class in translated children's literature. *Teachers College Record, 117*(2), 1–40.

Gardner, R. P. (2017). Unforgivable Blackness: Visual rhetoric, reader response, and critical racial literacy. *Children's Literature in Education, 48*(2), 119–133.

Gardner, R. P. (2020). The present past: Black authors and the anti-Black selective tradition in Children's literature. *Journal of Children's Literature, 46*(2), 8–18.

Gardner, R. P. (2022). Black Critical Theory in Children's Literary Analysis: Why It Matters. In K. Coats, D. Stevenson, & V.. Yenika-Agbaw (Eds), *A Companion to Children's Literature* (pp. 299-313). Wiley Blackwell.

Hunter, M. A., Pattillo, M., Robinson, Z. F., & Taylor, K.-Y. (2016). Black placemaking: Celebration, play, and poetry. *Theory, Culture & Society, 33*(7–8), 31–56. https://doi.org/10.1177/0263276416635259.

Jones, S. (2008). Grass houses: Representations and reinventions of social class through Children's literature. *Journal of Language and Literacy Education, 4*(2), 40–58.

Lei, R. F., & Bodenhausen, G. V. (2017). Racial assumptions color the mental representation of social class. *Frontiers in Psychology, 8*(519), 1–7.

McNair, J. (2021). Surprise, surprise! Exploring dust jackets, case covers, and endpapers in picture books to support comprehension. *Reading Teacher, 74*(4), 363–373.

McNair, J. C., & Edwards, P. A. (2021). The lasting legacy of Rudine Sims Bishop: Mirrors, windows, sliding glass doors, and more. *Literacy Research: Theory, Method, and Practice, 70*(1), 202–212. https://doi.org/10.1177/23813377211028256.

Moore, O. (1985). Picture books: The un-text. In D. MacCann, & G. Woodard (Eds.), *The Black American in books for children: Readings in racism* (pp. 184–191). Scarecrow Press.

Moynihan, D.P. (1965, March). The Negro family: The case for national action. The Office of Policy Planning and Research. United States Department of Labor.

Nopper, T. K., & Pattillo, M. (2021). Mary Pattillo's sociology of the Black middle class. *Critical Sociology, 47*(6), 1033–1041. https://doi.org/10.1177/0896920520928015.

Nyachae, T. M. (2021). Got diverse texts? Now what? Teachers as critical guides in the moment. *Literacy Today, 38*(6), 36–39.

Reay, E. J. (2020). Hands up! Close reading of the book and interview with Breanna J. McDaniel. *Bookbird, 58*(1), 77–82.

Richardson, E., & Ragland, A. (2018). #StayWoke: The language and literacies of the #BlackLivesMatter movement. *Community Literacy Journal, 12*(2), 27–56. https://doi.org/10.25148/clj.12.2.009099.

Children's Literature Cited

Clifton, L., & Barnett, M. (1975). *My brother fine with me*. Holt, Rinehart and Winston.

De la Peña, M., Robinson, C., & Thomann, R. (2015). *Last stop on market street*. G.P. Putnam's Sons.

Mitchell, K., & Ransome, J. (1993). *Uncle Jed's barbershop*. Simon & Schuster Books for Young Readers.

Mora, O. (2019). *Saturday*. Little, Brown.

Ringgold, F. (1991). *Tar beach*. Crown Publishers, Inc.

Roberts, D. E. (2002). *Shattered bonds: The color of welfare*. Basic Civitas Books.

Sims, R. (1982). *Shadow and substance: Afro-American experience in contemporary children's fiction*. National Council of Teachers of English.

Steptoe, J. (1970). *Uptown*. Harper & Row.

PART II

Reconsidering Methods of Inquiry: Children's Sensory Engagements and the *Resounding* Traces of Children's Lives

4

SITESENSING

Methods for Connecting to Young Children's Worlds

Amanda Reeves Fellner and Tran Nguyen Templeton

As former teachers of very young children (ages 5 and younger), we have long known that listening to the more-than-verbal is critical to entering young children's worlds. As children explore spaces, they do so with their whole selves, adapting and creating a dynamic social space (Corsaro, 2017) which evolves over time. Children's engagements with the world are embodied and emplaced, leaving traces (Ingold, 2007) of their actions throughout the spaces they inhabit. These traces engender memories of prior experiences (Stevenson, 2014) and impact the possibilities within environments by altering both the physical and social space (Christensen, 2003). Acknowledging the ways young children engage with/in space, researchers have recently begun to look more critically at the methods used to conduct research with this population (Fellner, 2020; Hackett, 2016; Hackett & Somerville, 2017; Yoon & Templeton, 2019). Ethnographic methods commonly used to study youth and adults, for example, may be sufficient in some ways to making sense of young children's movements through space, but wholly insufficient in other ways.

In this chapter, we discuss our explorations with ethnographic modes of inquiry inspired by children's sensory engagements within the places they inhabit. Because young children have distinct ways of knowing and being in the world, we join other critical scholars of early childhood who call for rethinking research methods that attempt to see children's worlds more completely. While observational tools are often used to annotate children's actions, we propose that a focused attention to the more-than-verbal worlds of young children can shed light on their unique ways of coming to know the spaces they inhabit. We discuss each of our approaches to understanding young children's movements through New York City streets and playgrounds. Through modes of inquiry

DOI: 10.4324/9781003399155-7

inspired by Pink (2009) and Ingold (2011)—such as tracing photographs and mapping movements—we suggest researchers' sensual encounters with data as a way to counter the adult-centric tendencies that play out within research with children. We start with discussing children's embodied ways of knowing the world around them, as well as how these ways contribute to children's placemaking.

Young Children's Embodiment

One foundational idea within critical childhood studies is that children experience the world differently from adults (Yoon & Templeton, 2019). In their engagements within different spaces, very young children construct knowledge through the sensorium before their capacities to communicate on adults' terms, catch up to their bodily modes of communication. Language, therefore, can convey only *some* forms of knowledge, which requires that we "acknowledge the existence of forms of knowing that escape the efforts of language" (Ellsworth, 2005, p. 156). Children's embodiment has to do with their being, making, and knowing; in children's movements—through force, action, and transformation—the body is constituted again and again as a knowing subject (Ellsworth, 2005).

The geographer Yi-Fu Tuan (1977) asserts that children attune to the world in more sensuous ways than adults do. In moments barely registered by adults, children might halt in the middle of a walk to wrap their fingers around wet soil, gasp at the sign of a squirrel, pounce onto a rain puddle, point upward at a distant plane. These attunements are how they come to know their place. Rather than being told what a place *is*, children *experience* it as socially and materially significant. Nondescript spaces like parking lots may be settings for cultural activities; routine walks to and from school may infuse more meaning into some city blocks over others; striking interactions with more-than-human life (flora and fauna) sediment children's memories of, and attachments to, place (Templeton, 2020). Children's experiences are felt through a "vitality for doing things" (p. 33) as their "living, moving, sensing bodies" (Ellsworth, 2005, p. 166) become entangled with the material and immaterial.

In other words, children's "physical experiences of places are central to their story" (Mills et al., 2013, p. 17), and while children may be very young, their stories are rich with layers. In Ingold's (2007) formulation, these narratives of place involve *relating* "occurrences of the past, retracing a path through the world that others, recursively picking up the threads of past lives, can follow in the process of spinning out their own" (p. 93). In this way, children's stories are intertwined with others'—human and more-than-human—such that "[t]here is no point at which the story ends and life begins." (p. 93). Therefore, to study children's meaning-making is to study how they inhabit their spaces.

Sensing Our Way through Spatial Worlds

Space is constructed not only of physical elements, but also of the intended desires and actual experiences of the people in those spaces (Lefebvre, 1991). Just as space[1] is constructed, children's worlds are ever entangled in the spaces they come to know, which influences their understanding of self. Never a neutral practice, the design of spaces for young children rarely takes into consideration the actual lived experiences of young children, particularly children from minoritized communities. Too often, these spaces privilege western, white notions of developmental progress (Pacini-Ketchabaw & Taylor, 2015) which minimize children's sensorial ways of being as they do not fit into this narrative of progress.

As children explore, they do so with their whole bodies, responding to the sounds, textures, tastes, scents, and movement around them. Young children (0–5 years), in particular, become entangled in the world around them through movement and physical exploration. Ingold (2007) describes this entanglement as an "enmeshment" that contains overlapping lines and traces of movement both physically and metaphysically. What is left is an altered space where children's previous actions influence future experiences; a flower moved from a branch might encourage another to explore or a street game created one day may be carried out in the future, adding to, and shifting, the social space.

While very young children's sociospatial practices are frequently overlooked, recent research places a critical lens on these complex engagements (Fellner, 2020; Hackett, 2016; Nxumalo et al., 2021; Templeton, 2020). These researches demonstrate children's multiple ways of knowing and being that push back against positivist notions of children as becoming and narratives of developmental progression (Burman, 2008). Focusing on children's actual lived experiences in space, allows for new understandings which influence how children are viewed, how their spaces are constructed, and what adults allow in those spaces.

The notion of paying attention to sensory worlds has been discussed by scholars across disciplines like anthropology and cultural studies (Low, 2015; Nakamura, 2013) but has recently informed more organized research methods within education (Pink, 2009). Pink (2009) explains that sensory ethnography is not about one way of viewing data or methods but instead focuses on multiple ways of knowing and knowledge construction. Further expanding on this, Mills and colleagues (2013) comment, "Sensory ethnography explicitly draws on geographical theories of place, place-making, and space in combination with philosophical and anthropological work on place and perception" (p. 13). Accounting for the sensorium in children's place-making acknowledges that their senses orient them to the world, thereby structuring place.

The Data in This Chapter

In the following sections, each of us discusses the sensory modes of research we deployed to get closer to how our young participants perceive and engage in their worlds. In Amanda's approach of mapping video footage of children's encounters on playgrounds in New York City (NYC), she advocates for methods that move beyond documenting children's behaviors to account for discrete tasks and toward methods that embrace children's embodied spatial practices. Tran's approach of tracing still images—specifically child-made photographs also created in NYC—is a way of grasping at the sensual dimensions of children's experiences and to unsettle the subjectivity of adult ways of seeing. In addition to observing and documenting participants' ways of being, we each sought "routes through which to develop experience-based empathetic understandings of what others might be experiencing and knowing" (Pink, 2009, p. 65). Johansson and Løkken (2013) emphasize the "idea of the embodied and intertwined existence of the child, the pedagogue, the researcher and the world" (p. 887). This suggests that data be analyzed not just at the site of language but also in the movements and sensations of participants *and* researchers.

Embodied Mapping as Method

> "…Footprints register emplaced movement. Far from staking a claim, the indigenous inhabitant leaves footprints in the ground as clues to his whereabouts and expectations, and for others to follow … Footprints are individual; paths are social."
>
> (Ingold, 2015, p. 63)

The data described in this section are from a larger study (Fellner, 2020), in which I (Amanda) focused on the ways 2-year-olds find meaning in, and take ownership of, playground spaces. In this study, children were asked to wear GoPro video cameras (attached to a helmet they wore) as they played in various playground spaces. GoPro cameras are worn by the user (in this case the children) and are set to continuously record the wearer's line of vision. These cameras are frequently used to experience a "first person" perspective and have been more recently adopted by researchers attempting to document the participant's perspective (Hackett, 2014; Nilson, 2017). Since the GoPro cameras were worn by the child and show the child's view of the playground space, they were chosen as a data collection instrument in an attempt to capture the embodied and emplaced ways of being of young children. As the cameras track the children's head turns, body positioning, speed, height, voicings, soundscapes, etc., GoPro's allowed me as a researcher to attend specifically to movement and to feel emplaced alongside them as I viewed the playground in a new way. The video data, produced by the children, captured aspects of the children's movement (head turns/speed/height/missteps/vocalizations) as well as interactions with the social and material space. Instead of the researcher choosing what to record or what was meaningful, GoPro cameras captured the world as the children moved through it. The challenge with this footage was how I might make sense of it. Engaging Ingold's (2007) framework on movement traces and Hackett's (2014, 2016) work with placemaking, I engaged mapping as a tool for investigating children's movement through space. Before I discuss my own approach to mapping, I situate it briefly in a larger discussion of maps.

The Power of Maps

Maps code spaces, leaving lasting impacts on the ways spaces are interpreted. Pickles (2004) explains that "maps provide the very conditions of possibility for the worlds we inhabit and the subjects we become," (p. 5) meaning the act of transcription, and the map produced, is political. If maps are not produced with a careful awareness of the spaces they are representing (in our case, children's spaces), they may limit our understanding, and the potentialities, of space and human worlds. Working off of Olsson's (1998) "lines of power" which reflect lived experiences on paper, Pickles explains, "The drawing and reading of a line, the historical emergence of cartographic reason, the production and circulation of a map, and lived experience are so thoroughly and historically intertwined and over-determined," (p. 5). In other words, the act of drawing maps has lasting impacts that can influence and restrict the ways spaces are seen and lived in. Just as prior experiences in space influence future action, so do physical representations of space.

More recent research looks at ways mapping can be a tool of resistance and can be used to bring to light ways of knowing and being that have been historically marginalized (Butler, 2018; Schmidt, 2011). Representing and co-constructing the ways space is viewed and experienced by Black girls (Butler, 2018) and queer students (Schmidt, 2011), is a start to acknowledging the various lived experiences that have been left out of the spatial discourse. Furthering this work, Hackett (2014, 2016) rethinks mapping with regard to very young children. The mapping of children's movements, according to Hackett (2014), should focus on moments of meaningful engagement with/in space; times when children are engaged in placemaking. This placemaking is often viewed by adults as erratic and lacking in intention as children's movements and intra/actions (Barad, 2007) with the world around them are not always predictable. However, when we focus on the lines of movement, the directionality, the changes, the pace, the routes of young children, they hold more intention than previously seen.

Transcribing Movement as Embodied Analysis

During data analysis, I watched the GoPro videos and began to grapple with how I might convey on paper the complexity of data this method produced. Sitting behind the screen, I viewed the playground in a whole new way and felt connected to the children's movements as they stopped, started, turned, focused, and ran. The whirlwind of their movement, the speed with which the playground zoomed past, and the ways the video jerked from side to side as they bounced and shifted throughout the space produced a feeling of emplacement that could not have been achieved through my own videoing. To start, I began mapping the children's movements on blank paper, tracing their motion from start to finish. These swirling lines, at times overlapping, mirror the children's traces (Ingold, 2007) created, and left to linger, in space. From here, I rewatched the videos and overlaid meaningful aspects of the environment, including physical, material, and social components, creating a map of the children's route through the playground.

The maps shown in Figures 4.1 and 4.2 illustrate two different ways of exploring the playground space, captured by Beckett (27 months) and transcribed/mapped by myself. The act of transcription, of drawing the lines as

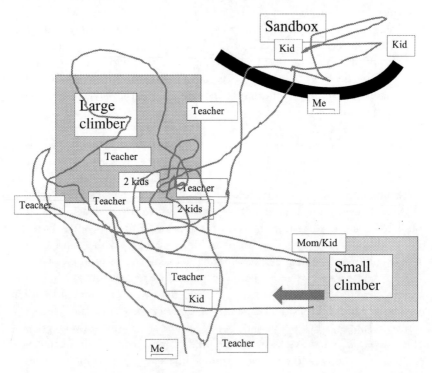

FIGURE 4.1 Map of Beckett's Movements with Points of Social Contact

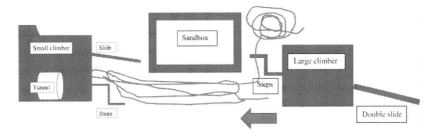

FIGURE 4.2 Map of Beckett's Movements between Structures

I watched his movement, allowed me to feel his movement in an embodied way. I felt the starts/stops, directionality, speed, and distance of his movement as my pen moved across the page. While one can never truly know another's understanding of place (Pink, 2009), the act of drawing alongside the videos produced a sensorial experience that helped me as a researcher to see Beckett's actions in a more complete way. Acknowledging that space is a co-construction of the social, material, and physical environments (Lefebvre, 1991; Massey, 2005), once the lines of movement were represented, I then layered on aspects of the physical, material, and social space that seemed meaningful to the child in each video. At times, these markers were people or social encounters as seen in Figure 4.1 and at others these were physical aspects of the playground like equipment or specific routes through space, as seen in Figure 4.2. Regardless, the production of the maps—starting with the movement and then overlaying aspects of the environment—valued the children's placemaking as a priority by visualizing aspects of the space that were meaningful in that moment, as opposed to beginning with a map of the playground. As Ingold (2015) states, "Ordinarily, the wanderer is not a walker of shapes or outlines, and his vision unfolds at ground level, as he goes along, rather than from a superior and stationary vantage point," (p. 60). Mapping the children's movements first privileges their embodied ways of exploring space and decenters it from my own adult perspective of the space.

As mentioned above, Beckett's movements in Figure 4.1 were tied to social encounters. Nearly every time the pen stopped as I drew his route through the playground, it was a moment of conversation or pause to observe some other individual. A moment where he participated in the (re)construction of the social space as his lines of movement intertwined with others.

In Figure 4.2, however, Beckett's movements become more about a route through the space that he traverses over and over again until his last final spin. This route of reductive movement (Ingold, 2007) changed the physical and metaphysical environments of the playground by leaving grooves of his footprints. These routes then inform future action, both by himself and others, which was seen as he embarked on similar routes on future dates relying on his emplaced knowledge of the playground. As I drew this route, my hand mimicked the grooves he created, leaving dents in the page from my pen. I could sense the impact he had on the environment through my own physical marking. This form of embodied mapping, whereby I translated Beckett's movements into map form, signifies the intentionality and awareness that is required when attempting to communicate the complexity of children's placemaking.

Touching Images: Tracing as an Analytic Tool

The data from this second case is derived from a study that I (Tran) conducted with young children ages 2–5 at the same childcare center where Amanda conducted her research. In this research, the young children made photographs using a digital camera; my intent was to learn about childhoods from children themselves. I've written about the details of this image-based process elsewhere (Templeton, 2020); in this section, I focus on tracing children's images as one kind of sensory approach that invokes a haptic relationship between myself and the children's photos. Though visual and participatory research with children intends to decenter the research's usual focus on the verbal and on adults' interpretations of children's actions, respectively, it does not necessarily allow us to perceive the physical and social world from children's positions. After all, photographs depend on seeing, and seeing is contextual, dependent on whose eyes are looking. Children simply *see* differently. "Vision" is not an isolated system, after all, but rather entangled with touch, smell, sounds, and movements (Ingold, 2002). Yet much of research is "marked by an ocularcentric bias" (Grimshaw, 2001, p. 7), guided by the researcher's eyes, despite how partially we ourselves are able to perceive. Further, what children see and how they look are affected by their stature/position in society, their own sensory development, and discourses that prevail in their everyday worlds (Rose, 2016).

In this work, children's ways of seeing were marked in practices of viewing photographs. After each child had a turn with the shared digital camera, I printed physical copies of photographs for children to audience, in one-on-one meetings and with classmates during morning meeting time. In these instances of viewing, I observed the children's encounters with the photographs: they traced the pictures with their fingers, ran the corners along their lips or the side of their faces, pressed the glossy side of pictures onto their faces until they stuck, bent them, looked very closely, and even licked the pictures. The children did not come to know images the way adults do; they did it as they do their ways of knowing—through oral, tactile, proprioceptive contact. During morning meetings where each assenting child showcased their "favorite" photos, my (and other adults') limited ability to view the elements of the children's images was apparent. The children attended to particular features within their own *and* others' photos. They noted details like younger siblings' diapers underneath the netting of a stroller, a plastic claw jutting out ever so slightly from a tunnel created out of wooden blocks, a pair of pajama pants resting against the arm of a couch, the lines on the sidewalk that marked where to stop. Some details I had coded for; others I did not even register, yet they were critical to understanding the children's emplaced identities. This realization forced me to reconsider whether I was seeing what I needed to see about the settings of the photos.

Trading Spaces, Tracing Places

It was this desire to get closer to children's visual worlds that led me to tracing the children's photos as a mode of inquiry, to uncover what I had previously been unable to perceive. Using the application Paper by FiftyThree, an iPad, and a stylus pen, I traced and applied digital watercolor to 14 of the children's photographs as a way to see and investigate the spatial contours of the images. Inspired by the work of Victoria Restler (2020), who traced the moving images of her participants' videos and rubbed the materials within teachers' classrooms as modes of inquiry, I attempted to bring myself closer to the photographs through this practice. Using the virtual tools available on the app (pencil, pen, watercolor), I outlined the shapes in the photographs and used the watercolor application to apply color that matched the color in the photograph itself. While doing so, I narrated the process using my phone's voice recording feature; this narration allowed me to note particular perspectives, textures, and surprises that arose during the process.

I followed up this practice with annotated memos where I described the images with painstaking detail and integrated my oral jottings from the voice recordings I made. The memos, as a reflexive engagement with the images, animated new pathways and questions toward understanding the children's everyday lives. These memos, which *had* previously included naming everything I saw in the photo (an approach common in visual research) then became about holding on to the feelings and sensations that tracing the scenes within the images provoked. Tracing a photo as seemingly simple as Saryu's (see Figure 4.3) put me in closer proximity not only to her as a research participant but also as a person who routinely inhabits the same spaces I did but with very different associations.

Saryu made her photograph in the morning (as indicated by the timestamp) near a familiar corner, about two blocks from the entrance to the school that she attended and where we both frequented. I walked along that same sidewalk every morning but I had not perceived it from the vantage point of a 4-year-old until my tracing. The perspective of looking up and outward—made more

FIGURE 4.3   Tracing of Saryu's Photograph

salient by the tapering lines of the sidewalk's contraction joints—accentuated the experience of being small in a big city. Though the photograph is a still image, the lines I sketched that followed the folds in the clothing of the two people closest to Saryu indicated that she had made this image while they were in motion. The gaze of the adult on the left to the person on the right demonstrated familiarity between the two pedestrians.

This image was one of five photographs Saryu had chosen to share with classmates, and before I traced it, it had been unclear to me why it had relevance to her (see Yoon & Templeton, 2019 for a longer discussion of the set of five images). In making note of the movement and the familiar glance between the two people within the image, I started to look more closely at the foregrounded figures. Though I had been in frequent interaction with Saryu's father, I had failed to recognize that he was featured in the picture. To the right was his father, Saryu's grandfather, who was visiting the family from India. This was not just any walk; it was an important daily ritual of care, conducted with her father and made more significant by the addition of a close family member. What's more, tracing allowed me to grasp the almost inverted quality of the image and of the relationship between Saryu and her caregivers. Looking *up* at the adults, while their backs were turned to the photographer, meant that Saryu was taking the photograph from behind her father and grandfather. The perspective signaled the adults' trust in Saryu to position herself in a way that she was not always within their line of sight.

Working from still images that children have made of their homes and encounters in public spaces required that I attempt to put myself in the scene as a way of "being there" (Johansson & Løkken, 2013). The children's pictures, are in and of themselves, "sensory, affective, and embodied experiences of their locality and activity through which to remember and imagine [their] worlds" (Pink, 2014, p. 419). As a 4-year-old, Saryu had gained a familiarity with the five city blocks that it took to get from her apartment to school, and this intimacy was situated in familial relations of care, further sedimenting her attachment to these five blocks as a place of importance. This frequent movement, between two addresses, with significant people, was key to her placemaking as locomotion is part of placemaking. Saryu's daily walk between school and home demonstrates how "the world can be perceived, not only through the mind, but also kinesthetically through the hands and feet" (Ingold, 2004 cited in Mills et al., 2013, p. 23).

Conclusion

Certainly, the fact that children become familiar with their neighborhoods or that they engage in multisensory ways of knowing, is neither novel nor revolutionary. What is worth attending to here is the way that we can be more attuned to how children might understand their own worlds. Working from Tishman's (2018) notion of "slow looking," tracing and mapping are "[ways] of gaining knowledge about the world" (p. 2) of children. Ingold (2011) writes about the interrelatedness of the visual, aural, touch, and feeling perceptions. Vision is often reduced to object, image, and interpretation (Ingold, 2011) when an active engagement with our worlds means that looking also includes other sensory modalities. As forms of sensuous scholarship (Stoller, 1997), tracing and mapping involve the movement of hands and eyes in coordination, a kind of mimesis of children's ways of moving, seeing, and looking. Tracing and mapping, in our formulations, are analytic modes of inquiry that force us as adults to ask how children's lines can guide us out of our adult senses and into children's.

Finally, while this chapter emerged out of our concerns for the ways that very young children are read and (mis)understood within classrooms, research, and our shared social worlds, we know that certain children are impacted more by this lack of understanding than others. That is, embodiment, as a way that our bodies are lived out, is critical to the way race is produced (Ahmed, 2002) so we must acknowledge the very real implications for this line of inquiry. Tuan's (1977) emphasis on children's "vitality for doing things" echoes Gail Boldt's (2021) invocation of psychologist Daniel Stern's writing on *vitality*. In discussing vitality as a manifestation of life and aliveness, Boldt emphasized the need to "attend less to language or representation and more to expressions of vitality" (p. 4) which provide information about children's bodily knowledge of their experiences. If we consider that vitality is a right that children should have, and dependent on knowing the world through the body, it seems dire to ensure that all children have these opportunities in school. Yet, the increasingly segregated, racialized politics of schooling in the United States means that young children of Color have fewer opportunities for embodied ways of meaning-making. White, middle-class children, for example, are more likely to attend progressive schools where freedom of movement (and, therefore, of being) are principles that guide the curriculum. The ongoing disembodiment and denial of the humanity of children from minoritized positions mean that their vitality and the ways they make meaning with their bodies, etc. are misunderstood and contained through punishing school systems (Boldt, 2021).

Note

1 Throughout this chapter, we differentiate place and space by the ways that space becomes bounded to become place. In Tuan's (1977) words, "What begins as undifferentiated space becomes place as we get to know it better and endow it with value" (p. 6).

References

Ahmed, S. (2002). Racialized bodies. In M. Evans & E. Lee (Eds.), *Real bodies* (pp. 46–63). Palgrave.

Barad, K. (2007). *Meeting the universe halfway: Quantum physics and the entanglement of matter and meaning.* Duke University Press.

Boldt, G. (2021). Theorizing vitality in the literacy classroom. *Reading Research Quarterly, 56*(2), 207–221.

Burman, E. (2008). *Deconstructing developmental psychology* (2nd ed.). Routledge.

Butler, T. T. (2018). Black girl cartography: Black girlhood and place-making in education research. *Review of Research in Education, 42*(1), 28–45.

Christensen, P. (2003). Place, space and knowledge: Children in the village and the city. In M. O'Brien & P. Christensen (Eds.), *Children in the city: Home, neighbourhood and community* (pp. 13–28). Routledge.

Corsaro, W. A. (2017). *The sociology of childhood.* Sage publications.

Ellsworth, E. (2005). *Places of learning: Media, architecture, pedagogy.* Routledge.

Fellner, A. R. (2020). Moving through playground spaces: Exploring the sensory, material, and embodied experiences of 2-year-olds in playground spaces (Doctoral dissertation, Teachers College, Columbia University).

Grimshaw, A. (2001). *The ethnographer's eye: Ways of seeing in anthropology.* Cambridge University Press.

Hackett, A. (2014). Zigging and zooming all over the place: Young children's meaning making and movement in the museum. *Journal of Early Childhood Literacy, 14*(1), 5–27.

Hackett, A. (2016). Young children as wayfarers: Learning about place by moving through it. *Children & Society, 30*(3), 169–179.

Hackett, A., & Somerville, M. (2017). Posthuman literacies: Young children moving in time, place and more-than-human worlds. *Journal of Early Childhood Literacy, 17*(3), 374–391.

Ingold, T. (Ed.). (2011). *Redrawing anthropology: Materials, movements, lines.* Ashgate Publishing.

Ingold, T. (2002). *The perception of the environment: Essays on livelihood, dwelling and skill.* Routledge.

Ingold, T. (2007). *Lines: A brief history.* Routledge.

Ingold, T. (2015). *The life of lines.* Routledge.

Johansson, E., & Løkken, G. (2013). Sensory pedagogy: Understanding and encountering children through the senses. *Educational Philosophy and Theory, 46*(8), 886–897.

Lefebvre, H. (1991). *The production of space* (D. Nicholson-Smith, Trans.). Blackwell.

Low, K. E. (2015). The sensuous city: Sensory methodologies in urban ethnographic research. *Ethnography, 16*(3), 295–312.

Massey, D. B. (2005). *For space.* Sage.

Mills, K., Comber, B., & Kelly, P. (2013). Sensing place: Embodiment, sensoriality, kinesis, and children behind the camera. *English Teaching: Practice and Critique, 12*(2), 11–27.

Nakamura, K. (2013). Making sense of sensory ethnography: The sensual and the multisensory. *American Anthropologist, 115*(1), 132–135.

Nilson, S. (2017). Use of a GoPro camera as a non-obtrusive research tool. *Journal of Playwork Practice, 4*(1), 39–47.

Nxumalo, F., Odim, N., & Smith, A. (2021). Black geographies in early childhood studies. *The SAGE handbook of global childhoods*, 192–203. SAGE Publications.

Olsson, G. (1998). Towards a critique of cartographical reason. *Ethics, Place and Environment, 1*(2), 145–155.

Pacini-Ketchabaw, V., & Taylor, A. (Eds.). (2015). *Unsettling the colonial places and spaces of early childhood education.* Routledge.

Pickles, J. (2004). *A history of spaces: Cartographic reason, mapping and the geo-coded world.* Routledge.

Pink, S. (2009). *Doing sensory ethnography.* Sage.

Pink, S. (2014). Digital–visual–sensory-design anthropology: Ethnography, imagination and intervention. *Arts and Humanities in Higher Education, 13*(4), 412–427.

Restler, V. (2020). Rubbing the room: Tactile epistemologies of teacher work. *Reconceptualizing Educational Research Methodology, 11*(2), 1–20.

Rose, G. (2016). *Visual methodologies: An introduction to researching with visual materials.* Sage.

Schmidt, S. (2011). Theorizing place: Students' navigation of place outside. *Journal of Curriculum Theorizing, 27*(1), 20–35.

Stevenson, A. (2014). We came here to remember: Using participatory sensory ethnography to explore memory as emplaced, embodied practice. *Qualitative Research in Psychology, 11*(4), 335–349.

Stoller, P. (1997). *Sensuous scholarship.* University of Pennsylvania Press.

Templeton, T. N. (2020). "That street is taking us to home": Young children's photographs of public spaces. *Children's Geographies, 18*(1), 1–15.

Tishman, S. (2018). *Slow looking: The art and practice of learning through observation.* Routledge.

Tuan, Y. F. (1977). *Space and place: The perspective of experience.* University of Minnesota Press.

Yoon, H. S., & Templeton, T. N. (2019). The practice of listening to children: The challenges of hearing children out in an adult-regulated world. *Harvard Educational Review, 89*(1), 55–84.

5

WHO GETS TO "PLAY"?

Play, Autism, and Possibilities for More-than-Human Young Childhoods

Emmanuelle N. Fincham

Western understandings of play rest primarily on Piaget's stages, which unavoidably link sensorimotor play with immaturity, infancy, and in/ability. Teachers of young children are expected to support them through this stage on their way to the preoperational stage, filled with coveted skills like language and pretend play that is more intelligible to adults. For many autistic children;[1] however, the stage-based developmental discourse deems their chosen ways of play invisible and diagnoses them as remaining too long in the sensorimotor stage, thus requiring often-intense intervention to "teach" them how to play in ways that are expected of a "typical" young child, most often not aligned with their interests and desires. In this chapter, I draw on critical childhood studies and critical disability studies to deconstruct this dominating perspective on the play, or presumed lack thereof, of autistic children. These areas of scholarship have shown how childhoods and disability are socially, historically, culturally, and discursively constructed (Goodley et al., 2019; Prout & James, 2014), bringing attention to the overwhelming reliance on norms rendered by developmental psychology in the study, as well as broad societal perceptions, of children. Then, I invite new materialist approaches and posthuman theories, as they are also emerging in critical disability studies and early childhood studies, as a way to think about the play of autistic children in new ways. Employing these perspectives to frame my own experiences working with young autistic children, I (re)engage with my teaching stories and memories to begin a process of (re)theorizing the play of one autistic child.

Assuming the social, historical, and discursive-material construction of childhood, questions of whose and what kind of childhoods count arise. The

DOI: 10.4324/9781003399155-8

play of Black boys, for instance, has been socially constructed as criminal and dangerous (Bryan, 2020), leading to an omittance of their childhoods from the wider perspectives of play that are steeped in historical discourses of racism, classism, and ableism. As most play literature in early childhood is based on the white, able, middle-class norms that have shaped developmental psychology, children of color, and disabled children are most often excluded from mainstream notions of "childhoods." The norms established for the "typically developing" child simultaneously construct the "problem" that is the disabled child (David, as cited in Curran & Runswick-Cole, 2014). As such, disabled children's childhoods, much like Black boyhoods, are rendered socially unimaginable, moreso, as these identities intersect (Dumas & Nelson, 2016).

Positioned as Other, Dumas and Nelson (2016) go on to describe perceptions of Black boys as "less than human, and therefore undeserving of the emotional and moral recognition accorded to those whose shared humanity is understood" (p. 29). Whereas societal perspectives often involve an adultification of Black boys, disabled children are commonly infantilized, assumed to be less than, less able, and less knowing than their typically developing peers throughout and beyond the presumed years of childhood. It is imperative, thus, to interrogate the ways conventional studies of childhood and the regime of truth that is developmental psychology have functioned to exclude certain children from having childhoods, or positioned them in spaces on the margins of "typical" childhoods. Drawing on both critical childhood studies and disability studies, Curran and Runswick-Cole (2014) promote a more specific "disabled childhood studies" that would position children not in the mainstream societal view as "*having problems*" but rather as "*having childhoods*" (p. 1).

Perceptions of the Young Autistic Child: A "Non-playing" Object

Autism spectrum disorder (ASD) comprises a wide variety of diagnostic characteristics, but consensus in the literature points to individuals with social and communicative difficulties as well as demonstrating behaviors that are repetitive or restrictive (APA, 2013; Barton et al., 2011). In classroom spaces, children with ASD are commonly referred to as having difficulties interacting with peers, forming attachments with adults, and participating in activities as their play is assumed to be more simplistic and repetitive than that of their "typically-developing" peers (Barton et al., 2011). The prevailing medical model of disability education pathologizes and positions autistic children as having deficits, which increase with their deviance from standard developmental measures. "Evidence-based" interventions like applied behavior analysis (ABA) are most heralded as discourses promoting a "cure" for autism permeate the field. However, for many children, these intense therapeutic approaches incur violence on the child as they are forced into a way of being that does not come naturally for their bodies or minds, expected to shape themselves and their behaviors into uncomfortable spaces (Douglas et al., 2021). Schooling, in general, is a "site in which childhood is constructed through the instruction, surveillance, and disciplining of children" (Dumas & Nelson, 2016, p. 33), but for children with autism, their childhoods are being constructed in a context where every aspect of their lives, especially their play, are coopted as sites of surveillance, intervention, and diagnosis (Goodley & Runswick-Cole, 2010).

I interned in a therapeutic children's center housed in a New York City hospital where the majority of children were bussed in from all over the city, specifically a classroom for 3- and 4-year-old children diagnosed with ASD in combination with multiple physical and cognitive disabilities. Of the seven children in the classroom, six were boys, six were children of color, only four were independently mobile, none were toilet-trained, none were considered "verbal," and they all received some level of feeding therapy, many unable to feed themselves or easily manage textured foods. For much of their 5-hour instructional day, the children were engaged in intense one-on-one therapies with the classroom teachers, assistants, or other specialized therapists. I participated in these interventions, mimicking the techniques of the classroom teachers and therapists as I learned the ins and outs of discrete trial training and ABA in practice.

First, the demographics of this tiny classroom reflect the intersectionalities of race, class, and ability that shape many intervention-focused centers such as this one (Goodley et al., 2019). Second, the description of the children's abilities illustrates many characteristics of the "disabled body" as it has been socially constructed. And third, the conditions of the school day for these children call attention to the fact that some children are located "outside the public imagination of what childhood means" (Dumas & Nelson, 2016, p. 30). Whereas other preschool children attend classrooms where they are expected to interact, play, and discover, the children in this classroom were given little if any opportunity to partake in those presumed elements of early childhood. Here, even mealtimes were a context for the intervention that was woven into every part of the day, except for the few minutes of "free play" they were allowed *only* in the times they needed to be moved out of the way in order for the teaching team to set up for the next round of instruction. At a very early point in their lives, these children were identified, as many disabled children are, as "nonplaying object[s] that [require] professional therapeutic intervention" (Goodley & Runswick-Cole, 2010, p. 499). Part of this intervention was promoted as "play" skills, although, the "play" consisted of training behaviors like putting puzzle pieces together or completing a shape sorter toy, all of which resulted in tangible rewards if done right. There was no reward for the children's own ways of playing.

A widely accepted "truth" in early childhood is that play, particularly pretend play, is crucial for children's cognitive and creative development (Russ, 2016). However, the "play" that has shaped policy and curriculum across early childhood does not represent some universal trait of childhood as it has been constructed (Lillard & Taggart, 2019). This is not to say that some children do not play, but rather, some children's play remains unintelligible or is named "inappropriate" within the constraints formed by the dominance of Western developmental psychology. As I endeavor to think differently about children's play, specifically for young children labeled as having autism, I am inspired by Goodley and Runswick-Cole's (2010) suggestion to reposition "play outside the grand narrative of developmental psychology" to dislodge it as "a site of diagnosis, intervention, and correction" (p. 509). Critical childhood studies brings the presumed right of the adult to intervene in children's play into question as we aim to pursue an understanding of childhood informed by children's own meanings. Accounting for the discursive control over children's bodies in educational settings, I acknowledge the forces that constrain children's abilities to express their ideas and act on their worlds in ways we are afforded to understand. Shifting then to new materialist approaches and positioning the child as posthuman subject allows us to build on our understandings of childhood as discursively constructed while also accounting for the materially based experiences of children's lived and embodied childhoods (Dumas & Nelson, 2016).

(Re)Constituting the Young Autistic Child: A Posthuman, Playing Subject

In a self-produced video widely available on YouTube, the late Mel Baggs filmed themself speaking in their "native language," which includes what could easily be read as stereotypical autistic behavior – repetitively fiddling with knobs, flapping hands, or pressing one's face into a book. In the second half of the video, Baggs translates for the viewer with the aid of assisted communication tools, and a computerized voice explains that "my language is not about designing words or even visual symbols for people to interpret. It is about being in a constant conversation with every aspect of my environment" (Baggs, 2007, 3:43). A prolific blogger and neurodiversity activist, Baggs opened a window for others into the often-misunderstood and dehumanized "disabled" body. Relatedly, a recent video storytelling project (Douglas et al., 2021) presented multimedia videos produced by both autistic persons and family members or others who work with autistic people. Like Baggs' video, these short films present new ways of knowing autism, beyond the biomedical, pathologized version so prevalent in educational discourses, and offer an alternative perspective on how communication is widely understood. As young children with a label of autism have likely not yet developed skills to communicate in these ways, looking to autistic adults or older children's telling of their experience provides insight for our attempts at understanding the young child's perspective.

Though habitual ways of knowing seek out intelligible representations, following Braidotti's (2011) positioning of the material body as the "embodiment of the subject" (p. 127), a posthuman subject is "not condemned to seek adequate representation of its existence within a system that is constitutionally incapable of granting due recognition" (p. 188). Multimodal ways of communicating as seen in these videos—art, assistive technology, relatings to objects, etc.—hearken a relationship with the more-than-human world that is often neglected in conversations around "typical" human development. According to Barad (2007), the posthuman subject is situated in a more-than-human ontology, the embodied subject in inextricable intra-action with nonhuman materialities. Autobiographical writing of autistic adults is another genre where the connection to posthumanism is evident as the authors make a case against "human exceptionalism" and convey a strong awareness of the embodied relationship with the more-than-human environment (Murray, 2013). Bergenmar et al. (2015) surveyed autobiographies of autistic adults and identified broad discursive positionings of autistic persons as nonhuman, both in the authors' construction of their own identities and in their perspective on society's view of them.

These frames challenge humanist understandings of the subject as fixed, identifiable, and categorizable. Challenging the anthropocentrism of educational research, inviting the posthuman, rather, allows for a subject that is emergent in a relational field, linked in intra-action with social-material and material-discursive contexts. Matter is assumed agential and a focus on the material body in intra-action comes to the foreground (Barad, 2007). Feely (2016) argues for more new materialist work in critical disability studies as a response to scholarship that has privileged discourse and language as modes of critique, circumstantially disembodying the material subject. Similarly, Goodley et al. (2019) note that new materialist theories provide a way to return focus to the material realities of disability, where previous theorizations have served to reduce disability to a discursive term. This, however, is not to throw out the usefulness of prior critique, but rather, to combine "a post-structuralist politics of critique with a new materialist politics of possibility" (p. 611).

A growing body of scholarship in early childhood studies is exploring applications of posthuman theories and new materialist approaches in studying young children's language development, considering a sensed intelligence about and with the more-than-human world as a way to challenge the anthropocentrism that centers spoken language and focuses on children's deficits (e.g., Hackett et al., 2020; MacRae, 2020). Using these frames, studies have illustrated how the discursive-material constructions of children's language development shift from classroom to more natural, outdoor spaces (Hackett et al., 2020) and how children's sounding and movement practices can contribute to new understandings of place, such as in museum spaces (Hackett & Somerville, 2017). Exploring intra-actions of children and matter, MacRae (2012) posited that classroom material, in this case, a babydoll, did not only animate desires and actions in children but that material was also animated by children's engagements. In other explorations related to what Barad (2007) terms "agential realism," MacRae (2020) and Hultman and Lenz Taguchi (2010) use new materialist analysis to examine children and sand in intra-action, working to decenter the child and position sand as a material with agency. These efforts shift attention away from children's perceived deficits, instead, amplifying their vast capacities in sensory ways of knowing. As in these studies, I am led in my (re)storying that follows by a "conscious effort to decenter the children and consider afresh the role of objects and spaces in what emerged" (Hackett & Somerville, 2017, p. 379). In doing so, it is possible to reframe autistic children's interests not as obsessive and inappropriate behaviors but rather as diverse forms of joyful play (Mitchell & Lashewicz, 2018), intra-actively entangled with the more-than-human world.

(Re)Storying the Spinning Plates

Drawing on autobiographical, narrative, and practitioner research practices, I share here one example of a (re)storying of one of my teaching memories. Writing memory is a process steeped in layers of historical and discursive fields that blurs the lines between data and interpretive analysis. It is mediated through years of experience, contexts of remembering, and shifts in ontological and epistemological beliefs (Richardson, 1997). Memories of teaching also engage affectual spaces as they are tied up with emotion, dreams, and sensory experiences—those aspects of our knowing that are usually unaccounted for in research (St. Pierre, 1997). This type of autobiographical inquiry brings my own discursively constructed self-knowledge under scrutiny, examining the historical, social, and cultural contexts that frame (or have framed) my understanding of young children's play and how young children are represented in relation (Smith & Watson, 2010). I choose to revisit and reexamine my own teaching stories and memories in order to imagine otherwise the ways in which teachers and other practitioners make sense of and engage with young children's play, specifically the play of young autistic children that begs for a reimagining within and against the developmental discourse.

Levi (pseudonym) was 2-years-old when he joined our toddler classroom. Assessed early as having severe language and communication delays, strong sensory aversions, a lack of eye contact, and repetitive and ritualistic behaviors like hand flapping, Levi was diagnosed as low-functioning with autism spectrum disorder before he even entered a school setting. He exhibited many of the stereotypical characteristics of what is often referred to as "severe" autism, spending much of his time in the classroom running back and forth, hand flapping, vocalizing nonspeech sounds, or finding round objects to spin. These behaviors, which he seemed to find much joy in, were automatically defined as in need of intervention due to his diagnosis. The guidance I and my co-teachers received from his therapists was to interrupt these behaviors and direct him to more "appropriate" play, leading to an adult-directed approach to play (Mitchell & Lashewicz, 2018).

Throughout my teacher preparation and first years of teaching, I was complicit in my beliefs that behaviors like these, termed "stimming" in the autism treatment world, could be detrimental to a child's development and need to be controlled in order for them to engage in learning. This is what I was taught, and this was the message I received from therapists that came to work with Levi in the classroom. Even using a therapy approach based in play, there was always an emphasis on helping him to stop "stimming" in order to focus on "productive" play, such as doing a puzzle, building with blocks, or putting food on the plate that he wanted to spin.

Spinning plates was one of Levi's favorite things to do in the classroom. As I was so deeply immersed in the medical, intervention-based discourses of disability back then, I had yet been able to understand Levi's plate-spinning as "play" even as I felt the tensions in my designated role as the teacher-intervenor in these moments. A co-teacher helped me begin to challenge this perspective one day when, instead of stopping the plate spinning, she chose to engage in it with him, with a goal of connecting through what he wanted to do, rather than what we were forcing on him. This shift, though seemingly so simple, was so different than the ways we had been told to support Levi in the classroom. However, making this change, I realized it was the first time we were supporting *him* in the classroom and not just the goals created for him. I no longer saw the plate spinning just as a behavior to stop, but I was able to attend to his body and the ways he engaged with the material more closely, noticing his skill, the fascinating aesthetic of a rapidly spinning blue plastic plate against a beige wooden table, and how his body related to this material in movement with its own rhythmic hand flapping, jumping, and sounding—aspects of his play that I recall and reframe in this memory.

> Levi made a few laps of the classroom, running and stopping in short bursts while vocalizing "ah-AH"s and "ooOO"s with tonal shifts impossible to represent in text. He made his way to the play kitchen and opened the cabinet he opened everyday to find the plastic plates. Lifting one plate off the top of the stack, Levi turned and, with seamless movement, travelled the several steps to the small kitchen table. He pushed items already inhabiting

the space to the side at almost the same time that the plate balanced on its edge against the table, held in place for a brief moment by Levi's hand. In a flash, Levi's hands moved swiftly to push the plate around on its axis and the plate spun. Smoothly gliding in its turns against the table surface until momentum slows just enough for gravity to take over and the plate's axis shifts and the base bangs repeatedly against the table as the spin rattles to a stop. In response, Levi's eyes focus intently on the spinning plate, his arms go out to his sides and his hands flap, hinged at his wrists. He voices a gutteral "ooo-ooo-ooo-ooo." His shoulders tense and release. A shudder, then stillness as he watches the plate come to a stop. A split second, a breath. He picks up the plate again. Repeat.

In my (re)storying of this memory, I chose to shift my observing gaze toward the plate as a way to challenge the anthropocentric view so ingrained in the way I have always observed children at play. By seeing the child as a posthuman subject in intra-action with the more-than-human environment of the classroom (Barad, 2007), I bring a new materialist analysis to this memory as a way to theorize play in ways that exist beyond the dominant narratives of the developmental discourse. My efforts at (re)theorizing play begin with decentering the child in a way that calls attention to Levi's intra-actions with the plate, his bodily responses with movement and sound, and the emergence of new ways of being a human subject in relation to material as part of his complex entanglements with the more-than-human world (Hackett & Somerville, 2017; MacRae, 2020; Olsson, 2009).

The developmental discourse, at first, would tell us that this obsessive, repetitive plate-spinning was inappropriate play for a 2-year old. Beyond that, a developmental perspective may note Levi's advanced fine motor skill and ability to make this plate spin—something even I found difficult to do. Refocusing my gaze with a new materialist lens, I am intrigued with Levi's hand in connection to the plate, not to investigate how the small muscles of his hand work but rather to view his touch, grasp, and manipulation as ways of knowing *with* the plate. Describing intra-action from the point of touch, MacRae (2020) writes, "as hands tender things, they are animated by what they touch, and simultaneously things are animated through the give and take of pulls and pushes of desire expressed as kinetic force" (p. 91). Seeing Levi and the plate relating in this way, they are each offering something to the other in a relational field. As Hultman and Lenz Taguchi (2010) suggest, the plate and Levi are posing questions to each other and thus, make themselves known to the other. Beings do not preexist these intra-actions, rather, it is through these relatings of touch and grasp that they come to constitute themselves and each other simultaneously (Haraway, as cited in MacRae, 2020). We might then ask not just what Levi is doing to the plate, but what the plate is doing to Levi. In this way, we not only think about humans as agentic but also see the nonhuman world and matter as having agency, what Barad (2007) terms agential realism.

Human exceptionalism in developmental theory is most prevalent in the hierarchical understandings of spoken language, as spoken language has been correlated with intelligence of the species. This perspective pathologizes humans who do not speak and constitutes a subject of presumed diminished intelligence. Levi was labeled as nonverbal, thus his ways of communicating were not perceived as mature or as skilled as other 2-year-olds who were beginning to speak words. Observing Levi in my memory of his play, I was drawn to the soundings and movements his body made in relation to the spinning plate: *He voices a gutteral "ooo-ooo-ooo-ooo." His shoulders tense and release. A shudder, then stillness.* What would typically be considered primitive or even nonhuman speech sounds, hold "an excess of meaning" (Hackett & Somerville, 2017, p. 380) as intra-actions between Levi, materials, and place happen without recognizable words. Attending closely to movement and sound, makes more-than-human qualities of communication perceptible in ways that would previously have been overlooked in the search for spoken language development (MacRae, 2020). I imagine Levi's movements and soundings in intra-action with the plate as similar to Bagg's (2007) description of their language being not about words or symbols but as a "constant conversation with every aspect of [the] environment" (3:43). In these ways, we might begin to view nonlinguistic sounding, rhythmic humming and gesturing, or unique movement not as separate from spoken language but as an element of language in a relational-material model of language development (Hackett et al., 2020).

Hackett and Somerville (2017) use movement and sound as a starting point in observations of children in an effort to decenter the human subject. In doing so, they noted how not just speaking, but also gesturing and sounding "were not so much about transmitting information or intentionally designed signs, but about embodied and sensory experiences in which communication about and in place occurred through the body being and moving in place" (p. 374). In this way, I recognize Levi's visible and audible reactions as ways of communicating about the place of the classroom and play kitchen, a situated knowledge intra-actively engaged with the material-discursive space of the plate, table, surrounding materials, and discourses of pretend play. This space is one in which "*non*-human forces are equally at play and work as constitutive factors in children's learnings and becomings" (Hultman & Lenz Taguchi, 2010, p. 527). Through the intra-actions of Levi and the nonhuman forces of the space, the play kitchen is no longer just a place for previously intelligible "pretend play" but a place of discovery, of intra-actions with humans and nonhuman material and forces. Levi contributes, with the plate, to "new versions of place" (Hackett & Somerville, 2017, p. 380), constituting new understandings of what is possible and what it means to be a subject in this classroom space.

To perceive Levi now as a posthuman subject requires a dismissal of the humanist notions of a fixed, stable, autonomous subject detached from their environment. The humanist subject of developmental science is positioned with presumed lack, only in process of becoming the ideal human (Lenz Taguchi, 2014). Rather, the posthuman subject is understood as always becoming-with, a dynamic, intra-active, interdependent process in which unfixed, permeable subjects emerge in relation across the human and nonhuman world (Haraway, 2008). Considering the posthumanist notion of *becoming-with*, I aim to let go of Levi's fixed identity as "autistic child" as it is read by intervention-focused discourses that seek to identify him in the same way across contexts. Rather, Levi, as a subject, is fluid, able to change and make himself intelligible in different ways when in intra-action with different environments. He is becoming subject alongside and simultaneously with his material-discursive surroundings. As we understand Levi in new ways, the plate is also becoming-with in ways that constitute itself differently, as a material with agency. All of this happens in intra-action and affects discourses of play, early childhood, and young children's learning and development. Viewing a child as a posthuman subject extends possibilities for their personhood, far beyond the limiting subject position of "disabled child."

Concluding Thoughts

Attending to play in new materialist and posthuman ways starts from a place of asking, what if we don't intervene? What if we let a child be? What if we perceive classroom materials, lights, sounds, and other bodies as having agency in relation to the child? Decentering the child here destabilizes human exceptionalism primarily defined through language and allows us to recognize and elevate children's sensed intelligence, rather than shaping the entirety of their schooling around their deficiencies (MacRae, 2020). This approach would not only benefit children labeled autistic or disabled, but all children, as our conventional, anthropocentric ways of knowing and assessing children come under scrutiny and possibilities emerge when children's learning and becoming are seen as fluid and emergent in a relational, more-than-human field (Olsson, 2009).

These shifts then push a reimagining of "inclusion" and what it looks like to include neurodiversity in ways that are not focused on interventions that seek to "normalize," letting go of the demand that inclusive educators are expected to be complicit with the dominant scripts around "fixing" autism (Douglas et al., 2021). If instead, we begin to presume the child as a posthuman subject and autism as a way of becoming and being-in-the-world, then the play of young children with autism might not need to be seen as merely a site for suppression and intervention. Rather, play could be emancipated from the realm of assessment and therapy by resignifying young children's "inappropriate" behaviors, such as rocking or hand flapping or plate spinning, as forms of play (Goodley & Runswick-Cole, 2010). It is through these "behaviors," which are so often marked unwanted and challenging, that children with autism are actively constructing their posthuman subjectivities by "escaping the confines of humanism" (van der Palen, 2014, p. 4) in intra-action with their environments through this sensory-material language and play.

Finally, I am reflexively called to examine my position as a teacher and researcher in line with my curiosity and fascination with children's play, particularly the play of autistic children. Employing posthuman theories not only in analysis but also in method and pedagogy, I work to decenter myself as a center of knowing. Data and memory, just as the material plate of Levi's play, take on an agentic role in this work as my own ways of making sense actively shifted throughout the process of writing this chapter. This is an important, and likely uncomfortable feeling for most teachers as we struggle against habits that naturally center the child (Lenz Taguchi, 2014) in order to allow for the opening of spaces that will likely upend our understandings and belief systems. At the same time, because I identify as a nondisabled person, I am mindful of my privilege in a society built on ableism and hold concerns about my production of scholarship *about* autistic children, wary of positioning disability as an "object of curiosity" (Goodley et al., 2019, p. 980). As I continue with related work in the future, I am eager to engage in research and the production of scholarship *with* autistic persons, their families, and those who work with and care for them, continuing to explore and discover new possibilities in conceptualizing play in ways that will serve to expand pedagogy and classroom practices while reimagining inclusive education.

Note

1 Like Mitchell and Lashewicz (2018), I prefer to use "autistic children" to reflect the preference of many in the autistic community to identify as "autistic." I do also use "children labeled with autism" to reflect commonly used terminology in the literature and to acknowledge that the very young children I have worked with do not yet make their ways of identifying themselves known.

References

American Psychiatric Association (APA). (2013). *Diagnostic and statistical manual of mental disorders* (5th ed.). APA.

Baggs, A. (2007). *In my language*. YouTube. https://www.youtube.com/watch?v=JnylM1hI2jc

Barad, K. (2007). *Meeting the universe halfway: Quantum physics and the entanglement of matter and meaning*. Duke University Press.

Barton, E. E., Reichow, B., Wolery, M., & Chen, C. I. (2011). We can all participate! Adapting circle time for children with autism. *Young Exceptional Children, 14*(2), 2–21. https://doi-org.tc.idm.oclc.org/10.1177/1096250610393681.

Bergenmar, J., Bertilsdotter Rosqvist, H., & Lonngren, A. (2015). Autism and the question of the human. *Literature and Medicine, 33,* 202–221. https://doi.org/10.1353/lm.2015.0009.

Braidotti, R. (2011). *Nomadic subjects: Embodiment and sexual difference in contemporary feminist theory* (2nd ed.). Columbia University Press.

Bryan, N. (2020). Shaking the bad boys: Troubling the criminalization of Black boys' childhood play, hegemonic white masculinity and femininity, and the school playground-to-prison pipeline. *Race Ethnicity and Education, 23,* 673–692. https://doi.org/10.1080/13613324.2018.1512483.

Curran, T., & Runswick-Cole, K. (2014). Disabled children's childhood studies: A distinct approach? *Disability and Society, 29,* 1617–1630. https:/doi.org/10.1080/09687599.2014.966187.

Douglas, P., Rice, C., Runswick-Cole, K., Easton, A., Gibson, M. F., Gruson-Wood, J. … Shields, R. (2021). Re-storying autism: A body becoming disability studies in education approach. *International Journal of Inclusive Education, 25,* 605–622. https://doi.org/10.1080/13603116.2018.1563835.

Dumas, M., & Nelson, J. (2016). (Re)imagining Black boyhood: Toward a critical framework for educational research. *Harvard Educational Review, 86,* 27–47. https://doi.org/10.17763/0017-8055.86.1.27.

Feely, M. (2016). Disability studies after the ontological turn: A return to the material world and material bodies without a return to essentialism. *Disability & Society, 31,* 863–883. https://doi.org/10.1080/09687599.2016.1208603.

Goodley, D., & Runswick-Cole, K. (2010). Emancipating play: Dis/abled children, development, and deconstruction. *Disability & Society, 25*(4), 499–512. https://doi.org/10.1080/09687591003755914.

Goodley, D., Lawthom, R., Liddiard, K., & Runswick-Cole, K. (2019). Provocations for critical disability studies. *Disability & Society, 34*(6), 972–977. https://doi.org/10.1080/09687599.2019.1566889.

Hackett, A., & Somerville, M. (2017). Posthuman literacies: Young children moving in time, place and more-than-human worlds. *Journal of Early Childhood Literacy, 17,* 374–391. https://doi.org/10.1177/1468798417704031.

Hackett, A., MacLure, M., & McMahon, S. (2020). Reconceptualising early language development: Matter, sensation, and the more-than-human. *Discourse: Studies in the Cultural Politics of Education, 20,* 3–12. https://doi.org/10.1080/01596306.2020.1767350.

Haraway, D. J. (2008). *When species meet.* University of Minnesota Press.

Hultman, K., & Lenz Taguchi, H. (2010). Challenging anthropocentric analysis of visual data: A relational materialist methodological approach to educational research. *International Journal of Qualitative Studies in Education, 23*(5), 525–542. https://doi.org/10.1080/09518398.2010.500628.

Lenz Taguchi, H. (2014). New materialisms and play. In L. Brooker, M. Blaise, & S. Edwards, (Eds.), *Sage handbook of play and learning in early childhood* (pp. 79–90). Sage.

Lillard, A. S., & Taggart, J. (2019). Pretend play and fantasy: What if Montessori was right? *Child Development Perspectives, 13*(2), 85–90. https://doi.org/10.1111/cdep.12314.

MacRae, C. (2012). Encounters with a life(less) baby doll: Rethinking relations of agency through a collectively lived moment. *Contemporary Issues in Early Childhood, 13,* 120–131. https://doi.org/10.2304/ciec.2012.13.2.120.

MacRae, C. (2020). Tactful hands and vibrant mattering in the sand tray. *Journal of Early Childhood Literacy, 20*, 90–110. http://dx.doi.org/10.1177/1468798420901858.

Mitchell, J., & Lashewicz, B. (2018). Quirky kids: Fathers' stories of embracing diversity and dismantling expectations for normative play with their children with autism spectrum disorder. *Disability & Society, 33*(7), 1120–1137.

Murray, S. (2013). Autism and the posthuman. In J. Davidson and M. Orsini (Eds.), *Worlds of autism: Across the spectrum of neurological difference* (pp. 53–72). University of Minnesota Press.

Olsson, L. M. (2009). *Movement and experimentation in young children's learning: Deleuze and Guattari in early childhood education.* Routledge.

Prout, A., & James, A. (2014). A new paradigm for the sociology of childhood? Provenance, promise and problems. In A. James & A. Prout (Eds.), *Constructing and reconstructing childhood: Contemporary issues in the sociological study of childhood* (pp. 6–28). Routledge.

Richardson, L. (1997). *Fields of play: Constructing an academic life.* Rutgers University Press.

Russ, S. W. (2016). Pretend play: Antecedent of adult creativity. *New Directions for Child and Adolescent Development, 151*, 21–32. https://doi.org/10.1002/cad.20154.

Smith, S., & Watson, J. (2010). *Reading autobiography: A guide for interpreting life narratives* (2nd ed.). University of Minnesota Press.

St. Pierre, E. A. (1997). Methodology in the fold and the irruption of transgressive data. *International Journal of Qualitative Research, 10*(2), 175–189. https://doi.org/10.1080/095183997237278.

van der Palen, T. (2014). *A cyborg autobiography: Autism & the posthuman* (Master's thesis, Utrecht University). dspace.library.uu.nl

6

THE "NO NOISE" CHAIR AND OTHER WILLFUL OBJECTS

Examining Young Children's Sonic "Moorings" and Animate Literacies in the Geographies of Play

Jon M. Wargo

Working at the axis of radical empiricism and posthumanism, this chapter engages what Snaza names "animate literacies" (Snaza, 2019) to examine the enmeshment of "affect" (Conradson & Latham, 2007) and mobility (Sheller, 2014) in early learning. In order to facilitate this demonstration, I discuss points of resonance and tension—a set of stacked stories—that emerged from a series of studies of young children "making space" to mobilize literacy learning. In so doing, I attend to the coproduction of sonic mobilities and literacy-related activities grafted onto two "willful" (Ahmed, 2014) objects, a masking tape square and a bike seat bolted to a wooden block.

The first story maps the iterative construction of material geographies by which Clayton, a so-called striving reader, was contained and built. Examining the imagined routes and rhythms of peers' movement in/through/around/ with his masking tape square, I trace the frictions that surfaced as students not only created playful subversions but also in the residual rhythms of disciplining and controlling Clayton as an animate subject. The second sketch focuses on an immobile bike seat, an anchor object on which three-year-old Charlotte was asked to sit during whole group instruction.

Following how these concepts and objects attach to subjects, I aim to address two interrelated inquiries:

1 How do "willful" objects of school-sanctioned control produce (im)mobilities in formal educational spaces?
2 What "permanences" (Harvey, 1996) or "moorings" (Hannem et al., 2006) underpin these "heard" mobilities? How might they enable and delimit particular ways of knowing, doing, learning, and being in the early years?

DOI: 10.4324/9781003399155-9

Thinking-with-Theory: Being Attuned to "Willful" Children

Feminist poststructural research in early childhood education has complicated the anthropocentric notion of the child as an autonomous learner detached from its environment. This literature and its focus on "thinking-with-theory" (Jackson & Mazzei, 2013) have reinscribed the child as simultaneously situational, contextual, and discursively inscribed. Although a growing body of literature examines the intra-actions of the material discursive in early childhood literacy (see, e.g., Hackett, 2021; Murris, 2016), few examine how the material technologies of classroom life work in tandem with the aural and felt atmospheres of play. In other words, little is known about how the social, spatial, and sonorous collide in early learning spaces.

Standing shoulder to shoulder with those colleagues following and forwarding the more-than-human turn in early literacy studies (Boldt, 2021; Dernikos, 2018; Dutro, 2019; Hackett & Somerville, 2017; Kuby et al., 2018; Leander & Ehret, 2019; Lenters, 2016; Truman et al., 2021), in this chapter I talk across three concepts (attunement, willfulness, and noise) and stitch together their meaning as it comes to inform issues of (im)mobility in early literacy learning.

Reading the "Noisy" Child as a Willful Subject

Drawing on the Brothers Grimm fairy tale "The Wilful Child," Sara Ahmed, in her book *Willful Subjects*, highlights how willfulness—as a space for vitality—"might not reside within a subject" (p. 12) alone but in objects as well. For example, in classroom spaces, one might refer to a *noisy child* as willful. From instructional practices structured to silence and quiet to more physical actions—a hand that rests on a shoulder as a teacher navigates around the room—the willful child is a sonic body. It is heard. It is felt. But what condition does noise—as a concept—hold as a condition of willfulness?

Noise is sound unmediated. More than sonic pollution that challenges mainstream aesthetics and ideologies, noise is an expressive index that symbolically and materially claims space. It refigures aural encounters of culture through communicative forms of more-than-human expression. Noise cannot be captured and constrained by definition (i.e., what it is), rather by what it does. As Hegarty (2021) details, "noise is nothing [...] or everything" (p. 1). Noise is the entanglement of subjectivity and objectivity. It is the "ineluctable noncoincidence of emission and reception" (Chow & Steintrager, 2011, p. 11). "Noise," as Malaspina (2018) writes, "reveals itself to be conceptually polymorphous because it has never been about types, classes, or measures of phenomena that qualify it as a particular type of disturbance, but about the relation between contingency and control" (Malaspina, 2018, p. 203). Noise is a philosophical optic.

In early literacy research, noise—and sound more broadly—has been featured as an element of multimodal design and material mattering. Whether investigating how emergent listening fostered new pedagogical spaces through "noisy" sonic play (Davies, 2014; Wargo, 2017) or attuning toward sound's capacity to foster a relational "withness" among humans and more-than-humans (Guzmán-Simón & Pacheco-Costa, 2021; Hackett & Somerville, 2017; Powell & Somerville, 2020; Wargo, 2018, 2019, 2021; Wargo & Alvarado, 2020), sound registered new insights regarding the cultural politics of early learning. Sound, in equal measure, also works systemically. As a form of meaning-making, sound incites us to rethink issues of affect, equity, and agency. Brownell (2019), for instance, used critical positioning theories to highlight how the sonic shaped and disrupted minoritized children's identities in a third-grade classroom. Dernikos (2020), similarly, turned up the volume on the aural to document how sound functioned and was affectively transmitted by, white-coded models of knowledge production in a reading classroom. Although these are but some of the many ways the sonic has been taken up in literacies research, these scenes of scholarship detail how the sound spotlights and silences particular bodies and voices. Regardless of focus or analytic approach, the sonic dimensions of children's learning continue to echo as critical issues in contemporary early years debates.

Attuning toward the Sounds and Silences of Early Learning

If, theoretically, we are to examine the noisy child as a willful subject, then we need the theoretical vocabulary to attune toward the sounds and silences of affective life. Attunement, as a concept, has many intellectual lineages in continental philosophy and social theory. Rather than talk across these divergent accounts or provide a summary of Heideggerian (1962) or Cavellian (1976) notions of the word, I want to use it here like Erin Manning does. Drawing upon the work of Daniel Stern, Manning foregrounds the unconscious aspects of the concept in linking her construction of attunement to affect. She writes in *Always More Than One: Individuation's Dance*:

> [A]ffective attunement is a preconscious tuning-with that sparks a new set of relations that in turn affect how singular events express themselves in the time of the event. Subtle and ongoing, affective attunements "give much of the impression of the quality of the relationship" (Stern, 1985, p. 141). Affective attunement makes felt the activation contours of experience, the intensity, as Suzanne Langer would say, of virtual feeling. This links affective attunement to affective tonality rather than either to empathy or to the matching of behavior. Stern defines this as a matching of feeling (p. 11)

Manning, unlike Heidegger or Wittgenstein, understands attunement not solely as a social practice or human phenomenon, but as a relationship between nonhuman things. She writes that

> ...affective attunement need not be solely located on a human scale. If conceived beyond human interaction, affective attunement might well describe the relational environment co-created by movement and sound .... Affective attunement: an open field of differentiation out of which a singularity of feeling emerges and merges. A tuning not of content, but of expression-with.
>
> *(Manning, 2013, p. 11)*

Expanding the scope and reach of the concept, Manning's understanding cultivates what she names "affective tonality" (p. 11), an assemblage of representation and affect that serves as a locating mechanism for feeling.

For this chapter, attunement operates as a relational analytic. It traces feelings of resonance and dissonance as affect registers across and with bodies. From this perspective, children (as "noisy subjects") and the objects that socialize, shape, communicate, and enforce particular disciplinary expectations of sonic disturbance and movement can be read as willful texts. Following Dernikos (2018), I understand a willful text "as an object that has the agentive capacity to stick to students' bodies, intra-act (Barad, 2007) with other social bodies and produce surging affects that shape a subject's will or agency" (p. 6). Leveraging Ahmed, Malaspina, and Manning's concepts as navigational guides, I will illustrate how these willful texts constituted tenuous "constellations of mobility" (Cresswell, 2010) with, for, and against young children's literacy learning.

Modes of Inquiry

Taking seriously that place—in part—is produced through how it is heard and materializes, this chapter uses a "stacked stories" (Burnett & Merchant, 2016) method to understand how the experiences of sound and willfulness crystalize into a collaborative co-authored text. Building on poststructural approaches to postqualitative analysis, a stacked stories approach extends baroque sensibilities in data representation. "A baroque sensibility," as Burnett and Merchant (2016) contend, "can help assert the messiness of educational experience and the contingent nature of meaning making that lie at the heart of ... learning" (p. 258). Because a stacked stories approach follows the six techniques of the baroque: knowing as distribution and movement, theatricality, boundlessness, heterogeneity, folding, and otherness (adapted from Law, 2011), I use an intra-active form of data analysis to read across/between/on these stories.

Using a stacked stories approach to data analysis examines play and early writing as an entangled matter, as an iterative becoming, not a thing but a doing and congealment of agency. Methodologically, I re-enter the data presented here with an acute awareness of the production of experience and the limited sensorium we have access to in the edited volume. The stories are drawn from my own empirical materials—interviews, field notes, observation, auto-ethnographic vignettes, sound recordings, and the discursive analysis of early learners' engagement with space. So stacked, they underscore how humans and the more-than-human are both the singular and plural, the oscillation and unfolding of intensities and literacy desirings that work through the material discursive. My goal in stacking is to highlight the felt emergence and contrastive desirings of "animate literacies."

Renderings

Two stories, juxtaposed and told from diverse perspectives and contexts, are stacked to evoke the possibilities of re-writing noise in early childhood research. As a literacies researcher, these stories are generated with the presupposition that sound can be read both as a heard decodable text and as a felt material, imbued with an affective capacity that moves, shapes, and transforms events. I present these stories in succession without comment or interruption to evoke partial takes, fragments of the complexity that raise questions and point to discontinuities about the possibilities of thinking with noise when guided by what Lenz Taguchi and St. Pierre (2017) called a "concept-as-method approach." Despite its importance, this impact of noise—audible and heard acoustic interference—is not what I am interested in exploring. Rather, by stacking these stories together, I invite readers to read my own witnessing of events with the caveat that I, of course, acknowledge the limitations of flattening the modal capacity here in form. The goal of these stories is neither triangulation nor is it to arrive at any form of truth concerning children's capacity for willful production in early teaching and learning. Instead, my goal is to incite dissonance, to read across and between these stories to consider what it may mean to take seriously the sonorous in early childhood research. How might sound open up (or close) our bodies in writing and desiring place as a co-authored text?

The Silent Square

"Where are the chairs?" This was the first question I asked Mrs. O'Toole when I entered her multi-age (7–9 years old) classroom in the 2016–2017 academic year. "What?" she responded inquisitively. "We don't need chairs," she replied. "We have flexible seating." Lined by beanbags, exercise balls, and slats of carpet, there was no visible chair outside of the 8 that lined the U-shaped table in the classroom. "We flood for guiding reading," she said. That's why we have those [chairs] right there. I don't want the other kids coming in not knowing what to do." Inquisitively, I walked over to a double-lined masking tape square glued down to the carpet. "And this," I asked. "Oh, that's the silent square. It's for our noisy friends."

Fast forward 4 months. The bell rings and Mrs. O'Toole's mix of 7, 8, and 9-year-olds begin snowballing into the room. Star, Isaiah, Theo, Grace, and Claire all circled me showing me their work. These five alongside six more are now focal participants to a larger study examining how young students leverage technology to write across genre. Together, they hurriedly move me over to the screen and I, by accident, step foot in the silent square. "You're dead," Isaiah—a white 8-year-old boy says laughing. He shoves me, almost to show me through his performative masculinity he's joking. "No, he's not," Clayton the white 7-year-old square occupant says. "You can sit in here with me." Mrs. O'Toole, seeing the interaction comes over. "Clayton," where should you be? "It's silent reading time, so it's silent square for you."

Star, Isaiah's Black 8-year-old peer picks up Isaiah's constructed idea of the 2-foot by 2-foot square. "It's lava Jon! The floor is lava" he shouts. You only have one-leg." Clayton grows visibly upset. "The square isn't bad. I'm not even making noise or talking now" he says. Clayton looks to Mrs. O'Toole who is situating materials for guided reading groups. I grow irritated with Star and Isaiah. I sit down next to Clayton, too large to occupy the square with him, and sit half in and half out. The square, although an inanimate object meant to mute, is now the center of attention. Seeing this, Clayton gets up. He starts pantomiming with one foot out of the square. Clayton toggles to his left, the side that is unbounded by the tape, and starts moving his mouth to signal that he is talking. He places his right foot in and SMACK. His palms hit the sides of his legs. Clayton now stands at attention. He laughs almost to encourage others to giggle at his bodied demonstration.

From the corner of the room, the boisterous hand-signal brings everyone to attention. "Clap, Clap, CLAP-CLAP-CLAP," Mrs. O'Toole loudly asserts. "Clap, Clap" the children respond. "No noise means don't move Clayton," she asserts. Mrs. O'Toole looks at me, shakes her head and finishes passing out whiteboards. Clayton asks me to finish the last chapter of Kate Messner's (2011) *Marty McGuire*. We read sitting alongside one another. "The silent square isn't bad Clayton," Mrs. O'Toole says walking over and kneeling next to us. "It's just something special. Something just for you." "And Jon," he retorts. "Yes," Mrs. O'Toole replies, "and Dr. Wargo."

The No Noise Chair

"Make your marker dance!" Following the tap-tap-tap-tap-uh-tap-tap of rain playing on the classroom loudspeakers, 13 young children begin making staccato dashes with watercolor markers. Charlotte, a younger Asian American 3-year old with bangs cut askew, grabs another child's arms. She lifts it up and down, watching not the child's exasperated look from being prodded, but the way her actions transform into scribed marks on the construction paper. The corporeal arm transduces felt sounds on white butcher paper. Ms. K, the white Pre-K teacher, raises her arm so as to shush the children. "Remember friends," Ms. K says. "My arm goes up; my mouth goes shut." The children hold both hands over their mouths signaling the surrounding silence the classroom now encases. The music continues. The track changes. The classroom refrain responds. Charlotte, now hearing the BONG BONG of the bass drum playing on the CD, starts screaming on beat. Bong. **Bong**. Bong! Her low bass timbre mixes with felt laughs. She looks on, almost asking why the other children are not joining in. The melodic form takes over and the other children rush to the carpet and sit in their squares silent.

"Charlotte," Ms. K, implores. "Do you need the no noise chair?" She walks over to the library station and relocates what looks to be a neon green bike seat. Ms. K places the seat on the floor in front of me and Melita, my graduate student research assistant who now looks horrified at the found artifact. Melita mouths the words "What is this?" to me. We have come to know Ms. K for several years now. We have never seen the no-noise chair before. Reacting quickly to our widened eyes, Ms. K notifies us that "It's from the occupational therapist. This isn't my idea."

Charlotte, standing firm, resolutely responds with a "No." Ms. K walks over to Charlotte and gestures with her hand. "Here, come join me. Everyone is reading before lunch." Cece, a white red-haired 3-year-old, echoes "Come read Charlotte." Charlotte, now looking at Melita and I, defiantly screams. A visceral sounding that is felt on our collective body.

Ms. K walks over to the classroom boom box and hits play. Sung to the nursery rhyme of Frère Jacques, a voice rings out: "eyes are watching, ears are listening, voices quiet, bodies calm. This is how we listen, this is how we listen, at group time, at group time." Melita and I stand up from our criss-cross position just behind the carpet and look onto Ms. K. Charlotte runs toward the bike seat and turns it over. With two arms on the shaped spine of the chair, she works—begrudgingly—and slowly forwards the piece of furniture to the back of the room. "It doesn't go by the water table," Kieffer—a Latino 3-year-old—details. "OK, Charlotte, I guess I will be your no noise chair." Ms. K walks over to the child and physically embraces her. "My arms can be your straps." Charlotte continues to cry, but she now holds Ms. K and returns the embrace. Yusef, a white peer of Charlotte's stands up, walks over to the chair, and sits in the bike seat. He carefully slips his small arms through the straps and leans back so as to snap the clip in tight. "It's OK Charlotte, I can be quiet for you."

Reading Across

To take affective and posthumanist critiques of early literacy seriously requires a shift in the theoretical vocabulary and methodological imaginary. Indeed, we need new lexicons for expressing the vibrancy and volume of young children's sonic (im)mobilities. For some, you may ask how these two stacked stories operate. Why does this matter? What might this teach us about diverse childhoods? Who (or what) should we blame? For me, sound centers praxis.

If classrooms and other learning spaces serve as sonic hosts to children's bodies, a more robust understanding of the "noisy" child as a willful subject is necessary. Outside of the always already racialized, gendered, sexed, and classed ways of recognizing "noisy bodies" as those to assign blame to, so too must we recognize how noisy children are classified as willful, an affective expression forwarding feelings of rejection and enclosure. Noise, as refracted through Clayton and Charlotte, was unwieldy. It was insubordinate. As subjects, their willfulness/noisiness became a difference to discipline. Albeit implicitly, the move to silence sedimented ready-known instructional and interactional practices—a hand on the shoulder, a holding hug. Sedimented over time, silence became one of the few routes through which Clayton and Charlotte moved in their classrooms. Their once willful bodies—communicated through shouted screams and choreographed movements—became compliant. Whereas each story, independently, highlights how noise became punitively disciplined, together they tell the tale of the noisy "troublemaker," a heard category that not only reproduces stratified social hierarchies but labels a stunted social identity.

As a concept and practice, attunement yields insight into investigating the acousmatic diversions of sonic objects, material conceits, and ideological productions of noise that act as the carapace to the willful child. It helps widen the methodological angle we come to know children and childhood in classroom life. Analytically, attunement reorganized the representational logics of language to eschew a theoretical account of the senses that one could control or discipline. It advanced new forays for willing what Boldt (2021), drawing from Stern, describes as vitality, the "feel of flowing and aliveness" (Stern, 2010, p. 23). Willful sounds and subjects—refracted here through silent squares and no-noise chairs—transformed "the cartography of the perceptible, the thinkable, and the feasible" into what Rancière (2010) introduced as "a multiplicity of folds and gaps in the fabric of common experience" (p. 3). Attuning toward and with the sonic, as this chapter suggests, incites new ways to hear the harmonies and noisy transgressions of teaching and learning.

(In)Conclusion

To end, I want to close by parsing the precarity and politics of "animate literacies" in early schooling and gesture toward a more integrated approach to examining young children's movement and play—one that resists attempts to bracket off the senses and silences noise for one that is both inclusive of and responsive toward the sonic. Indeed, as Springgay and Truman (2018) note, affect refuses to be captured. It, instead, "proposes problems rather than seeking solutions" (Springgay & Truman, 2018, p. 208). Hence, rather than provide exhaustive remarks, I want to chart two provocations, problem spaces that can be picked up or left behind during your read of this text. First, how are sonic (im)mobilities produced in spaces and places of early learning? What moments of (intra-)action do we—as educators and researchers of young children—turn up the volume on and which do you silence? How do we reproduce (in)equality by disciplining difference? Second, how are injustices—heard, felt, and/or silenced—(re)inscribed in the same willful objects meant to dismantle them?

References

Ahmed, S. (2014). *Willful subjects*. Duke University Press.

Barad, K. (2007). *Meeting the universe halfway: Quantum physics and the entanglement of matter and meaning*. Duke University Press.

Boldt, G. (2021). Theorizing vitality in the literacy classroom. *Reading Research Quarterly, 56*(2), 207–221.

Brownell, C. J. (2019). Sound the alarm!: Disrupting sonic resonances of an elementary English language arts classroom. *Curriculum Inquiry, 49*(5), 551–572.

Burnett, C., & Merchant, G. (2016). Boxes of poison: Baroque technique as antidote to simple views of literacy. *Journal of Literacy Research, 48*(3), 258–279.

Cavell, S. (1976). *Must we mean what we say? A book of essays*. Cambridge Press.

Chow, R., & Steintrager, J. A. (2011). In pursuit of the object of sound: An introduction. *Differences, 22*(2–3), 1–9.

Conradson, D., & Latham, A. (2007). The affective possibilities of London: Antipodean transnationals and the overseas experience. *Mobilities, 2*(2), 231–254.

Cresswell, T. (2010). Towards a politics of mobility. *Environment and Planning D: Society and Space, 28*, 17–31.

Davies, B. (2014). *Listening to children: Being and becoming*. Routledge.

Dernikos, B. P. (2018). "It's like you don't want to read it again": Exploring affects, trauma and "willful" literacies. *Journal of Early Childhood Literacy*. https://doi.org/10.1177/1468798418756187.

Dernikos, B. P. (2020). Tuning into rebellious matter: Affective literacies as more-than-human sonic bodies. *English Teaching: Practice & Critique, 19*(4), 417–432.

Dutro, E. (2019). How affect theory can support justice in our literacy classrooms: Attuning to the visceral. *Language Arts, 96*(6), 384–389.

Guzmán-Simón, F., & Pacheco-Costa, A. (2021). "Like, I'm playing, but with this". Materialization and affect in early childhood literacy. *Journal of Early Childhood Literacy*. https://doi.org/10.1177%2F14687984211068117.

Hackett, A. (2021). *More-than-human literacies in early childhood*. Bloomsbury.

Hackett, A., & Somerville, M. (2017). Posthuman literacies: Young children moving in time, place and more-than-human worlds. *Journal of Early Childhood Literacy, 17*(3), 374–391.

Hannem, K., Sheller, M., & Urry, J. (2006). Mobilities, immobilities, and moorings. *Mobilities*, *1*(1), 1–22.

Harvey, D. (1996). *Justice, nature, and the politics of difference.* Blackwell.

Hegarty, P. (2021). *Annihilating noise.* Bloomsbury Publishing.

Heidegger, M. (1962). *Being and time* (J. Macquarrie & E. Robinson, trans.). Blackwell.

Jackson, A. Y., & Mazzei, L. (2013). Plugging one text into another: Thinking with theory in qualitative research. *Qualitative Inquiry*, *19*, 261–271.

Kuby, C. R., Spector, K., & Thiel, J. J. (Eds.). (2018). *Posthumanism and literacy education: Knowing/becoming/doing literacies.* Routledge.

Law, J. (2011). *Against method: Mess in social science research.* Routledge.

Leander, K. M., & Ehret, C. (Eds.). (2019). *Affect in literacy learning and teaching: Pedagogies, politics and coming to know.* Routledge.

Lenters, K. (2016). Riding the lines and overwriting in the margins: Affect and multimodal literacy practices. *Journal of Literacy Research*, *48*(3), 280–316.

Malaspina, C. (2018). *An epistemology of noise.* Bloomsbury Publishing.

Manning, E. (2013). *Always more than one: Individuation's dance.* Duke University Press.

Messner, K. (2011). *Marty McGuire* (B. Cloca, Illus.). Scholastic.

Murris, K. (2016). *The posthuman child: Educational transformation through philosophy with picturebooks.* Routledge.

Powell, S., & Somerville, M. (2020). Drumming in excess and chaos: Music, literacy and sustainability in early years learning. *Journal of Early Childhood Literacy*, *20*(4), 839–861. https://doi.org/10.1177%2F1468798418792603.

Rancière, J. (2010). *Dissensus: On politics and aesthetics.* Continuum.

Sheller, M. (2014). The new mobilities paradigm for a live sociology. *Current Sociology Review*, *62*(6), 789–811.

Snaza, N. (2019). *Animate literacies: Literature, affect, and the politics of humanism.* Duke University Press.

Springgay, S., & Truman, S. E. (2018). *Walking methodologies in a more-than-human world: WalkingLab.* Routledge.

Stern, D. N. (1985). *The interpersonal world of the infant.* Basic Books.

Stern, D. N. (2010). *Forms of vitality: Exploring dynamic experience in psychology, the arts, psychotherapy and development.* Oxford University Press.

Taguchi, H. L., & St. Pierre, E. A. (2017). Using concept as method in educational and social science inquiry. *Qualitative Inquiry*, *23*(9), 643–648.

Truman, S. E., Hackett, A., Pahl, K., McLean Davies, L., & Escott, H. (2021). The capaciousness of no: Affective refusals as literacy practices. *Reading Research Quarterly*, *56*(2), 223–236.

Wargo, J. M. (2017). Rhythmic rituals and emergent listening: Intra-activity, sonic sounds, and digital composing with young children. *Journal of Early Childhood Literacy*, *17*(3), 392–408. https://doi.org/10.1177%2F1468798417712573.

Wargo, J. M. (2018). Writing with wearables? Young Children's intra-active authoring and the sounds of emplaced invention. *Journal of Literacy Research*, *50*(4), 502–523. https://doi.org/10.1177%2F1086296X18802880.

Wargo, J. M. (2019). Sounding the garden, voicing a problem: Mobilizing critical literacy through personal digital inquiry with young children. *Language Arts*, *96*(5), 275–285.

Wargo, J. M. (2021). "Sound" civics, heard histories: A telling case of young children mobilizing digital media to write (Right) injustice. *Theory and Research in Social Education,* *49*(3), 360–389. https://www.tandfonline.com/doi/full/10.1080/00933104.2021.1874582?src

Wargo, J. M., & Alvarado, J. (2020). Making as worlding: Young children composing change through speculative design. *Literacy,* *54*(2), 13–21. https://doi.org/10.1111/lit.12209.

7

(RE)SOUNDING CHILDREN'S WORLDS

Making a Case for Methods that Tune in

Cassie J. Brownell

"This is Francisco and Allen.[1] *This is the water falling from the drink thingy majigger."*

"What the?! … oh, the water fountain!" fourth-grader Francisco—a Latino boy—exclaimed over the giggles of Allen, his first-grade buddy, whose voice described the "thingy majigger" on a recording they collaboratively created.

"Yeah," the still giggling Allen—a Black boy—said, rocking back-and-forth between his chair's armrests. Exchanging smiles, both boys laughed as Francisco told me, "Oh, yeah, I keep forgetting the names [of things]."

Clustered around my computer at their elementary school, the two young boys and I listened together to their audio recording, made in previous days. Their collective recording was a part of a research inquiry I engaged in with their two teachers to consider how, for children's ears, the sounds of schooling (and community) might differ from sounds attuned to by adults.

In my experience with Francisco, Allen, and their peers, I quickly realized just how dissimilar children's and adults' listening experiences could be. One such example came a few moments after the boys' chuckling subsided.

"Well, what do you think about the water fountain?" I asked Francisco and Allen. "I don't know," said Allen, with his arms outstretched on the table. Leaning back in his chair, Francisco commented, "I think it was … I don't know. Gargling?" shrugging his shoulders. Allen hurriedly chimed in, "Yeah, like, hnnnnnnnn …," lifting his chin to make the sound effect. "You know? Like when you press the button?" Allen clarified.

DOI: 10.4324/9781003399155-10

Catching on to what Allen was indicating, I asked if "hnnnnnnn" was representative of the motor mechanism's hum that ensured each fountain sip was cold. As we continued, Allen made clear how numerous sounds—the motor, the flowing water both down his throat and that which fell to the fountain—collided as he drank. Then, the boys listed for me the numerous times they drank from the fountain daily, including after gym and being outdoors.

For many readers, the nuanced sounds of the water fountain recording and the additional sounds described by the boys might be easily dismissed, perhaps even considered unimportant. Yet, this single instance of listening demonstrated for me how the audible sounds of schooling children recorded differed from those of adult hearers, including me—a white woman—in the space of their urban elementary school in the Midwestern United States.

On (Re)Learning to Listen

As an adult hearer, I had spent nearly a decade amongst the sounds of elementary schools when I conversed with Francisco and Allen, including 5 years teaching in New Orleans followed by 5 years as a researcher in the boys' Michigan school. As a novice educator, my understanding of the sounds of schooling largely reflected an aversion to "noise." Especially since my teacher training depicted "loud" classrooms as representative of "out-of-control" or chaotic spaces, I spent my first year teaching trying to restrict or constrain particular reverberations, fearing how my colleagues or administration might read me as an educator.

However, in shifting from lead teacher to an early year's researcher, I no longer interpreted sounds I heard only as echoes of tumultuous commotion. Instead, I grew to understand the rumblings and reverberations I once qualified as "noise" in more nuanced ways. I recognized as a researcher the need to retrain my body to "be more aware, alert, and attuned to sonic events in all of their complexity" through what Ceraso (2014) calls "multimodal listening" (p. 103). As I fine-tuned my skills related to ambient sounds, I shifted from simply being a *hearer* to becoming a full-body *listener*, aware of the tonal qualities of sound and the felt vibrations and affective capacities of the sonic.

Cumulatively, my experiences relearning to listen led me to consider new questions and new research methods. For instance, as I attuned my ears to the ambient acoustics of everyday school life, I wondered, what might adults learn from listening alongside children to understand more about their lived (schooling) experiences? In turn, I became more attuned to the aural geographies of schooling. Simultaneously, I began to ponder how it was that sound—as "medium, method, and modality" (Wargo et al., 2021, p. 316)—might offer alternative means for understanding children and their social worlds.

Attuning to Children's (Sonic) Experiences of Schooling

While many critical childhood scholars have inquired about how children and adults form relationships within school-sanctioned spaces (Corsaro, 2003; Dyson, 2021), most have utilized ocular-centric methods for doing so. Fewer scholars have asked how children's sonic encounters might elucidate distinct understandings (Wargo & Morales, 2021). In part, the latter remains nascent in the literature, perhaps because what one sees often appears more concrete and simultaneously less ephemeral than what one hears. Moreover, scholarly findings from visually based studies typically provide actionable, adult-oriented tasks for adults. Especially in the neoliberal era, easily measurable tasks are favored by policymakers and practitioners alike, despite long-standing critiques (Dahlberg et al., 1999; Genishi & Dyson, 2012). Frequently, within early childhood and elementary education research, this can include everything from disciplinary referrals (Boonstra, 2019; Ferguson, 2000) to adult documentation (Cowan & Flewitt, 2020, 2021; Graue, 1993) and standardized curricular evaluations (Yoon, 2013). Put simply, adults endure in their positioning as the knowledge bearers in schools and as the individuals with agency and the ability to act (or, control; Dumas & Nelson, 2016). Comparatively, children's perspectives remain, at best, peripheral in school, society, and much of the wider literature (Brownell & Parks, 2021; Paley, 1986; Yoon & Templeton, 2019), including children's sonic experiences of schooling.

In considering the disparity between the inherent valuing of adults' perspectives and visual modes over children's aural experiences, my larger inquiry centered on children's listening. Aligned with calls for a sensory turn in educational studies (Mills, 2016), I turned up the volume of children's experiences by asking, *How do children hear the world? How might their listening attune adults to the real and imagined sounds of (school) community?* In this chapter, I zero in on a series of audio recordings Francisco, Allen, and their classmates made in response to the prompt *What sounds are most important for a new student or a visitor to hear to understand our school community?* To begin, I connect my inquiry to previous research. Next, I use examples garnered from this final inquiry during my 5-year research partnership with Francisco and Allen's school to highlight how a sonically grounded, child-centered methodological approach helped children not just show but also make audible their understandings of their worlds (Clark, 2011; Dyson & Genishi, 2005). Then, I call attention to how children's listening differed from what I (and, likely, other adults) traditionally considered the sounds of schooling. Ultimately, I use this chapter to challenge colleagues to reimagine possible qualitative methods for coming to know, to be, and to be known alongside children in schools.

Tuning in to the Sounds of Schooling

While on the one hand, the expansion of smartphones has afforded many people a personalized sound system, so too has listening become a more individualized experience than before (Krukowski, 2017). Especially prior to the COVID-19 pandemic, few public arenas appeared untouched by the proliferation of headphones, as adults popped in earbuds for daily commutes and workouts. Nevertheless, primary classrooms remained one public venue that seemingly escaped the personal listening movement. Even as the prevalence of digital composing in schools and the wider world continues to increase, many children are only just beginning to be afforded opportunities to compose digitally; fewer still are asked to do so with sound as the primary mode (Wargo, 2018).

Furthermore, most children have little acoustic or bodily autonomy in public institutions, including schools, because regulatory authorities (e.g., teachers, other adults) often control children's movements and sounds (Milner et al., 2019). Within school walls, limited opportunities exist for children to linger in spaces or monitor their volume without oversight from adult authorities (Burke & Grosvenor, 2011; Gallagher, 2011). For instance, in many North American schools, children are usually expected to move at a particular pace, in a single row, with eyes forward, hands at their sides, and *quiet* mouths. Traditionally, learners who fall out of line face disciplinary action. In this way, children's movements and sounds in schools—a heavily institutionalized setting—are typically scrutinized and surveilled (Adair & Colegrove, 2021). This is particularly true for racialized children, especially since sound is socioculturally and sociopolitically situated (Dernikos, 2020). As such, sound remains undergirded by histories of white supremacy (Stoever, 2016; Weheliye, 2014). Although some children do resist such norms, their sonic experiences often remain *unheard* in school discourse and educational research (Brownell, 2019).

In response to the dearth of scholarly and practical knowledge about young children's sonic experiences of schooling, I sought to amplify children's encounters by positioning them as authorities as they shared school sounds that resonated with them. Specifically, I presented fifty children in first and fourth grades the opportunity to write digital compositions by recording a modified soundwalk—a walk during which the primary purpose is listening (Schafer, 1994; Westerkamp, 1974). As noted by Drever (2009), as compositions, soundwalks can be seemingly composed along a linear trajectory or, alternatively, as "extemporized performance, contingent on the vicissitudes of the environment in correspondence with the whims of the composer as sherpa" (p. 163). Still, no matter the form of a soundwalk, everyday life remains its central feature.

Historically, sound studies scholars and artists have intentionally incorporated sound with movement to teach concepts about sound and critically consider space, place, and community (Rousell et al., 2018). Soundwalking, then, can be a research and pedagogical method that potentially enables children's acts of resistance in public venues. Further, because children's movements *are* marked and regulated within most public spaces, including schools, the need to cast children as documenters of school experiences is all the more imperative in order to create new publics.

Across the disciplines, scholars have identified sound as one tool to amplify how power operates within publics, including institutions like schools, prisons, and in society writ-large (Gallagher, 2011; Rice, 2016; Stoever, 2016). Grounded in the notion that the ear is capable of troubling "some of our most entrenched clichés" (Erlmann, 2010, p. 24), I was curious how soundwalks might amplify children's experiences of school—a public place that, arguably, serves as children's "town square" in their early years. I wanted to gauge how children understood this public and its associated acoustic territories. Since "one of the underpinning goals of soundwalking is about circumnavigating habituation, in a process of de-sensitization and consequently re-sensitization, in order to catch a glimpse (un coup d'oreille) of the 'invisible, silent and unspoken' of the everyday" (Drever, 2009, p. 166), I hoped a child-led soundwalk might help adults attune to children's listening in publics differently by calling attention to both "the ordinary" and "what was yet unheard" (Ihde, 2007, p. 49).

Recording the "Hear" and Now of School

Initially, I worked separately with children in one first-grade and one fourth-grade classroom within Community School J—the focal school. In their respective homerooms, children completed read alouds and associated learning experiences that provided shared background knowledge for children to work with their "buddies" (e.g., a peer they were paired with from the opposite classroom) for the project's culminating days. These experiences shaped the foundation for the child-produced recordings because the lessons introduced children to the process of soundwalks and offered them opportunities to explore ambient sounds (Brownell, 2021). For instance, one afternoon, after reading a story focused on sounds in nature, children ventured outdoors to listen and jot notes about what they heard. After attuning themselves to ambient sonic experiences, they put language (or drawings) to these sounds.

Day one of collaboration between the classrooms began with first- and fourth-grade buddy pairs brainstorming possible locations for their soundwalk. As a pedagogical event, the teachers and I presented the soundwalks to children as a new potential for sensorial engagement with the school's geographies. Duos brainstormed using a map. Most children used images to represent sounds and spaces, and nearly all incorporated alphabetic text (Wargo et al., 2021). Children completed the maps prior to walking to guide them in their listening.

FIGURE 7.1   Christopher and Destroyer's Recording of Footsteps on Sidewalk [QR Code]

On their second day together, we divided buddies into five adult-facilitated groups (10 children/five pairs per group). With their smaller group, the buddies walked through spaces inside and outside the school, capturing sounds using an iPad. Although pairs mapped their intended route the day prior, most did not strictly follow their plans. Children added stops and sounds based on what they noticed at the moment. Their recordings, then, illuminated what sound artist Brown (2017) argued when he suggested: "soundwalks map the present," particularly because walking "produces embodied knowledge through direct physical contact with an environment" (n.p.).

Two Black boys who were buddies—fourth-grader Christopher and first-grader Destroyer—provided an example of what Brown (2017) described as they took to recording their footsteps. Together, the boys recorded the consistent pattern of their sneakers hitting the concrete pathway surrounding the playground and the sudden squeak such shoes produced on the indoor gym's wooden floor (to hear an excerpt, scan Figure 7.1's QR code). Similarly, two white boys—fourth-grader George and first-grader Knuffle Bunny (K.B.)—recorded the familiar crunch of wood chips colliding as children's feet traversed the high-traffic understory of the playground. Children's recording of these sounds required active listening to capture what was "a unique series of moments in time and space" (Brown, 2017, n.p.). Hence, in many ways, the soundwalks were a mapping practice of their own.

Amplifying Dissonant and Euphonic Phenomena

As a life force for world-making, many scholars underscore sound as a sensory force that can seemingly shift between fringe or focal phenomena due to our culturally informed habits of sonic filtering (Ihde, 2007). For instance, the hum of the motor Allen focused on in his recording of the water fountain is typically a fringe phenomenon for me as an adult-hearer in schools because I tend to focus on the hustle and bustle of children in the hallway as they await their turn to drink. However, for Allen, the motor was a focal sound of schooling, and thus, it demanded attention and was therefore granted a place in his recording with Francisco.

Another child, Andy—a fourth-grade Latino boy—offered additional examples of diverse filtering of phenomena during his retrospective interview (adapted from Dalton et al., 2015). Andy noted that the initial recording he made with his first-grade buddy, Kitty Bottom, was in another fourth-grade classroom. Here, Andy and Kitty Bottom—a first-grade white boy—wished to record children walking and talking in the space. As we listened back, however, Andy noted frustration because the sound of the "heater" (e.g., the school's air system) was quite prominent to him within the boys' recording. Not only was the "heater" something I did not tend to in their recording, but it was also not a sound I recalled attuning to in my daily experiences as an adult in the school. However, as I reviewed the child-produced lesson artifacts and maps again, I noted the "heater" was a recurring sound many children noted. Thus, like the hum of the water fountain, the "heater" was yet another focal sound for children while remaining seemingly unheard by the filtered ears of adults.

Additionally, children's recordings amplified different focal phenomena than what many adults heard. For instance, children focused on the consistent whir of the classroom projector, the impromptu brushing of hands against eraser dust and desks, and the muffled flush of the toilet behind the door to the in-classroom washroom. As I shared children's noticings with their teachers—both of whom were only in their second year as educators—they too were taken aback by the sounds children framed as irritating. To me, the marked differences between what seemed within earshot of children and adults represented the relationality of sound: it is informed by and informs worlds we inhabit (Feld, 2015).

In addition to the contrasting reports of what was heard by children and adults, I also noticed the ways children recorded soundwalks contrasted with research about observed soundwalks of adolescents or adults. Whereas older youth and adults tend to have more agency over where and how they move, children typically have constraints imposed on their movements by teachers or other adults. However, in my inquiry, the children took advantage of the opportunity to disrupt "schooled" notions of walking as they scurried about the hallways, playground, and other sites. Bodies not only walked, but ran, jumped, skipped, and skidded. Their gait varied as they scrambled from one location to the next, sometimes tip-toeing to get close to another living creature on the garden wall and other times sprinting to capture the sound of "wind" in the grassy field adjacent to the school.

FIGURE 7.2 Andy and Kitty Bottom's Recording of Swings [QR Code]

While feet took primacy as children moved throughout school spaces, their fingers and hands also played intricate roles within the soundwalk. Children used their hands in conjunction with their feet to maneuver peers on playground equipment and swings. Numerous pairs recorded the familiar rhythms of a chain-linked swing (to hear an example, scan Figure 7.2's QR code). To do so, children positioned one person on the swing's seat with the iPad while the other took to pushing their peer from behind. By, quite literally, inserting their bodies into the landscape of the public school space, the children generated and captured unplanned sounds. Simultaneously, they also seemed to mark the spontaneous nature of the playground.

In addition to the swings, children made recordings that required multiple bodies to document their desired sounds. Children's collective action was especially evident on the playground. Here, teams of children lifted another child's body off the ground so one child's feet could dangle. Then, while that child's hands gripped the metal handle of the glider, two more children pushed them across the wood-chipped landscape, while another child recorded the interaction on an iPad. Listening back to the children's recording, the scratchy sounds of the metal zipline, overlayed by children's heavy breathing and giggling alongside the crunch of wood chips, became a clear example of the temporality, sociality, and, importantly, the playful improvisation of the playground as a public space where controlled walking was not the only way to "move."

Disharmonious Discord amongst (Peer) Participants

Children had complete control of the iPads during the soundwalks; collectively, they negotiated how they used the iPad with their peer-partner. At times, frictional moments unfolded when the buddies' desires for the soundwalk and what sounds the iPad should record differed. In other moments, I noted strained discussions between buddies about how (and where) they could use the iPad. The verbal excerpt from K.B. and George's shared recording on the playground provides an example of such tensions:

K.B.:   It's that place! It's … Let's go up here! I wanna go up here. [*metal ding on a pole*] Let's go up here! Let's both go down the slide. [*metal swings creaking back and forth*].

George: I can't go down the slide. I'm holding this [iPad].

K.B.:   I'll beat you down! [*low rattling thud of footsteps on the slide*].

The duo's differing desires complicated their seemingly autonomous movements. Despite my conceiving of their task as one laced with freedom not typical of school, the children remained immersed in the political fabric of control.

Conflicts like the one between K.B. and George foreground how power differentials persist in school spaces, even amidst child-led learning. Not only did many fourth-graders like George maintain authority over their buddies, but so too did the ever-pervasive authority of adults appear to undergird children's actions. Across nearly all children's soundwalk recordings, listeners could hear supervising adults' voices in the background. Moreover, adults' verbal commands and their physical ushering of children predicated many movements and events of the children's soundwalks. Thus, despite my intentions for this sensory inquiry to be primarily child-led, it remained one wherein adults still informed the temporal rhythm of children's soundwalks. As illuminated in George's comment and as represented by his control of the iPad, the pervasiveness of power differentials in schools—between children and undergirded by the persistent presence of supervising adults—likely informed at least some of the recording decisions children made. Such discord also likely constrained the children's soundwalk itself.

Outro: Insight/Inciting Action

My primary goal in this chapter was to detail my noticings about elementary-aged children's soundwalk experiences. Through my brief sharing of children's sonic compositions, I called attention to classroom rhythms and frequencies that often go unheard in school-based research. Particularly, I sought to emphasize the dissonance between how this group of young children heard in schooling compared to adult counterparts like myself. By offering concrete examples of what sounds children considered salient, I wished for readers to gain insights into the possibilities of contemplating *and* centering early learners' sonic experiences of schooling. Ultimately, I contended for what Erlmann (2004) termed the "resurgence of the ear" (p. 2).

Throughout the multiweek unit, the focal teachers and I positioned children as experts in listening. We encouraged children to learn to listen in context and cultivate an "ethnographic ear" (Clifford, 1986, p. 12) as they considered the sounds of their school community. To assist children in undertaking this task, the teachers and I collaboratively stitched together a pedagogy of aurality to provide children across grades a shared foundation and support their collective writing with the sonic. We did so by grounding their listening in sound-centered picturebooks[2] followed by shared listening activities, the sum of which were crafted through shared planning meetings. In such discussions, the teachers remained open to the possibilities of sound work; our shared curiosity fueled our creativity to think outside of the box as we designed lessons to facilitate children's ability to see the world and, in turn, hear it (see, Brownell, 2021).

The practice of putting iPads in the hands of children and asking them to compose a soundwalk also demonstrated the potential for sound as a mode for writing community with early learners. In turn, we gave children opportunities for choice (where/what to record), which is sometimes lacking in early grades. Hence, the children's final products, alongside their postrecording commentary, provided novel contributions and considerations for child-led sensory methodologies.

However, a lingering challenge of sound work is explicating for others the nuances of the soundwalk itself. Because children recorded the soundwalk, these sounds of schooling can be played in part or in full for future audiences whenever desired. Yet, as children's recordings play, they largely remain decontextualized; the sounds listeners hear are disconnected from the time and space in which children recorded them. Furthermore, the sounds are detached from the children who listened as they walked their school campus to make the recording. Thus, while the sound of playground swings may be reminiscent for many listeners, the documented squeaks and creaks exist differently than when the children heard them.

As evidenced across the various soundbites shared herein, *listening* with children can provide new understandings about children's experiences (of/with/in schooling). But learning to listen requires a paradigmatic shift for many critical researchers and practitioners alike, especially since children's perspectives in everyday spaces typically remain marginalized (Templeton, 2018). To incite such action, I encourage my colleagues to use insights I gained from this inquiry to gauge for themselves how children understand and experience schooling and its associated acoustic territories. In particular, I suggest readers consider how children's perspectives and realities of school are not just overlooked, but they often remain *unheard*, due to the dominance of taken-for-granted (adult) notions of schooling and society. This chapter highlighted one way for adults to turn an ear to children's sonic experiences, particularly of schooling. Yet, others may opt to tune in to acoustic territories of children's social worlds beyond the perimeter of school grounds. Foci might include the sounds of children's figured worlds, or, conversely, the absence and/or erasure of children's listening in society. Such listening ventures, as LaBelle (2010) contended, can help us to better understand acoustics as "territorial and deterritorial processes shaped by the social and political tensions at the heart of listening" (p. x).

Of course, the listening of Francisco, Allen, and their peers that I described here was from the time before the COVID-19 pandemic dramatically shifted lives of adults and children, the full impact of which we will likely continue to learn of in years to come. Thus, amidst and following the COVID-19 pandemic, it is essential to consider how, if at all, the sounds of schooling have changed. How might children write sounds of the "hear and now" of schooling today? In what ways might their writings resonate with or differ from primary children's experiences globally?

As I walked and listened with children, I noticed how they engaged in listening practices differently than I anticipated or than I did myself. For me, the postwalk conversations with buddy pairs made clear to me the differences in what sounds I filtered and how, often, the frequencies that were fringe sounds for me were focal sounds for children. Ultimately, I argue that by attuning to what children hear in the space of school, adults can begin to finetune their ears. Further, adults might "yield new and richer kinds of ethnographic data" and encourage a rethinking of "a broad range of theoretical and methodological issues" (Erlmann, 2004, p. 2). In doing so, they can perhaps more readily work to disrupt commonplace narratives about who children are as people in the world and what they are capable of knowing, doing, and understanding. So too might adults then facilitate alternatives for the inequitable power relations which dominate school culture and spaces.

Notes

1 All names are pseudonyms children self-selected.
2 In each class, we first read aloud two picturebooks authored by Helen Borten (1959, 2016) entitled, *Do You See What I See?* and *Do You Hear What I Hear?* Then, we read several other texts wherein ambient sound and listening were central elements, including *Too Much Noise* (McGovern, 1957), *Oscar and the Bat: A Book about Sound* (Waring, 2006), and *The Listening Walk* (Showers, 1961). For more about how these books were used in the classroom and for additional details about the associated lesson activities, see Brownell (2021).

References

Adair, J. K., & Colegrove, K. S. S. (2021). *Segregation by experience: Agency, racism, and learning in the early grades.* University of Chicago Press.

Boonstra, K. E. (2019). *First time out: An ethnographic multiple case study of kindergarten discipline* (13897361). [Doctoral dissertation, University of Wisconsin-Madison]. ProQuest.

Borten, H. (2016[1959]). *Do you see what I see?* Flying Eye Books.

Brown, A. (2017). Soundwalking: Deep listening and spatio-temporal montage. *Humanities, 6*(3), 69. https://doi.org/10.3390/h6030069.

Brownell, C. J. (2019). Sound the alarm!: Disrupting sonic resonances of an elementary English language arts classroom. *Curriculum Inquiry, 49*(5), 551–572. https://doi.org/10.1080/03626784.2019.1671137.

Brownell, C. J. (2021). Seeing the world to hear it: A case study of young children learning to listen through visual observation. In Park, H. & Schulte, C. M. (Eds.), *Visual arts with young children: Practices, pedagogies, and learning* (pp. 123–128). Routledge. https://doi.org/10.4324/9781003020776.

Brownell, C. J., & Parks, A. N. (2021). When the clips are down: How young children negotiate a classroom management system. *Anthropology & Education Quarterly, 53*(1), 5–26. https://doi.org/10.1111/aeq.12400.

Burke, C., & Grosvenor, I. (2011). The hearing school: An exploration of sound and listening in the modern school. *Paedagogica Historica, 47*(3), 323–340. https://doi.org/10.1080/00309230.2010.530273.

Ceraso, S. (2014). (Re)Educating the senses: Multimodal listening, bodily learning, and the composition of sonic experiences. *College English, 77*(2), 102–123.

Clark, C. D. (2011). Introduction: Valuing young voices. In C. D. Clark (Ed.), *In a younger voice doing child-centered qualitative research*. Oxford University Press. https://doi.org/10.1093/acprof:oso/9780195376593.003.0001.

Clifford, J. (1986). Introduction: Partial truths. In J. Clifford & G. E. Marcus (Eds.), *Writing culture: The poetics and politics of ethnography* (1–26). University of California Press.

Corsaro, W. A. (2003). *We're friends, right? Inside kids' culture*. Joseph Henry Press.

Cowan, K., & Flewitt, R. (2020). Towards valuing children's signs of learning. In C. Cameron & P. Moss (Eds.), *Transforming early childhood in England: Towards a democratic education* (pp. 119–133). UCL Press.

Cowan, K., & Flewitt, R. (2021). Moving from paper-based to digital documentation in early childhood education: Democratic potentials and challenges. *International Journal of Early Years Education*, 1–19. https://doi.org/10.1080/09669760.2021.2013171.

Dahlberg, G., Moss, P., & Pence, A. R. (1999). *Beyond quality in early childhood education and care: Postmodern perspectives*. Falmer Press.

Dalton, B., Robinson, K. H., Lovvorn, J. F., Smith, B. E., Alvey, T., Mo, E. … Proctor, P. (2015). Fifth-grade students' multimodal compositions: Modal use and design intentionality. *The Elementary School Journal, 115*(4), 548–569.

Dernikos, B. P. (2020). Tuning into 'fleshy' frequencies: A posthuman mapping of affect, sound and de/colonized literacies with/in a primary classroom. *Journal of Early Childhood Literacy, 20*(1), 134–157.

Drever, J. L. (2009). Soundwalking: Aural excursions into the everyday. In J. Saunders (Ed.), *The Ashgate research companion to experimental music* (pp. 163–1920). Routledge.

Dumas, M. J., & Nelson, J. D. (2016). Re)imagining black boyhood: Toward a critical framework for educational research. *Harvard Educational Review, 86*(1), 27–47. https://doi.org/10.17763/0017-8055.86.1.27.

Dyson, A. H. (2021). *Writing the school house blues: Literacy, equity, and belonging in a child's early schooling*. Teachers College Press.

Dyson, A. H., & Genishi, C. (2005). *On the case: Approaches to language and literacy research.* Teachers College Press and the National Council for Research on Language and Literacy.

Erlmann, V. (2004). *Hearing cultures: Essays on sound, listening and modernity.* Berg Press.

Erlmann, V. (2010). *Reason and resonance: A history of modern aurality.* Zone Books.

Feld, S. (2015). Acoustemology. In D. Novak & M. Sakakeeny (Eds.), *Keywords in sound* (pp. 12–21). Duke University Press.

Ferguson, A. A. (2000). *Bad boys: Public schools in the making of black masculinity.* University of Michigan Press.

Gallagher, M. (2011). Sound, space and power in a primary school. *Social & Cultural Geography, 12*(1), 47–61. https://doi.org/10.1080/14649365.2011.542481.

Genishi, C., & Dyson, A. H. (2012). Racing to the top: Who's accounting for the children? *Occasional Paper Series, 27*(6), 18–20.

Graue, M. E. (1993). Ready for what: Constructing meanings of readiness for kindergarten. SUNY Press.

Ihde, D. (2007). *Listening and voice: Phenomenologies of sound.* SUNY Press.

Krukowski, D. (Host). (2017). *Ways of hearing* [Audio podcast]. *Showcase.* https://www.radiotopia.fm/showcase/ways-of-hearing

LaBelle, B. (2010). *Acoustic territories: Sound culture and everyday life.* Bloomsbury Publishing USA.

McGovern, A. (1957). *Too much noise.* Clarion Books.

Mills, K. A. (2016). *Literacy theories for the digital age: Social, critical, multimodal, spatial, material and sensory lenses.* Multilingual Matters.

Milner, R., Kestenberg, E. G., Delale-O'Connor, L., & Cunningham, H. B. (2019). *"These kids are out of control": Why we must reimagine "classroom management" for equity.* Corwin.

Paley, V. G. (1986). On listening to what the children say. *Harvard Educational Review, 56*(2), 122–132. https://doi.org/10.17763/haer.56.2.p775487x30tk69m8.

Rice, T. (2016). Sounds inside: Prison, prisoners and acoustical agency. *Sound Studies, 2*(1), 6–20. https://doi.org/10.1080/20551940.2016.1214455.

Rousell, D., Gallagher, M., & Wright, M. P. (2018). *Becoming Listening Bodies: Soundwalking as a Pedagogy of Sensation.* In 5th Conference on Arts Based Research & Artistic Research Provoking Research and Social Intervention, 13–15 March 2018, TATE Liverpool.

Schafer, R. M. (1994). *The soundscape: Our sonic environment and the tuning of the world.* Destiny Books.

Showers, P. (1961). *The listening walk.* Harper Collins.

Stoever, J. L. (2016). *The sonic color line: Race and the cultural politics of listening.* NYU Press.

Templeton, T. N. (2018). *"I know how to take a picture": Young children's photographic practices and the construction of identity.* [Doctoral dissertation, Columbia University]. Columbia. https://doi.org/10.7916/D8VH759Q

Wargo, J. M. (2018). Writing with wearables? Young children's intra-active authoring and the sounds of emplaced invention. *Journal of Literacy Research, 50*(4), 502–523. https://doi.org/10.1177/1086296X18802880.

Wargo, J. M., Brownell, C. J., & Oliveira, G. (2021). Sound, sentience, and schooling: Writing the field recording in educational ethnography. *Anthropology & Education Quarterly, 52*, 315–334. https://doi.org/10.1111/aeq.12365

Wargo, J., & Morales, M. (2021). Young children experimenting with sound art: Painting the politics of noise. In H. Park & C. M. Schulte (Eds.), *Visual arts with young children* (pp. 85–99). Routledge. https://doi.org/10.4324/9781003020776

Waring, G. (2009). *Oscar and the bat: A book about sound*. Candlewick Press.

Weheliye, A. G. (2014). *Habeas viscus: Racializing assemblages, biopolitics, and black feminist theories of the human*. Duke University Press.

Westerkamp, H. (1974). Soundwalking. *Sound Heritage, 3*(4), 18–27.

Yoon, H. (2013). Rewriting the curricular script: Teachers and children translating writing practices in a kindergarten classroom. *Research in the Teaching of English, 48*(2), 148–174.

Yoon, H. S., & Templeton, T. N. (2019). The practice of listening to children: The challenges of hearing children out in an adult-regulated world. *Harvard Educational Review, 89*(1), 55–173. https://doi.org/10.17763/1943-5045-89.1.55.

PART III

Rethinking the Relationships between Children and Adults: Intergenerational Intersections, Crossings, and Interactions

8

EXPANDING NOTIONS OF CHILDREN'S TRANSNATIONAL LIVES AND THE PHENOMENOLOGY OF MIGRATION

María Paula Ghiso

How can educators be attuned to the linguistic and cultural resources that young children from immigrant backgrounds bring to classrooms without homogenizing or co-opting their experiences? How can our pedagogies be affirming of children's legacies while also inviting inquiry into broader socio-political histories that shape the complexities and contradictions of (im)migrant identities?

These questions are central to efforts seeking to address educational inequities, including those impacting immigrant communities. Children of color and from immigrant backgrounds often enter schools that hew to unexamined white monolingual norms and devalue their transnational funds of knowledge and community cultural wealth (Yosso, 2005). High-stakes testing and the accountability paradigm have exacerbated the focus on individual achievement starting at the earliest levels of schooling, to the exclusion of systemic critiques that call into question such metrics and make visible their roots in racial hierarchies (Willis, 2015). When schools do focus on equity and inclusion, many initiatives become depoliticized, with a proliferation of race-evasive multicultural celebrations and best practice strategies that homogenize student experiences (Ladson-Billings, 2014). Within and against these challenges, educators have sought to remake classrooms to learn from and honor students' knowledge and community legacies of activism and resistance (e.g., Campano, 2007; De los Ríos & Molina, 2020; Ghiso, 2016).

This chapter draws on data from two related studies with Latinx and immigrant-background children that sought to use children's image-making (photography, videos, drawings, mapping) to unsettle normative assumptions of what experiences are valued in school literacy curricula. Through

DOI: 10.4324/9781003399155-12

intergenerational exchange, I spotlight children as makers who, in dialogue with their families, authored their own experiences of migration and fore-grounded the nuances of their culturally situated lives. The family narratives contest homogenizing depictions of migration and the "commodified inclusion" (Walia, 2021, p. 15) children of color often experience in school and invite teachers to learn from and alongside them and their families.

Framing Migration, Children, and Schooling

This research is informed by feminist of color thinkers who consider migration as part of global capitalist systems (e.g., Mohanty, 2003; Walia, 2021). Walia (2021) provides an important reframing of the border not as a natural boundary but as "an ordering regime" (p. 2). In examining the experiences of migrants and refugees from a global perspective, she emphasizes the *production* of borders and traces how imperialism and racial capitalism create "crises of displacement and immobility, preventing both the freedom to stay and the freedom to move" (p. 3). Centering the perspectives of communities vulnerable to global displacement—what Mohanty (2003) refers to as "read[ing] up the ladder of privilege" (p. 511)—can provide a vision for global justice that is attentive to communities' material realities as well as their advocacy and resistance. The experiences of (im)migrant children and families can help us to better understand our shared world and to reform educational institutions and practices (Campano, 2007).

Orellana et al. (2001) note the centrality of children's participation in family migration processes, arguing that "children help constitute and reconfigure transnational social fields, and transnational practices, in turn, shape the contours of particular childhoods" (p. 572). Children with (im)migrant backgrounds have long been a focus of educational priorities across a range of paradigms, from assimilationist interventions and deficit-oriented school categories like "English learner" (Martínez, 2018) to asset-based pedagogies recognizing children's transnational funds of knowledge (Kwon et al., 2019). This chapter seeks to elevate children from (im)migrant backgrounds as "cosmopolitan intellectuals" (Campano & Ghiso, 2011) whose border-crossing languages, literacies, networks, and vantage points can unsettle bounded conceptions of the nation-state and provide global perspectives on (in)equality. There is much intergenerational learning that happens in transnational families. Mangual Figueroa (2012), for example, documents the microlevel linguistic practices of mixed-status families as children and their parents/caregivers navigate exclusionary policies and plan for contingencies such as family separation amid the militarization of the border. Within activist communities, children and parents work in tandem to organize for their rights, enacting communal practices of resistance (Rusoja, 2022). Families—children and elders together—engage in intergenerational learning as they critically engage educational challenges posed by existing systems and advocate for greater opportunities (Ghiso et al., 2022). Given colonial histories and current detention practices of family separation that have been leveraged by the nation-state to terrorize (im)migrant communities, it is essential that children and their learning be understood as integrated within the family unit.

Story of the Question

The genesis of the research featured in this chapter lies in dissonances I encountered working alongside teachers of emergent bilingual children in two first-grade, dual-language classrooms as we noticed—and sought to challenge—the ways that a deficit discourse of language remediation and being "at-risk" was produced through implementation of literacy curricula upholding monolingual norms and white middle-class experiences. The teachers and children were policed through these accountability measures, yet together we wondered how we might work within and against these constraints. Over the span of 3 years, with the support of the school principal and in partnership with my colleague Patricia Martínez-Álvarez, we set about creating classroom openings that honored children's languages, racial identities, and migration histories, and which leveraged these experiences as a site of inquiry into social justice issues. We centered cameras as a mediating tool for children to frame their own stories: to record and make decisions about aspects of their lives they wanted to share in the classroom space and bring to the attention of their peers and teachers. In an iterative design process, guided by principles from the practitioner research movement (Cochran-Smith & Lytle, 2009) which emphasize how educational knowledge can be generated from classrooms and those most impacted by educational policies and practice, the curriculum was cocreated with teachers and children and continually revised in response to children's meaning-making, their interests, and their priorities.

In the third year of implementation, we were inspired by the children, who often surreptitiously used the video features in their cameras to capture moving images. We invited them to conduct video interviews with parents or community members about their perspectives on migration and their transnational experiences. Having noticed how children's discussions of their images continually surfaced issues of equity, such as, for example, language access or economic precarity, we also directly asked them to consider notions of (in)justice as they documented experiences in their lives and neighborhoods to make what had heretofore been implicit an explicit area of inquiry. In a second cycle of inquiry, Dr. Martínez-Álvarez and I partnered with a city community organization to scale up the project, which would be facilitated by teachers in several afterschool programs in NYC, in a historically Latinx neighborhood (see Ghiso et al., 2019). In this iteration of the project, children in grades two and three engaged with a more codified version of the curriculum, and we also worked with teachers to support their implementation, reflection, and curricular designs. Most of the children in the two interrelated studies were Latinx, of Mexican Central American, and Caribbean descent and with families of varying immigration status. There were also a smaller minority of participating children who came from other cultural and linguistic backgrounds.

Curricular Invitations Focusing on Video Interviews

As part of the overall curriculum, children were invited to see their neighborhoods, families, and communities as an epistemic resource for exploring issues of social justice and resisting the assimilationist norms of schooling. Designed to deepen children's reading and writing not as stand-alone skills but hand-in-hand with centering transnational communities' experiences, the children received cameras to document what mattered to them, with a focus on language, culture, migration, and justice. Once children brought in images that they had chosen to capture, these were utilized as a platform for discussion and inquiry. Given that school-based texts often fell short in capturing the complexity and nuance of children's culturally inflected experiences, children's photo and video productions were themselves treated as texts that we could "read-aloud" together. These invitations were situated within thematic explorations that viewed photography as agentic and as a means of making visible oppressions and social hierarchies.

For the video interviews, the children selected a family member or someone in their community and asked a series of questions regarding their migration histories, their transnational perspectives, and the issues of justice that were relevant to their lives. They were provided sample questions but also encouraged to design their own (see Figure 8.1).

Data Sources and Analysis

Data collection for this qualitative study included children's discussions and multimodal compositions that leveraged their linguistic and cultural resources for meaning-making. Researchers (myself, my coresearcher, and participating graduate students) also took reflective fieldnotes on the sessions, documenting children's engagement with these texts and their social interactions with each other, situating children's multimodal artifacts within sociocultural factors such as the classroom pedagogy, children's relationships, and their worlds outside the classroom. Our larger study, for example, made note of broader xenophobic discourses of immigration prevalent in the media or policing/ICE surveillance as well as the advocacy of community organizations and local

INTERVIEWS WITH PARENTS AND RELATIVES

Use the camera to interview someone who was born in another country and who remembers his or her experience in that country. First, ask them to share information about the culture in that country. Then, ask them to talk about the differences they notice between life in the country where they were born and here in New York. Finally, ask them to tell you about something unfair in their lives or in the world. Some questions could be:

- **How are your community and your life different in the country where you were born and in New York?**
- **What is something unfair in your life or in the world in relation to your experience?**
- **Is there someone who has a different opinion about this?**
- **If you'd like, you can add your own question here:**

_____

_____

Bring the camera with your videos back to school on

_____

FIGURE 8.1   Explanation and Instructions for Video Interviews

asset-based Latinx representations in the neighborhood. Elsewhere, I have argued that community spaces, or what I refer to as transnational locals (Ghiso, 2016), are sites of learning where children come to understand themselves as part of global dynamics, and where they can cultivate childhoods centered on an ethos of interdependence.

This chapter focuses specifically on analysis of the children's videos created as part of the curricular invitations described above. As these were framed around migration and issues of justice, they were particularly suited for understanding these ideas as reflected in and produced through family exchanges. The videos were one mode where families' perspectives and their transnational histories and emotional entanglements were made explicit, and thus warranted

more focused consideration. The analysis combined attention to semiotic features of these texts and children's design choices (Kress & van Leeuwen, 2020),
dimensions of multimodal production that were interpreted alongside "historical, cultural, and political theories of literacy curriculum, teaching, and learning" (Siegel & Panofsky, 2009, p. 99). I transcribed the videos and noted the
multimodal choices, such as setting, camera movements, which actors were featured and how, the inclusion of artifacts within the video, and the foreground-
ing, backgrounding, or positioning of different elements. I paid attention to the
content of the video interviews (e.g., how children and parents characterize life
in Latin America and in the United States, how they refer to the process and
politics of immigration) as well as the interactions among participants, such as
the dynamic among interlocutors or the roles taken up by children and family
members. Insights from this focused analysis of video interviews were triangu-
lated with findings from the broader set of study data.

Findings

In the sections that follow, I spotlight two interviews conducted by Latinx
children Daniel and Leilani (names are pseudonyms). Daniel was a 7-year-
old Mexican child attending a first-grade dual language program in a Queens
public school, where myself and my coresearcher designed and facilitated instruction during the literacy block. Leilani was an 8-year-old Puerto Rican
child who grew up in Manhattan. She took the video as part of her afterschool
program, which was facilitated by an Afro-Caribbean teacher and a Puerto
Rican Assistant teacher. Below, I first discuss each of the child-parent interviews individually to showcase their ideas within real-time intergenerational
dynamics and then talk across these moments to discuss the potentials of child-
family interactions as sites of transnational learning.

Missing Convivir: Troubling Asymmetrical
Renditions of US Immigration

Daniel looks directly at the camera, a hairbrush microphone in his hand. Off
to the side, his father sits in a chair, the camera lens positioned so that both
interviewer and interviewee are equally in the frame. The scene resembles
a news program, with Daniel as an anchor and his father the invited guest.
Daniel confidently states, in Spanish, "Voy a entrevistar a mi papá" [I'm going
to interview my dad]. He then turns to face his father and reads the first question from the interview assignment sheet, asking him to compare his life in
Mexico and in the United States.

In his response, Daniel's father characterizes life in these two locations as
"muy diferente" [very different] and draws on his transnational vantage point

to challenge representations of migration as an unequivocal advancement. He notes:

> La vida en mi país era … más tranquila. Convivía yo más con mi familia y estaba un poco más, más relajado. En cambio aquí, en Estados Unidos, es más estresante, siempre anda uno corriendo para acá y para allá.

> [Life in my country was … more tranquil. I used to convivir more with my family and I was more, more relaxed. Instead here, in the United States, it's more stressful, one is always running from here to there.]

Daniel's father emphasizes the relational aspect of life—the convivir—as a central signifier of a good life. Later, when his child asks him which of the countries he prefers, he returns to this theme.

> Hablando económicamente me gusta más aquí, este país, porque aquí se trabaja y se gana dinero, trabajo hay y siempre hay el dinero en la casa, para comprar, creo que vivimos mejor en este aspecto. Pero si decimos en lo personal o en lo físico, yo creo que diría en mi país, porque ya estaría yo más relajado, más viviendo, conviviendo con mis papas y estaría bueno.

> [Talking economically I like it more here in this country because here one can work and make money, there is work, and there is always money in the house, to buy, I think we live better in that aspect. But if we talk about the personal or the physical, I think I would say in my country, because there I would be more relaxed, more living, conviviendo with my parents, and it would be good.]

Literally translated as to "live with," convivir implies more than simply cohabiting. It represents being in community, spending time with one another. Daniel's father contrasts this with the capitalist pace of the United States, which in his view does provide more economic stability, but at a cost. At the heart of his testimony are different definitions of what it means to "vivi[r] mejor"—to "live better." By naming the relational practices that nurtured personal and physical well-being in Mexico, these comments contest narratives of immigration as a categorical improvement. One recurring theme in the family interviews was the replacement of romanticized notions of US opportunities with bilateral narratives that emphasize the affordances of life in the Global South. Parents' descriptions of preferred ways of being in their countries of origin raised questions about what is lost in the search for productivity and economic security. Such narratives can potentially be mobilized for imagining forms of sociality and community outside of racial capitalism.

When Daniel turns to questions of justice, his father focuses specifically on the issue of immigration:

> Algo que es injusto yo creo que es la inmigración. Por ejemplo, si hablamos de inmigración, por qué tenemos, o por qué tendríamos que, por qué tendría que haber, yo sé que son las leyes, pero por qué uno tendría que tener algún papel o algún, algo, por ejemplo una visa, para poder estar en los Estados Unidos. Si yo creo que ante los ojos de Dios todos somos seres humanos y merecemos estar en cualquier parte del mundo. Creo que la tierra no es de nadie, no le pertenece a nadie.

> [Something unjust I think is immigration. For example, if we talk about immigration, why do we have to, or why would we have to, why does there have to be, I know that they are the laws, but why would one have to have a paper of some, something, for example, a visa, to be able to be in the United States. I believe that before God's eyes we are all human beings and we deserve to be in any part of the world. I believe the Earth is no one's, it does not belong to anyone.]

Daniel's father pauses and beings to hand off the "microphone" to his son but then changes his mind, taking it back and continuing to elaborate:

> Y sí, hay muchos que tienen diferentes opiniones, hay gente que está en contra de la comunidad inmigrante y que siempre está tratando de hacerle la vida imposible. ¿Por qué? Porque piensa que uno viene a quitarles el trabajo a esas personas.

> [And yes, there are many who have different opinions, there are people who are against the immigrant community and who are always trying to make their life impossible. Why? Because they believe that one is coming to take jobs away from them.]

Daniel's father pinpoints immigration as a site of contestation and grounds the transnational dynamics children and families are grappling with daily within the political and economic decisions of the nation-state. He chooses his words carefully and reformulates his statements to highlight that the issue is not with laws per se, but with the ways land is owned by nations and mobility policed through "papers." As Vieira (2016) underscores, texts like immigration documents and educational certificates—the products of institutional power—legitimate or curtail participation in the so-called American Dream, with communities differentially able to access these as impacted by race, class, and migration pathways. Daniel's father goes on to assert that "the Earth's is no one's, it does not belong to anyone," offering a reservoir of ancestral values that critiques the colonial appropriation of land and racialized capitalism. Tracing the interconnection of anti-Indigenous and anti-Black violence in what she terms border imperialism, Walia (2021) notes that "forcing Indigenous people to relinquish collective land title and assimilate into the capitalist economy of the white settler state, citizenship was thus dependent on the legal regime of private property" (p. 24). This colonial history is buried in both liberal and right-wing characterizations of immigrants aptly called up by Daniel's father as either contributing to the economy or "tak[ing] jobs"—complementary perspectives that "treat immigrants as commodities to be traded in capitalist markets" (Walia, 2021, p. 19). It is through intergenerational exchanges that children learn collective histories of resistance and counterframings of policies that circumscribe their families' well-being.

"It's Beautiful, One Day I'll Take You": Figuring Puerto Rico

The camera pans to a mom dressed in a vibrant purple shirt. Second-grader Leilani, her daughter, is off-camera but directing the action. The conversation unfolds as they walk home from the day's afterschool session, where Leilani had received the interview questions she begins to read, haltingly, to her mother. In response to the opening query about the differences between New York and the country where she was born, Leilani's mother, who identifies as Puerto Rican, instantly unsettles this dichotomy. "I was born here," she notes. "Manhattan is in New York. Next question." Her comments suggest how characterizations of children and families, even within asset-based curricula, can homogenize identity and obscure migration differences and colonial histories. As Puerto Ricans/Nuyoricans, Leilani and her family's realities are entangled with the paradoxes of border politics—experiencing "relative security" (Caronan, 2015, p. 15) in mobility as contrasted with other Latinx groups due to Puerto Rico's status as a commonwealth, yet also under threat due to racialization on the mainland and subject to economic and environmental exploitation. In rejecting the home-country/host-country binary, Leilani's mom expands our visions of children's transnational backgrounds over multiple generations.

Undaunted, Leilani initiates a dialogue about her mom's Latinx heritage, asking a series of unscripted questions that lead to more and more details of a Caribbean homeland Leilani has never physically visited.

Leilani: Where do your parents come from?
L's Mom: My parents come from Puerto Rico, my mother and my father.

Leilani:	Have you been to Puerto Rico?
L's Mom:	Oh yes, plenty of times. My family, all my family lives in Puerto Rico.
Leilani:	What it is in Puerto Rico? How does it feel?
L's Mom:	It feels wonderful [small smile to the camera] It–
Leilani:	[interrupts]—Could you tell me your experience?
L's M:	Wow, I haven't been there in so many years. So, I don't know, I like it. It's different from here. The environment is different, it's always hot. I love it. … The food is better, it's always hot. Love it [smiles at camera]. Then you got the little coquís which are little frogs that make noise, they say "coquí coquí" [in high voice]. Don't let you sleep but [smiles] yeah, I like Puerto Rico, I'd rather be there than here.

A few conversational turns later, Leilani returns to the topic of the Island, asking for further details and continuing to probe, excitedly, when she finds the answers too vague for her liking.

Leilani:	What goes on in Puerto Rico?
L's Mom:	What goes on in Puerto Rico? Oh, a lot of things.
Leilani:	Like what?
L's Mom:	Everybody hangs out in front of their house, they play dominos, they make lechón. Lechón is a big pig.
Leilani:	A big pig?
L's Mom:	Yeah, a big pig.
Leilani:	Wow.
L's Mom:	A lot of things goes on in Puerto Rico. It's different, like I said. There's a lot of things to do out there. Like I said, the environment is different. At least out there you could be outside. You could hang around, do things. It's beautiful, one day I'll take you.

The conversation between Leilani and her mom makes visible the complex transnational geographies in children's hearts and minds. Navigating multiple worlds of Latinx heritage does not require physical migration but can take the form of affective reverberations and embodied memories passed down through generations. The emotional resonance of Puerto Rico is evident in the stories shared by Leilani's mom—the way her tone shifts, how she smiles, repeatedly, toward a faraway point off-camera. These moments of early childhood education between family members foster a critical nostalgia for other places and communities—a nostalgia that has political import. Such encounters call forth different types of social worlds and, in doing so, may enable children to embody futures beyond their current locations.

Leilani guides the conversation to inquire about equity, rephrasing the assigned question to prompt specific comments:

Leilani: Tell me what's unfair in New York.
L's mom: Everything is unfair. The cost of living. Everything is expensive. There's a lot of crimes. That's why I want to leave.

As part of US imperialism, Puerto Rico occupies a liminal space "between inclusion and independence" with clear economic links between the island and mainland (Immerwahr, 2019, p. 257). Caronan (2015) argues that this "semblance of sovereignty"—with a local governor but limited voting representation in Congress and lacking the rights of statehood—"belie[s] Puerto Rico's economic dependence on the U.S." (p. 7). With the highest poverty rate in the United States by far, an effect of colonial occupation and unfavorable treaties, many Puerto Ricans are displaced to the mainland. This mobility, as Leilani's mom describes, comes at the cost of separation from family; her comments also suggest that the economic stability that fueled migration is not necessarily realized. Despite these challenges, there is also an inherent collective agency in reproducing Puerto Rican culture in New York City in the ways Leilani and her mom do through their conversation. As Curanon notes, "culture provides a space where critiques of institutionalized narratives, such as that of US exceptionalism, can emerge" (p. 9). And emerge they do, with Leilani's mom puncturing the meritocratic narrative of migration, being explicit about US shortcomings and declaring her desire "to leave" and her preference for "there"—Puerto Rico.

Learning Transnational Lives

The interviews by Daniel and Leilani, alongside those of their peers, showcase intergenerational exchanges as sites of learning about migration and global justice, and children as active directors of these dialogic moments. Daniel sets the scene and manipulates the microphone to create a space for politicized funds of knowledge (Gallo & Link, 2015) to surface. Leilani revises the provided questions and asks many pointed follow-ups, steadfast in her determination to get to know Puerto Rico and how it "feel[s]." They both use their multilingual resources to elicit and/or make sense of these stories. Through the video interviews, families surfaced a more complicated picture of their migration histories with embedded political critiques. Children are learning and navigating these accounts, often within and against the status quo of school, where such knowledge are misrepresented or altogether missing from historical renderings that uphold US exceptionalism.

Families' narratives also challenge us to interrogate homogenizing categories and the embedded assumptions in our curricular invitations. Daniel and Leilani's lived experiences cannot be subsumed to a pan-ethnic "latinidad" but invite further inquiry into the differences and overlaps among migration experiences. As educators, we need to learn from families like those featured in this chapter that identifying as Latinx may involve different languages (e.g., English, Spanish, Mixteco and other indigenous languages), movement across multiple generations, and different relationships to documentation status, the "nation," and the politics of migration. The narratives also expand the contours of school discussions about migration, such as how economic precarity and immigration policies shape day-to-day realities and critiques of aspirational and one-sided notions of the American Dream. These portraits can help educators learn from the lived experiences of children to design curricula that hinge on, rather than gloss over, the particularities of migration, and which invites families to take the lead in authoring their own stories of justice.

Misreadings and Missed Opportunities: An Epilogue

I am in one of the second grade after school classrooms during a session in which the children and teacher are going to watch Daniel's interview with his father and discuss it together. We are delayed because of technical issues—the video isn't working and the teacher did not have time during her busy day to prepare the set-up so as to minimize downtime. After a long school day, the children are understandably restless. With technical difficulties finally resolved, Daniel's video plays on the screen. Time is running out before dismissal so opportunities for discussion are cut short. The teacher summarizes the video by noting that Daniel's father experienced lots of hardships and that he was really thankful and lucky to be in the United States. Then, it is time to pack up and go home. I am not sure whether the teacher or students ever returned to Daniel's video beyond that day.

When we are in a hurry and perhaps even when we are not, it is easy to interpret children's experiences through dominant discourses and our own situated assumptions. Certainly, Daniel's father felt thankful to be in the United States, but reducing his narrative to one of thankfulness reinforces notions of American exceptionalism, erasing the critique of border policies impacting transnational communities and the texture and benefits of life elsewhere. And the curriculum I co-created was itself too narrow, assuming migration experiences and inscribing there/here dichotomies that families like Leilani's had to push up against. Inviting children and families to share their knowledge with school contexts is only as successful as our abilities to learn from them by decentering our perspectives, questioning what it is we think we know about children and families, and putting different narratives in conversation with each other. The transnational stories of a child's family can help educators know more about their particular histories and the nuances of navigating cross-border lives. Collectively, the stories can help all members of a classroom community cultivate global perspectives of justice and call into question the enactment and enforcement of borders themselves.

References

Campano, G. (2007). *Immigrant students and literacy: Reading, writing, and remembering.* Teachers College Press.

Campano, G., & Ghiso, M. P. (2011). Immigrant students as cosmopolitan intellectuals. In S. Wolf, K. Coates, P. Enciso, & C. Jenkins (Eds.), *Handbook of research on children's and young adult literature* (pp. 164–176). Routledge.

Caronan, F. (2015). *Legitimizing empire: Filipino American and U.S. Puerto Rican cultural critique.* University of Illinois Press.

Cochran-Smith, M., & Lytle, S. L. (2009). *Inquiry as stance: Practitioner inquiry for the next generation.* Teachers College Press.

De los Ríos, C. V., & Molina, A. (2020). Literacies of refuge: "Pidiendo posada" as ritual of justice. *Journal of Literacy Research, 52*(1), 32–54.

Gallo, S., & Link, H. (2015). "Diles la verdad": Deportation policies, politicized funds of knowledge, and schooling in middle childhood. *Harvard Educational Review, 85*(3), 357–382.

Ghiso, M. P. (2016). The laundromat as the transnational local: Young children's literacies of interdependence. *Teachers College Record, 118*(1), 1–46.

Ghiso, M. P., Martínez-Álvarez, P., Clayton, E., Álvarez, F., & Gutiérrez, M. (2019). Critical inquiry in the literacy curriculum: The community as a transnational resource. *Language Arts, 97*(2), 97–104.

Ghiso, M. P., Campano, G., Thakurta, A., & Vazquez Ponce, O. (2022). Community-based research with immigrant families: Sustaining an intellectual commons of care, resistance, and solidarity in an urban intensive context. *Urban Education.* https://doi.org/10.1177/00420859221082676

Immerwarh, D. (2019). *How to hide an empire: A history of the greater United States.* Farrar, Straus and Giroux.

Kress, G., & van Leeuwen, T. (2020). *Reading images: The grammar of visual design* (3rd ed.). Routledge.

Kwon, J., Ghiso, M. P., & Martínez-Álvarez, P. (2019). Showcasing transnational and bilingual expertise: A case study of a Cantonese-English emergent bilingual within an afterschool program centering Latinx experiences. *Bilingual Research Journal.* https://doi.org/10.1080/15235882.2019.1589605.

Ladson-Billings, G. (2014). Culturally relevant pedagogy 2.0: Aka the remix. *Harvard Educational Review, 84*(1), 74–84.

Mangual Figueroa, A. (2012). "I have papers so I can go anywhere!": Everyday talk about citizenship in a mixed-status Mexican family. *Journal of Language, Identity & Education, 11*(5), 291–311.

Martínez, R. (2018). Beyond the English learner label: Recognizing the richness of bi/multilingual students' linguistic repertoires. *The Reading Teacher, 71*(5), 515–522.

Mohanty, C. T. (2003). Under western eyes revisited. *Signs, 28*(2), 499–535.

Orellana, M. F., Thorne, B., Chee, A., & Lam, W. S. E. (2001). Transnational childhoods: The participation of children in processes of family migration. *Social Problems, 48*(4), 572–591.

Rusoja, A. (2022). "Our community is filled with experts": The critical intergenerational literacies of Latinx immigrants that facilitate a communal pedagogy of resistance. *Research in the Teaching of English, 56*(3), 301–327.

Siegel, M., & Panofsky, C. P. (2009). Designs for multimodality in literacy studies: Explorations in analysis. In *58th yearbook of the national reading conference* (pp. 99–111).

Vieira, K. (2016). *American by paper: How documents matter in immigrant literacy.* University of Minnesota Press.

Walia, H. (2021). *Border and rule: Global migration, capitalism, and the rise of racist nationalism.* Fernwood Press.

Willis, A. I. (2015). Literacy and race: Access, equity, and freedom. *Literacy Research: Theory, Method, and Practice, 64*, 23–35.

Yosso, T. (2005). Whose culture has capital? A critical race theory discussion of community cultural wealth. *Race, Ethnicity and Education, 8*(1), 69–91.

9

STACKED CHILDHOODS

(Re)Membering as Pedagogical Practice

Muyanwi Lum Fube and Haeny Yoon

Lily was one of the first children that struck Haeny when she entered the inclusive kindergarten classroom in New York City. She was friendly—someone who was going to be a great "kid ally" to the goings-on of the classroom. Lily was one of three girls, partly due to the reduced class size: 13 children altogether. Lily's family were immigrants from Haiti—her father immigrated as a child while her mother came later and still had family there. Lily's mother, Natalie, still spoke with a French-infused accent, given her Haitian roots. Though born in the United States, Lily visited Haiti and exhibited strong connection and love for its culture, evidenced as the year progressed. During a map activity, Lily located the Haitian flag, found Haiti on the world map, encompassed the area with her arms and embraced the small island on the 2D map, declaring, "I *want* Haiti. I want Haiti. Here's Haiti!" Her unflappable enthusiasm made way for her mother's planned visit to the classroom early in the school year. On that day, she pretended to harbor a joyous secret, whispering to others, "Spoiler alert, spoiler alert," referring to her mother's arrival.

We amplify Lily's voice, demonstrating that children's lives are increasingly transnational, mobile, and digitally mediated. A rich body of work highlights the diverse practices of immigrant communities across the United States—their linguistic and communicative sophistication (Ghiso, 2016), carework and contributions to everyday life (Orellana et al., 2001), and the digital and social practices that transnational communities display and embody (Kwon, 2019). Building from this line of inquiry, we emphasize the role of children as teachers and mentors to unpacking the child within all of us. How are identities shaped by childhood experiences? How does this frame adult/child interaction

DOI: 10.4324/9781003399155-13

in classroom spaces? We argue for a more dynamic, learning stance in how we understand children in the present.

We place our stories and identities in conversation with Lily's, to reflect, "re-member," and reconnect with the hidden parts of ourselves. In understanding how one young girl moved through the world confidently as a Black, first-generation child of immigrant parents, we uncover the stories that bring the three of us (Lily, Lum, and Haeny) in conversation with each other. We demonstrate both the connections and fissures that occur when we juxtapose our immigrant experiences with children. On one hand, the weight of belonging and marginalization provide particular insight into structures and obstacles that barred us from assuming multiple identities. On the other hand, our memories and moves to belong come with preconceived notions and assumptions we make about children who are like us. Yet, Lily reminds us to widen our frames and disrupt static notions of what it means to be a child, girl, immigrant, and cultural being in contemporary times. We frame memories within immigrant/transnational experiences, return to Lily's interactions with others in the classroom, and reflect on our childhood memories.

Becoming: Stacked Identities and the Childhoods(s) within

Twenty Something, a short Pixar film, features a 21-year-old Gia who enters her first-ever dance club alongside her older sister. She experiences many *firsts* in the transition from "childhood" to "adulthood": entering the bar/club with her new ID card, ordering her first drink, flirting with boys. Clearly, she is not comfortable in comparison to her older more experienced sister who seems self-assured and worldly. Literally and figuratively, Gia still feels the accumulated insecurities of her child self-creep into how she positions herself in this new space. The viewer sees that underneath her trench coat, there are three different versions of Gia awkwardly walking, talking, and moving through the dance club—the 10-year-old is on top while the 1-year-old and 16-year-old remain hidden underneath the coat. The stacked Gias come out in moments of uncertainty—sometimes the 16-year-old tries to be "too cool" to mask insecurities, the 1-year-old gets fussy at inconvenient times, the 10-year old is prone to frustration and acts out. After a series of mishaps, the three Gias lock themselves into the bathroom and begin to cry, as her older sister assures her that "being an adult is always a mess." Before 21-year-old Gia reemerges from the bathroom stall, she glances in the mirror to see a reflection of all three Gias looking back at her. They are a reminder that the "tugs of memory, and the child within" (Thorne, 1993, p. 23) are always a part of how we situate ourselves in the world. These lived experiences, replete with our insecurities, fears, and uncertainties, frame our ideologies and perspectives. The "stacked" children within us are instructive and critical to our identities, as always *becoming* (James, 2009).

Childhood Memories and Identity: Re-entering the Transnational Experience

As adults, our memories are a reconstructed act, simply because of our status as no longer children. We cannot go back in time and literally relive the moments passed. However, like Gia, the children "stacked" within us awaken affective emotions of pain, joy, uncertainty, and excitement (Zembylas, 2003). As educators, in particular, we filter our lived experiences through childhood memories as lenses by which we encounter and interpret children's lives. Children disturb those memories and urge us to work through salient moments where "traces of past pains and letdowns" (Farley et al., 2020, p. 9) continue to re/frame our identities in relationship to the current social, cultural, and political contexts (Alsup, 2006; Britzman, 2003; Haddix, 2010). Chang-Kredl et al. (2016) studied the narrated memories of early childhood teachers, illustrating how teachers' longings influenced how they saw children—in need of protection, vulnerable, innocent, and naïve. Other times, perspectives are mediated by an *absence* of freedom, structure, and agency, influencing what we assume children might need and the subsequent role of teachers in school spaces. In other words, *how* we talk about our memories and *what* assumptions emerge about children informs our pedagogical choices, "fractured by the intersection of activities, judgments, emotions, and desires" (Zembylas, 2003, p. 124). As researchers and teachers, we benefit from "holding past and present together" (Elbaz-Luwisch, 2004, p. 396) as we negotiate spaces for children.

Our specific memories and revelations, as two immigrant women of Color, are also filtered by "transnational social fields" (Basch et al., 1994; Orellana et al., 2001) or the linkages between our countries of origin and settlement. While we have now spent a majority of our lives in US contexts, we use transnational to illustrate the cultural practices extending beyond geographic location. For instance, a range of daily activity from the food we eat, to the languages we speak, to the community spaces we inhabit (e.g., church, heritage language schools, ethnic enclaves) "construct and sustain multilayered linkages, interconnections, and mobility" (Kwon, 2020, p. 101) for many immigrants like ourselves. Therefore, border crossing goes beyond physical borders but highlights the movement of transnationals between language, customs, and practices (Alexander & Mohanty, 2013; Anzaldúa, 1987; Nagar & Swarr, 2010). In our own memory work, we frequently share school memories where belonging felt like a binary of American versus foreigner. Our stories are remnants of marginalized experiences where cultural differences elevated social tensions, heightened unwanted visibility, and limited access to the cultural and social capital for school success (Yoon & Llerena, 2020). We reenter our stories of cultural loss with the shifting social and political conditions of contemporary childhood via Lily.

Although Lily was born in the United States and only visited Haiti once, her understanding of self was multisited and mobile (Tolia-Kelly, 2010). Birthed through her mother's stories, her transnational identity and diasporic citizenship transported and solidified her sense of home and pride. Her citizenship was not defined by her physical presence in Haiti but inherited kinship through oral stories and cultural materials (El-Haj, 2009). The map and flag of Haiti signaled Lily's mobile, cultural memory, from Haitian ethnic enclaves in Brooklyn to Michel Martelly (a.k.a. Sweet Mickey) as then president of Haiti. Therefore, transnationals embody memories through both first-hand experiences and second-hand knowledge, passed down generationally and absorbed through repeated re-tellings. Memories are the cumulative interaction of the personal, communal, material, and cultural; they are ecological (Mitchell et al., 2010; Tolia-Kelly, 2010).

The "ecologies of citizenship" (Tolia-Kelly, 2010) are also constituted through visual and material culture—artifacts that make up our domestic landscape: photographs, artwork, iconographies. Like Tolia-Kelly (2010), we believe identity extends beyond "the skin, nationality, economic status, political citizenship, or religion" (p. 7). Identity is mediated by the materials, sensory memories, and the stories we employ to locate ourselves in the world. We *remember*, not as time or location specific, but "touched, accessed, or mediated through sensory stimuli" (Tolia-Kelly, 2010, p. 87). Lily's childhood connections to the ecological landscape of Haiti inspire our journey to the material, visual, and sensorial memories of childhood.

Indigeneity and (Re)Membering: Lum and Her Grandmother's Picture

Lily's mother, Natalie, explained the complex history of language in Haiti.

> Yes, they do [speak English] but it is not the official language. The language, when I was there, it used to be French. And everyone had to speak, but you also speak Creole. The lower class speaks Creole. I remember when I was younger, my dad found me speaking Creole. It was a big thing because you go to school, you are not supposed to speak Creole, but now they change it. They make Creole also an official language because that's our original language. But the last time, I went in December, French is still, you have to (imitates talking). So, then if you speak French fluently, you are really educated. So, if you don't it means you didn't get to the level you are supposed to be to learn.

Natalie's account of language and schooling immediately transported me (Lum) to a photograph of my grandmother and me during her 90th birthday

FIGURE 9.1   Lum with Her Grandmother on Her 90th Birthday

(Figure 9.1). My earliest childhood memories are situated in my grandparents' compound in Manji, Bafut, Cameroon. I remember my grandmother leaning over the fire pit and stirring a large pot smiling and telling me a funny story. My grandmother only spoke our native tongue, Bafut, and I became fluent while spending time with my grandmother in the village. I associate this memory with the precise but fleeting second when the first drops of rain merged with the soil, releasing a distinct smell that lingered only for a moment, until the torrential downpour washed it away. On this particular day, it was raining and I was sitting on my grandmother's kitchen floor, laughing and smiling.

I often think about how I lost my fluency over the years in my indigenous language—the inevitable effects of colonial schooling. Similar to Natalie's experience in Haiti, English was the official language in school in Bamenda, and Bafut was spoken at home with my grandmother, mother, and other select relatives. I understood from a young age that Bafut was an unofficial language while English was the language of access and power (Baker-Bell, 2020; Rosa & Flores, 2017). Ngugi Wa Thiong'o (2011) describes this as colonial alienation resulting in "a society of bodiless heads and headless bodies" whereby one is conditioned to dissociate themselves from the reality of their surrounding community while acquiring a reality or worldview removed from their own context. In Cameroon, French and English are the language of currency, fraught with complicated colonial histories. When I immigrated to the United States and became more "educated" and advanced in my studies, an emphasis was placed on my mastery of English at the expense of maintaining my native language.

Cynthia B. Dillard (2012) asserts that "all too often, we have been seduced into forgetting (or have chosen to do so)" (p. 4) and further maintains, "learning to (re)member is about recognizing and examining our seductions: Those irresistible moments of when we have been enticed away from ourselves, led away from our duties, and have accepted others' principles or notions of identity and proper conduct as our own" (p. 15). The picture of my grandmother and me symbolizes a return to self. Years ago, I was asked to talk about my first teacher and I immediately thought about my first schooling experience. However, recently, as I've engaged in the work of (re)membering and doing away with the seductions, I now answer that my first and primary teachers were my mother and grandmother. I carry the picture of my grandmother and me almost everywhere. It's the background image for my phone and tablet, and a reminder of the price of my "education"—distanced from my indigenous ways of knowing and being. Encapsulated by my grandmother, I find myself returning to her kitchen on days that are especially cumbersome. My "re-memorialization" of the moment in the kitchen with my grandmother is now an ancestral sanctuary where I journey for strength and connection to those who came before me, traveling between the present and past in recognition of the connection between the histories and stories bridging the past, present, and future (Bhattacharya, 2020).

The Intersection of Culture, Race, and Gender:
Haeny and Her White Doll

These memories and experiences also exist at the intersection of race/ethnicity, gender, and citizenship. How do I (Haeny) locate myself in the present and past as I look back on my experience in light of Lily? As Toni Morrison (1984) reminds us, memory is an unreliable witness, a "willed creation" to illustrate what these moments *do* for us as intersectional beings. I consider the ways that Lily moved—willingly and literally embracing her own racial and ethnic identity, confidently voicing her abilities, and rejecting fixed ways of being. She was maternal and playful, assertive and soft, funny and thoughtful, boisterous and compliant. As a young girl whose status as a Black immigrant might steer her towards assimilation and invisibility (like it did for me as an Asian immigrant), Lily's story fills me with both longing, sadness, and renewal. I would never *embrace* Korea like Lily embraced Haiti; instead, I desired sameness, content on making my Korean heritage invisible.

This photograph (Figure 9.2) of me and my white doll at 3 years old illustrates the merging of multiple cultures: a heavily frosted "American" birthday cake with a giant, wax candle on top; a tin jar of Korean candies that I consumed as a child; a bowl of fruit which was more traditional of Korean birthday celebrations. Slowly, I saw the vestiges of that Korean heritage slip—English became my dominant language, American food became my preferred choice,

FIGURE 9.2   Haeny's Third Birthday with Her White Doll

my traditional customs became caricatures at school "multicultural" fairs, and what I played fit into traditional gender norms that elevated whiteness, despite the fact that I would never look the part.

Contrastingly, Lily's fluid movement between cultures also extended into how she viewed her gendered identity. In a conversation with Evan, she "challenged" him to a physical duel:

Lily: Like, like, like, I'm more flexible than him because I can do a split and a cartwheel.
Evan: I can do a cartwheel.
Lily: Well, you can't do a split. I can. I can do a handstand.
Evan: No, you—
Haeny: Well, I have seen Lily do the splits. I haven't seen you do the splits yet (to Evan).
Lily: Well, I can do a split with my jeans.
Haeny: With your jeans? Wow.

She was confident in her abilities and competitive, and many times, eager to prove her claims were true. As mentioned above, she did a front split during one of the morning movement breaks, and switched back and forth to side splits. All the students, including Evan were impressed by her ability to move so flexibly.

This kind of flexibility was not only a physical trait, but a social and ideological one as well. When children chose worksheets—one featuring a king and one featuring a queen—Lily challenged others, Evan included, who insisted on following gendered choices. Lily's response was more fluid, declaring that boys can be queens and, "all girls can be kings." She was consistent in these flexible gender roles throughout the school year. On one occasion, several children in the class firmly declared that boys cannot wear pink, should not be called "pretty," or play with "girls' stuff." In response, Lily revealed that her father wore pink shirts and in fact, liked that color. She acknowledged playing with boys' and girls' stuff, despite the response from Xavier, "Ew, you're disgusting. That's gross." Lily's inter/actions made her visible, central to the conversation and prone to ridicule and backlash. In observing Lily over the school year, I learned that visibility and vulnerability gave her cultural capital, a trait I had always assumed would exclude me from my peers. These moves signaled to me (at an early age) that conflict was undesirable and the outcomes of this would never be good. I learned from Lily that productive tensions and conflicts are a benefit and asset to classroom life. She took up space and commandeered respect from her peers.

Unlike Lily, my perceptions of race and gender were often binaries of Black and white, boy and girl, feminine and masculine, English and non-English speaking. I put myself in categories that I recognized, complicit in letting others do the same to me. What drew me to Lily is not simply her willingness to play across gendered and raced constructions of play and being, but her practices and affiliations were multiple and disentangled with binary thinking. By all accounts, she loved typically feminine things—she wore ornate dresses, participated in a lot of kitchen and cooking scenarios, and loved dressing up during play. Even when she played cops and superheroes, she somehow defaulted into a nurturing role and fixed up a hero's injury. She was "both and" (Enriquez et al., 2016), moving between lines that felt like dueling opposites. Contrastingly, I saw rules, lines, and norms as *the* most important aspect constituting play rather than only one of many things encircling play.

It has been a long journey of shifting how I thought about myself in relationship to whiteness and girlhood. I see the ideologies of whiteness taking shape in the photos I analyze as an adult, the childhood memories I cull together, and the haptic memories that I recall. My doll or toy served as a mentor—she shaped what I thought was possible, what I aspired to be, who I admired, and how I chose to present myself in the world. That is, toys and by extension, the material world, represented how space was occupied (Mitchell et al., 2010; Tolia-Kelly, 2010). For example, a white girl with a porcelain face and feminized features occupies a privileged space, un/consciously making my play raced and gendered. I applied these conditions to who I saw as desirable in early childhood and found pleasure in being small, cute, and "doll"-like. After many years of unpacking the feelings populating my notions of race and culture, I struggle to reconcile both my American and Korean identities, rather than acculturate into the blended term Korean American which inevitably leans towards American (Hong, 2020).

Memory as a Pedagogical Tool

Anthropologist Barrie Thorne (1993) illustrates the "chain of remembering" (p. 24) while engaging in her own ethnography of children's gendered play in first grade. As researchers who are also attuned to children's lived experiences in and out of school, we attest to the feelings and emotions that tug at us when we interact with certain children. Some remind us so much of ourselves, and others (like Lily) remind us of who we could have been. However, like Thorne, we are also cognizant of how we ignore or dismiss children's ideas and passions, particularly when we do not find them interesting. We stand guilty of distancing ourselves from children that we do not find a natural affinity for, and center our attention to children like Lily who expand our own standpoints and worldviews. Our memories are both a "distortion [and] insight [having] lived that world in another time or place" (Thorne, 1993, p. 26), evoking strong feelings of dis/connection. We assume these same feelings arise for educators in classrooms: who captures our attention, who do we gravitate towards, who do we connect with, who do we have difficulty relating to? Children are also astute observers of how teachers situate and position certain students in classrooms, influencing how Black boys, for example, are overly surveilled and disciplined (e.g., Bryan, 2020; Dumas & Nelson, 2016; Powell & Coles, 2021). In our actions or lack thereof, teachers are in the background and foreground "approving, disapproving, reacting to, and being reacted to" (Paley, 2007, p. 155). Therefore, the answers to these questions also need to be juxtaposed with our own childhood memories, knowing our experiences offer one standpoint out of a multitude, particularly when we engage with children and families whose cultural or ethnic practices vary widely from our own. We misinterpret and misunderstand because our experiences limit our vision.

As we unpack our childhood memories, we might want to (re)consider those scenarios that give us pause, that create dissonance in our worldviews, that make us uncomfortable, or force us to recall something that (re)traumatizes us. These moments are inevitable, yet what we consider and do in these moments matter. Thorne felt this in her own work—making excuses to avoid the company of specific children; making assumptions about how children's social worlds worked by filtering it through her own memories of it; rifling through notes realizing how "obsessed" she was with a specific child over others. Clearly, we must confront the limitations of our own adult gaze. The presumptions we make, the memories that we bring to the forefront, and the ideological standpoints by which we look can have both beneficial and deleterious effects.

Reflexivity: Reflecting Toward Social Action

True reflexivity arises when our reflective practices lead to social action. Many of us who became teachers excelled in school, afforded opportunities and access that led to our success. However, many of us from nondominant communities accomplished this at the cost of our own ethnic and cultural heritages. Haeny is less fluent in Korean and had to be intentional in tracing back her Korean heritage as an adult. Her relationship with her parents is often fractured as their stories were dismissed with disdain and contempt as obstacles barring her from real inclusion. To this day, it is clear that she grew up more *American* at the cost of knowing what it really meant to be *Korean*. Lily, on the other hand, blended her home life and school, partially through the space the teacher provided. Lily's mother visited the classroom not for any special occasion, but as an ad-hoc, spontaneous activity during everyday activity. Her culture was less a spectacle and more an extension of who she was in the classroom.

While beyond the scope of this chapter, we believe Lily's teacher created this space through her own vulnerability and humility. As a woman of Color, she was intentional about sharing literature about Puerto Rican community members, discussing her own migration journey to the United States. She connected children's interests with that of her two young sons' and sharing the materials/toys from her own home with the kindergartners. She willingly admitted uncertainty and discomfort around "controversial" topics of race, gender, politics; she took time to process children's words; she tabled discussions and returned to them after thoughtful consideration. Her pedagogical moves lead us to ask: How seriously do we take the moments when students evoke memories and stories in us? How do we view these provocations as an opportunity for vulnerability and humility? How do we attune to the ways in which our storied past influences our present, specifically in pedagogical practices and curriculum design?

While reflecting on her experiences as a transnational woman of Color in academia, Bhattacharya (2016) argues that vulnerability provides an opportunity to disrupt social inequities, enabling joy and creativity in oppressive spaces. Lily resurfaced parts of Lum's identity she never brought into the classroom, awakening the buried identities connected to her transnational experiences, both as a child and a teacher. Over years, Lum compartmentalized her transnational identity, keeping it neatly and safely tucked away, to escape the exoticization and negative assumptions encountered as an African immigrant. As an early teacher, Lum's self-imposed compartmentalization (unconsciously) limited the parts of herself she shared with students and vice versa. Students and families were invited to participate and share their experiences, but their participation and sharing centered around predetermined and restrictive curricular goals, curtailing the ways in which they could creatively and authentically express their stories. In an effort to play the role of the teacher "correctly," Lum created distance between her cultural self and her professional self—something we argue she learned as a young child. Her indigenous language, her cultural practices, and her ways of being were relegated to unofficial, nonschool spaces. She learned to do the same as a teacher, believing that cultural identities should be respected but separate from curricular and pedagogical practices.

We share these memories in conversation with Lily to illustrate how our childhood memories filter into our practices as educators and researchers. They broaden and limit what we think is possible in classrooms, specifically when we turn the gaze on ourselves. Rather than claim memories as "accurate or reliable containers of experience" (Chang-Kredl et al., 2016, p. 271), these critical moments filter how we see children and their childhoods. As we demonstrate, children's identities as raced and gendered beings are complex negotiations, mis/guided by adults who facilitate these spaces. Even as adults, our *becoming* is not complete as we confront the limitations of our own experience. By extension, we enter classrooms with our own baggage and worldviews, some of which can act as tools of oppression while others work for more equitable futures.

References

Alexander, M. J., & Mohanty, C. T. (Eds.). (2013). *Feminist genealogies, colonial legacies, democratic futures*. Routledge.

Alsup, J. (2006). *Teacher identity discourses: Negotiating personal and professional spaces*. Routledge.

Anzaldúa, G. (1987). *Borderlands/La Frontera: The new mestiza*. Aunt Lute Books.

Baker-Bell, A. (2020). *Linguistic justice: Black language, literacy, identity, and pedagogy*. Routledge.

Basch, L., Schiller, N. G., & Blanc, C. S. (2020). *Nations unbound: Transnational projects, postcolonial predicaments, and deterritorialized nation-states*. Routledge.

Bhattacharya, K. (2016). The vulnerability academic: Personal narratives and strategic de/colonization of academic structures. *Qualitative Inquiry, 22*(5), 309–321.

Bhattacharya, K. (2020). Connecting with water spirits: An autoethnography of home and higher education. In R. M. Boylorn & M. P. Orbe (Eds.), *Critical autoethnography* (pp. 103–117). Routledge

Britzman, D. P. (2003). *Practice makes practice: A critical study of learning to teach*. SUNY Press.

Bryan, N. (2020). Shaking the bad boys: Troubling the criminalization of Black boys' childhood play, hegemonic white masculinity and femininity, and the school playground-to-prison pipeline. *Race Ethnicity and Education, 23*(5), 673–692.

Chang-Kredl, S., Wilkie, G., & Ghaznavi, S. (2016). Circling a memory: A layered reflective method for generating subjective knowledge about childhood and teacher identity. *Reflective Practice, 17*(3), 270–283.

Dillard, C. B. (2012). *Learning to (re)member the things we have learned to forget: Endarkened feminisms, spirituality, & the sacred nature of research and learning*. Peter Lang Publishing, Inc.

Dumas, M. J., & Nelson, J. D. (2016). (Re)Imagining Black boyhood: Toward a critical framework for educational research. *Harvard Educational Review, 86*(1), 27–47.

Elbaz-Luwisch, F. (2004). Immigrant teachers: Stories of self and place. *International Journal of Qualitative Studies in Education, 17*(3), 387–414.

El-Haj, T. R. A. (2009). Becoming citizens in an era of globalization and transnational migration: Re-imagining citizenship as critical practice. *Theory into Practice, 48*(4), 274–282.

Enriquez, G., Johnson, E., Kontovourki, S., & Mallozzi, C. A. (Eds.). (2015). *Literacies, learning, and the body: Putting theory and research into pedagogical practice*. Routledge.

Farley, L., Sonu, D., Garlen, J. C., & Chang-Kredl, S. (2020). Childhood memories of playful antics and punishable acts: Risking an imperfect future of teaching and learning. *The New Educator, 16*(2), 106–121.

Ghiso, M. P. (2016). The laundromat as the transnational local: Young children's literacies of interdependence. *Teachers College Record, 118*(1), 1–46.

Haddix, M. (2010). No longer on the margins: Researching the hybrid literate identities of Black and Latina preservice teachers. *Research in the Teaching of English, 45*(2), 97–123.

Hong, C. P. (2020). *Minor feelings: An Asian American reckoning*. One World.

James, A. (2009). Agency. In J. Qvortrup, W. A. Corsaro, M. S. Honig, & G. Valentine (Eds.), *The Palgrave handbook of childhood studies* (pp. 34–45). Palgrave Macmillan.

Kwon, J. (2019). Third culture kids: Growing up with mobility and cross-cultural transitions. *Diaspora, Indigenous, and Minority Education, 13*(2), 113–122.

Kwon, J. (2020). The circulation of care in multilingual and transnational children. *Literacy Research: Theory, Method, and Practice, 69*(1), 99–119.

Mitchell, C., Strong-Wilson, T., & Pithouse, K. (2010). *Introducing memory and pedagogy.* Routledge.

Morrison, T. (1984). Memory, creation, and writing. *Thought, 59*(235), 385–390.

Nagar, R., & Swarr, A. L. (2010). Theorizing transnational feminist praxis. In A. L. Swarr & R. Nagar (Eds.), *Critical transnational feminist praxis* (pp. 1–20). SUNY.

Orellana, M. F., Thorne, B., Chee, A., & Lam, W. S. E. (2001). Transnational childhoods: The participation of children in processes of family migration. *Social Problems, 48*(4), 572–591.

Paley, V. G. (2007). HER classic: On listening to what the children say. *Harvard Educational Review, 77*(2), 152–163.

Powell, T., & Coles, J. A. (2021). 'We still here': Black mothers' personal narratives of sense making and resisting anti-Blackness and the suspensions of their Black children. *Race Ethnicity and Education, 24*(1), 76–95.

Rosa, J., & Flores, N. (2017). Unsettling race and language: Toward a raciolinguistic perspective. *Language in Society, 46*(5), 621–647.

Thorne, B. (1993). *Gender play: Girls and boys in school.* Rutgers University Press.

Tolia-Kelly, D. P. (2010). *Landscape, race and memory: Material ecologies of citizenship.* Ashgate Publishing, Ltd.

Wa Thiong'o, N. (2011). *Decolonizing the mind: The politics of language in African literature.* Boydell & Brewer Ltd.

Yoon, H. S., & Llerena, C. L. (2020). Transnational friendships and fluid boundaries in early childhood classrooms: The possibilities of (un)productive play in teacher–researcher collaborations for equity. *Urban Education, 55*(6), 865–891.

Zembylas, M. (2003). Interrogating "teacher identity": Emotion, resistance, and self-formation. *Educational Theory, 53*(1), 107–127.

10

TRANSNATIONAL FLOWS AND LINGUISTIC FLUIDITY IN AN ETHNIC PUBLIC SPACE

The Experiences of a Young Emergent Bilingual

Jungmin Kwon and Lindsey Allene Hall

This chapter features Sujin, a 6-year-old emergent bilingual born into an immigrant household in the United States. Sujin's parents and grandparents own a Korean supermarket in a predominantly white area located in a Midwestern state. After her first day of the first grade, Sujin's mother and Jungmin, the first author, had a conversation in the back corner of the family's supermarket. Wearing a perplexed look, the mother recalled a small encounter that had happened at the school playground that day when she and her daughter, Sujin, were there:

> We were playing in the playground after school. Do you know Ms. Brown? She is an ESL teacher. She came to us and asked, "Where are you from?" I said, "We are from Korea." And Sujin said, "Mom, I am from here." The teacher seemed so surprised and said, "You were born here? Oh, you are American?" Maybe she asked us because there are many international families in this school? I don't know. She is an ESL teacher.

Sujin's parents and grandparents were immigrants who left South Korea—their country of origin—for better economic and educational opportunities, yet Sujin and her older sibling were born and raised in the Midwestern state where they lived, and had never visited South Korea, though they wished to do so someday. Sujin's interjection of "I am from here" serves to indicate her strong tie to place of birth though never having physically stepped foot there. In this chapter, we position Sujin as a transnational child who maintains a strong connection to both the United States and South Korea.

DOI: 10.4324/9781003399155-14

The back corner of the Korean supermarket was filled with artifacts that demonstrated Sujin's multilingual and transnational expertise. There was a pile of books and stickers; many of them were written either in Korean or English, the languages that Sujin proudly speaks, and she often sorted them out by language. During the global pandemic and school closure, Sujin made artifacts that entailed multiple languages, such as a storybook, letters to her aunts and grandparents, and a drawing of a Korean flag. Each artifact encapsulated stories and memories—a chalkboard that another immigrant family gave to Sujin's family, a doll with an English and Korean name, and stickers that her maternal grandmother in South Korea had sent to her. The small corner in the Korean supermarket was her playground, library, and second home, where she would draw, write, and create crafts, many of which showed her translingual practices and transitional identity as someone linked to two countries. In this space, she even expanded her multilingual repertoire by interacting with signs, products, and music that entailed multiple languages, as well as people such as her family members and customers.

Just like Sujin, many Asian American children are connected to multiple languages, cultures, and nation-states. Even at a young age, they, as multilinguals, are well aware of who they are, where they are tied to, and how and for what purposes they can make use of their linguistic and cultural knowledge. They also have a wealth of knowledge that spans across countries and is shaped by their transnational experiences. The reality is, however, that these children are often considered as "perpetual foreigners" (Lee et al., 2017), and frequently encounter the question, "Where are you from?" which leads to surprised comments of, "Oh, you are American?" Such moments then create questions and tensions for the children and further marginalize both the children and their parents. Like Sujin's mother, who pushed herself to legitimize the question from an ESL teacher as having had good intentions, many parents feel the burden of navigating racialized stereotypes and deficit views on immigrants for themselves and their children.

In this chapter, we take a "trans-"perspective (Hawkins & Mori, 2018) and focus on Sujin's transnational funds of knowledge—a wealth of linguistic, cultural, and experiential knowledge grounded in transnational networks. Reading and interpreting the Korean supermarket as a classroom, we then focus on how Sujin's transnational knowledge was built, expanded, and mobilized in this ethnic public space, which we conceptualize as "transnational local" space (Ghiso, 2016). By sharing how languages and literacies were represented, taken up, and observed in this space, we illustrate what early childhood educators may learn from meaningful interactions in ethnic public spaces when interpreting the transnational and multilingual experiences of immigrant children and families with asset and resource-based orientations (Ruiz, 1984).

Immigrant Children's Transnational Funds of Knowledge

Transnationalism, or "the movement of people, media, language, and goods between distinct nation states" (Jiménez et al., 2009, p. 17), involves intricate processes of negotiating temporal, social, and physical spaces (Compton-Lilly et al., 2019). For immigrant families engaged in such complex negotiations, the advancement of technology has brought "more affordable travel, mobile communication devices, social media, and online connectivity" (Darvin & Norton, 2014, p. 113), which allow them to more seamlessly maintain and strengthen connections between their countries of birth and present nation-state location (Basch et al., 1994). In doing so, immigrant children and families become interwoven in complex transnational networks (Lam & Warriner, 2012) that yield economic, political and cultural implications (Darvin & Norton, 2014). In this chapter, we particularly attend to Sujin's own funds of knowledge, which have been shaped by her transnational connections and experiences in the ethnic public space. According to Moll et al. (1992), funds of knowledge are "historically accumulated and culturally developed bodies of knowledge and skills essential for household or individual functioning and well-being" (p. 133). Furthermore, immigrant children and their families utilize their transnational funds of knowledge as they experience flows of "people, money, labor, goods, information, advice, stories, languages, care and love" (Sánchez, 2007, p. 260) across temporal, social, and physical space. It should be no surprise that Sujin's funds of knowledge can be thought of as transnational, despite her being "from here" and never having stepped foot on her familial homeland. Given that movement across borders forges unique repertoires for navigating the world that extend temporally across generations, Sujin can be viewed as a child navigating the creation of a unique cultural and linguistic repertoire situated in both "here" and "there" simultaneously.

That a child can be both here and there culturally and linguistically stands in sharp contrast to monolingual ideologies that situate the distinct separation of named languages as both nature and ideal, and the power and privilege accorded to specific named languages normalized and unexamined (Rosa & Burdick, 2016). However, the flexible, creative use of linguistic repertoires is common in the everyday life of multilingual communities (García, 2009; García & Otheguy, 2019; Kwon, 2019). With increasing recognition of this, recent years have witnessed a significant shift in how cultural and linguistic repertoires are conceptualized in both scholarly and practitioner-based education circles. Originating in bilingual Welsh/English classrooms, the concept known as translanguaging was conceptualized as a pedagogical practice in which classroom language usage was navigated flexibly (Galante, 2020). In more recent years, translanguaging has gone beyond a pedagogical practice to now represent "the notion that multilingual individuals do not 'have' or 'know' two

or more separate languages, but rather have at their disposal a complex linguistic repertoire where languages interact and can be drawn upon fluidly"
(Galante, 2020, p. 553 citing Otheguy et al., 2015). For example, Martínez-
Álvarez and Ghiso (2017) found that when bilingual children engage in translanguaging, their "meaning-making encompasses varied linguistic modalities
and extends to embodied knowledge of community spaces, metalinguistic
awareness, global influences, and multilingual and transnational knowledges"
(p. 685). Translanguaging thus acts as a "mediating artifact" (Martínez-Álvarez
& Ghiso, 2017) across the interactions and collaborative activities of bilingual
children, enabling them to draw upon their transnational funds of knowledge
in enacting creative, critical and transformative learning experiences (Kwon,
2019; Martínez-Álvarez & Ghiso, 2017).

Ethnic Public Space as Transnational Local Space

For immigrant families, then, these inherent boundaries of power are navigated when they create places that validate their transnational identities while
also supporting their economic survival. As Butler and Sinclair (2020) note,
"Places are cultural products with different meanings for different people. The
attachments people develop to places and the meanings they make of places
may vary greatly depending on one's cultural background and positionality"
(p. 67). Thus, places that may seem purely economic and mundane, such as
laundromats and grocery stores, carry significant cultural meanings and opportunities for transnational connections within their physical walls. Building
on Mignolo's idea (2000) of a "transnational localism," Ghiso (2016) contends that such places "are contact zones where young children negotiate languages, literacies, and cultural values in ways that are at the forefront of global
dynamics—constructing new social practices and identities" (p. 34). In other
words, these community sites can play roles as areas to understand young immigrant children's language, literacies, and agency.

In a study focusing on the literacy experiences of Spanish-English bilinguals in New York City, Ghiso (2016) conceptualized laundromats as "transnational local" spaces and argued that these public spaces are not "simply a
site for transactions, but also for affective, cultural, and linguistic exchanges"
(p. 19). In the study, young immigrant children engaged with multilingual
signs, supported one another, and built relationships with community members in the laundromat. Other scholars (Orellana, 2016) whose attention to
immigrant children's everyday lives and transnational literacies also emphasizes the importance of considering community spaces as important sites for
learning about the children's language, literacy, and identity. These studies
corroborate with Souto-Manning and Yoon's argument (2018) that children

engage in rich language and literacy practices in neighborhoods and communities. While these spaces have been widely studied through the perspectives of economists, sociologists, and criminal justice scholars (Min, 2017), little is known about the languages and literacies represented within them, or how people, particularly children and families, engage in language and literacy practices in these spaces.

Methods

Participant and Context

Sujin (pseudonym), a 6-year-old at the time of the study, is a second-generation immigrant child born in the United States. At home, Korean was primarily used among her family members, yet it was noticed over the year that Sujin came to speak English more often with her older sister. Sujin's parents were committed to supporting their children's heritage language (HL) learning, given the crucial roles that language plays in intergenerational relationships and immigrant children's identity. Her parents and paternal grandparents moved from South Korea about 20 years prior to the study, and 3 years prior, the family had become owners of a Korean supermarket after years of working temporarily at different stores. The family lived in a predominantly white county in a Midwestern state. As of 2019, the total population of the county was estimated at just over 290,000 people (U.S. Census Bureau, 2019a). Of these individuals, over 19,000 or approximately 6.8% were Asian. Approximately 1244, or 0.4% of the total population of the county, identified as Korean. Though the overall Asian population estimates grew from 5% to 6.8% between 2010 and 2019, the percentage of Koreans decreased from 0.8% (2308 people) to 0.4% (1244 people) during this same period (U.S. Census Bureau, 2019b).

In this community, the Korean supermarket is one of the few ethnic public spaces available, which include an Indian restaurant, a Chinese grocery store, and a few interethnic stores. While Sujin's family's store was much smaller in size than the ones located in ethnic enclaves in meta-metropolitan areas such as Chicago and New York City, it played an important role for many people in the community who were tied to the Korean language and culture. It was not only a place to find goods and services, but also to connect with other Korean immigrants. For Sujin, the place played an important role, particularly during the pandemic, as she spent most of her daily time. The back corner of the store was where Sujin's playhouse was located, and next to the house was her library where she would read books and draw. The supermarket, which people would consider a public space, was a space filled with love and care for Sujin, where she would interact with and support her older sibling, parents, and grandparents.

Data Collection and Analysis

We used an ethnographic case study approach (Dyson & Genishi, 2005) to understand the focal child's transnational funds of knowledge and how they were constructed, expanded, and shared in a Korean supermarket. The following sources of data were collected: child-generated artifacts (including writings, drawings, and crafts), video-recordings of Sujin's Korean class, audio-recordings of informal conversations with the child and her mother, child-centered interview activities, and fieldnotes. The fieldnotes included what the first author had noticed and observed during the first few months of getting to know Sujin's family and visiting the supermarket, before "the unfamiliar aspects of a new site" became "familiar" and "taken for granted" (Dyson & Genishi, 2005). After completing the data collection, iterative reading, open coding, and line-by-line coding were used to identify codes and categories, which were developed into the three major themes that we describe below.

Findings

In this chapter, we discuss how the focal child engaged in the crossing of languages, cultures, and countries in the Korean supermarket, a site that we consider to be a "transnational local" space (Ghiso, 2016). We highlight how the children drew on their linguistic, cultural, and transnational knowledge and engaged in transnational practices in the space. We also discuss the collaborative efforts that the children and their family made in the space to resist language shift and maintain their HL and culture (Tse, 2001a).

Transnational Flows and Translanguaging in and Across the Space

As Dyson and Genishi (2005) note, "Any educational setting—a classroom, a school, a family, a community program—is overflowing with human experiences and with human stories" (p. 12). The supermarket, which we conceptualize as a "transnational local" space (Ghiso, 2016), overflows with transnational experiences and human stories, and it served as an educational setting for Sujin. There, Sujin was exposed to and interacted with multilingual signs and brochures, Korean food products, Korean popular music, and the multilingual and transnational experiences that people—Sujin's family members, customers, visitors, etc.—embody and bring to the space. For instance, the stack of bilingual brochures promoting local ethnic stores and churches was intentionally placed next to the entrance door to share information, resources, and care, which also seemed to intensify the visitors' and Sujin's family's transnational affect—stronger attachment to their HL, culture, and country (Jo & Lee,

2016). The supermarket was not just a place where money and goods flowed, but also where first- and second-generation Korean immigrants drew on their multilingual repertoires and engaged in meaningful exchanges of advice, care, and love.

Spending most of her daily life in the space seemed to help Sujin build and expand her transnational funds of knowledge (Kwon, 2019, 2021) but also her linguistic repertoires. When customers entered the store, Sujin and her mother greeted them by crossing named languages (Korean and English), utilizing gestures (bowing and waving), and making use of linguistic features (honorific expressions). When encountering challenges, Sujin and her family members in the space cocreated and negotiated their exchanges through drawing on their linguistic assets and care. For example, when Sujin's mother encountered challenges in communicating with a customer, Sujin served as a language broker (Tse, 1996), mediating the interactions using her multilingual repertoire by suggesting English translations and encouraging the mother to use an online dictionary. On another occasion, when one of the customers had difficulty translating the Korean recipe attached to the product, multiple interlocuters (the owner, the customer, and the first author) used a digital device, drew on our multilingual repertoires, and helped the non-Korean-speaking customer. Observing and being involved in these multilingual interactions were part of Sujin's everyday lives. When young children visited the store, it even turned into a site for play, where the children navigated different aisles and played hide and seek, engaged in conversations about different snacks, and interacted with multilingual labels and signs. On one occasion, Sujin, her older sibling, and a Korean child who visited the store were observed drawing and coloring pictures together, during which they added words in English and Korean and invited each other to guess what the pictures were portraying. Their conversations involved multiple named languages, characters from Korean and American cartoons, multimodal resources, and more importantly, their playfulness. In other words, Sujin orchestrated multilingual and multimodal resources for meaning-making and interacting with others in the space, and her translanguaging practices further expanded through the transnational flow and the circulation of care, goods, information, and people.

Transnational Funds of Knowledge Shaped in the Local Space

Though advancements in technology have indeed made cross-border travel more feasible for many immigrant families (Kwon, 2017), this is not a guarantee for most due to inequitable distributions of various forms of capital, manifested as tenuous immigration status and insufficient financial resources for example (Oliveira, 2018). However, frequent deficit-based perspectives surrounding the discussion of cultural capital in communities of color have been critiqued and countered with the theory of community cultural wealth (Yosso, 2005). In this theory, communities of color are seen to nurture "cultural wealth through at least six forms of capital such as aspirational, navigational, social, linguistic, familial, and resistant capital" (Yosso, 2005, p. 77). Indeed, flows of cultural wealth can be observed in the focal child's family. For Sujin, almost everything she knew about her parental homeland was shaped by what she had seen, learned, and heard locally, in her home and the Korean supermarket. Observing Sujin and her literacy practices and interactions with others revealed that her funds of knowledge was shaped by "sustained and meaningful flows of people, money, labor, goods, information, advice, care, and love" (Sánchez, 2007, p. 493) in and across the space.

When Sujin was invited to create an artifact (Figure 10.1) showing what she knew about her parental homeland, she first added Taeguk, the red and blue circle that is in the middle of the Korean national flag, and put down words associated with the culture. These words showed her understanding of Korean popular culture (콩순이 [Kongsuni—the name of a Korean cartoon character], BTS) and conglomerates (삼성 [Samsung], 기아자동차 [Kia Car]). She then added names of foods (김밥, 김치) and ingredients (김, 멸치) and explained that these are Korean but could be found locally in her family-owned supermarket.

FIGURE 10.1 Sujin's Drawing about Her Parental Homeland

In her community-based HL class, Sujin often shared what she had noticed in the store, which created a space for other children to discuss how Korean language and culture are represented or erased in different community spaces. For example, when the children in the class were asked to share a place that is meaningful to them, Sujin selected the Korean supermarket and said it was because the store has Korean food, drinks and "신문" [newspapers]. Her sharing evoked a discussion among other Korean immigrant children about different neighborhoods and communities. Jihoon, who lived 45 minutes away from the area, mentioned that there is no ethnic public space in his neighborhood. Gayoung mentioned that her Taekwondo academy does not have any signs written in Korean, nor does it display the flag, which she found unusual. On another occasion, when the children engaged in a writing assignment to share what they want their peers in US schools to know about their culture, Sujin created a chart (Figure 10.2) with the help of her older sibling in the supermarket. Using two languages (Korean and English) and symbols, she highlighted the different ways that people greet one another, dress up and eat on special occasions, and count age in the United States and South Korea. She then elaborated on how she learned the culture-specific knowledge about wearing "한복" and eating "송편" on "추석" from her older sibling. In other words, her comparative perspectives and transnational understanding were shaped in the ethnic public

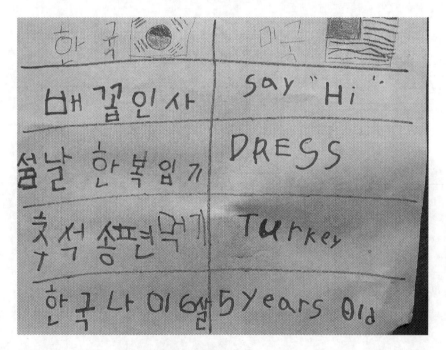

FIGURE 10.2 What Sujin Would Like Her Peers to Know about Korea

space, and the knowledge she gained in the space was shared with her peers beyond the supermarket.

Transmission of Heritage Language

According to Tse (2001b), immigrant parents play a key role in exposure to and maintenance of HL and culture by "speaking the heritage language to their children at home, providing access to institutions and practices that use the language, and enrolling their children in HL programs" (p. 681). As evident earlier, Sujin maintained her HL while expanding her multilingual repertoires and flexibly crossing named languages including English and Korean. In her case, HL was maintained through the deliberate efforts that Sujin's family members and the community members made in the supermarket. For example, multilingual artifacts in the supermarket (i.e., brochures promoting Korean HL schools) reflected the efforts that the community was making to challenge monolingual ideologies and resist language shift among second-generation immigrants. Sujin's mother intentionally provided children's literature written in Korean and English, so that Sujin could not only expand her multilingual repertoires, but also expand her understanding of different cultural contexts.

Sujin's mother, who felt the importance of promoting Korean language and culture among Korean immigrant families in the community, even placed a bookshelf in the store and invited the customers to circulate the different literacy materials they had (Figure 10.3). While the sign "Free Books," written in English, demarcated its audience as English speakers, almost all books that were donated, displayed, and shared were literature, history books, and children's books written in Korean and published in Korea. The way that these books, which were written and published in Korea, were circulated through this "free library" space in the store corroborates what existing studies say about how immigrant parents receive and send HL literacy materials from their home countries (Kwon, 2017).

The efforts that Sujin's mother and the customers make in promoting biliteracy (Tse, 2001a) through sharing literacy resources show that the store is not "simply a site for transactions, but also for affective, cultural, and linguistic exchanges" (Ghiso, 2016, p. 19). It also shows how immigrant parents utilize their navigational and linguistic capitals (Yosso, 2005) to overcome the limited HL resources they have as linguistically minoritized families, cocreate commonalities with others, and "align themselves with those who share similar dispositions and investments" (Darvin & Norton, 2014, p. 113). This example expands the ongoing dialogues on immigrant children's transnational experiences by showing how children and families who are unable to engage in physical border-crossing experiences, due to constraints of economic capital, still manage to foster and preserve transnational connections through transnational local spaces.

FIGURE 10.3 "Free Books" at the Store

Implications and Conclusion

This chapter provides implications for researchers and teachers who seek to understand immigrant children's out-of-school language and literacy practices by turning attention to ethnic public spaces. These spaces overflow with immigrant children's and families' multilingual and transnational experiences. Sujin's case shows how the studied ethnic public space, or the child's experiences in the space, reflects the language, literacy, and identities of immigrant children and families, as well as the collaborative resistance capital (Yosso, 2005) that immigrant parents form in opposition to language shifts and monolingual ideologies. As shown in this paper, when we take a learner stance and "analytic eye" (Dyson & Genishi, 2005) toward spaces that are part of our everyday lives, we come to realize the stories, experiences, and knowledge constructed and shared in these spaces that are often overlooked. Hence, we argue that it is important for early childhood educators to consider community spaces as opportunities to learn more about the lives and literacies of immigrant children and families. As a counternarrative to deficit-based perspectives which assume the experiences of children of color outside of school to be negative, educators must acknowledge, support, and come alongside members of ethnic public spaces to bridge the gap between communities and schools. We also encourage early childhood educators to create learning opportunities that involve, highlight, and partner with different local ethnic community sites and spaces where children can engage in transnational literacies. It is also important to note that no single ethnic public space is homogenous or identical (Ho & Seow, 2013). Different ethnic public spaces can teach us various transnational experiences that immigrant children bring to the spaces, as well as the transnational flows that we take part in. As Kim et al (2021) argue, taking on "community, collaborative, and translanguaging perspectives" (p. 20) can open up possibilities for multilingual families to engage in complex literacy practices and freely share their funds of knowledge through utilizing their full repertoires.

References

Basch, L., Schiller, N., & Blanc, C. (1994). *Nations unbound: Transnational projects, postcolonial predicaments and deterritorialized nation-states.* Gordon and Breach.

Butler, A., & Sinclair, K. A. (2020). Place matters: A critical review of place inquiry and special methods in education research. *Review of Research in Education, 44*(1), 64–96.

Compton-Lily, C., Kim, J., Quast, E., Tran, S., & Shedrow, S. (2019). The emergence of transnational awareness among children in immigrant families. *Journal of Early Childhood Literacy, 19*(1), 3–33.

Darvin, R., & Norton, B. (2014). Social class, identity, and migrant students. *Journal of Language, Identity & Education, 13*(2), 111–117.

Dyson, A. H., & Genishi, C. (2005). *On the case: Approaches to language and literacy research.* Teacher's College Press.

Galante, A. (2020). "The moment I realized I am plurilingual": Plurilingual tasks for creative representations in EAP at a Canadian university. *Applied Linguistics Review, 11*(4), 551–580.

García, O. (2009). *Bilingual education in the twenty-first century: A global perspective.* Wiley-Blackwell.

García, O., & Otheguy, R. (2019). Plurilingualism and translanguaging: Commonalities and divergences. *International Journal of Bilingual Education and Bilingualism*, *23*(1), 17–35.

Ghiso, M. P. (2016). The laundromat as transnational local: Young children's literacies of interdependence. *Teachers College Record*, *118*, 1–46.

Hawkins, M., & Mori, J. (2018). Considering 'trans-'perspectives in language theories and practices. *Applied Linguistics*, *39*(1), 1–8.

Ho, L. C., & Seow, T. (2013). Teaching geography through "Chinatowns": Global connections and local spaces. *Social Education*, *77*(1), 36–41.

Jiménez, R. T., Smith, P. H., & Teague, B. L. (2009). Transnational and community literacies for teachers. *Journal of Adolescent and Adult Literacy*, *53*(1), 16–26.

Jo, J. O., & Lee, S. (2016). Heritage language sustainability and transnational affect: The case of second-generation Korean American. In X. L. Rong, & J. Hilburn (Ed.) *Immigration and education in North Carolina: The challenges and responses in a new gateway state* (pp. 221–240). Sense Publishers.

Kim, S., Dorner, L. M., & Song, K. H. (2021). Conceptualizing community translanguaging through a family literacy project. *International Multilingual Research Journal*, *15*(4), 293–316.

Kwon, J. (2017). Immigrant mothers' beliefs and transnational strategies for their children's heritage language maintenance. *Language and Education*, *31*(6), 495–508.

Kwon, J. (2019). Parent-child translanguaging among transnational immigrant families in museums. *International Journal of Bilingual Education and Bilingualism*, *25*(2), 436–451.

Kwon, J. (2021). Mobilizing historical knowledge through transcultural play: A multi-sited ethnographic case study of an immigrant child. *Early Child Development and Care*, *191*(4), 624–639.

Lam, W. S. E., & Warriner, D. S. (2012). Transnationalism and literacy: Investigating the mobility of people, languages, texts, and practices in contexts of migration. *Reading Research Quarterly*, *47*(2), 191–215.

Lee, S. J., Park, E., & Wong, J. S. (2017). Racialization, schooling, and becoming American: Asian American Experiences. *Educational Studies*, *53*(5), 492–510.

Martínez-Álvarez, P., & Ghiso, M. P. (2017). On languaging and communities: Latino/a emergent bilinguals' expansive learning and critical inquiries into global childhoods. *International Journal of Bilingual Education and Bilingualism*, *20*(6), 667–687.

Mignolo, W. (2000). *Local histories/global designs: Coloniality, subaltern knowledges, and border thinking*. Princeton University Press.

Min, P. G. (2017). Transnational cultural events among Korean immigrants in the New York-New Jersey area. *Sociological Perspectives*, *60*(6), 1136–1159.

Moll, L., Amanti, C., Neff, D., & González, N. (1992). Funds of knowledge for teaching: Using a qualitative approach to connect homes and classrooms. *Theory into Practice*, *31*(2), 132–141.

Oliveira, G. (2018). *Motherhood across borders: Immigrants and their children in Mexico and New York*. NYU Press.

Orellana, M. F. (2016). *Immigrant children in transcultural spaces: Language, learning, and love*. Routledge.

Otheguy, R., García, O., & Reid, W. (2015). Clarifying translanguaging and deconstructing named languages: A perspective from linguistics. *Applied Linguistics Review*, *6*(3), 281–307.

Rosa, J., & Burdick, C. (2016). Language ideologies. In O. Garcia & N. Flores (Eds.), *The Oxford handbook of language and society* (pp. 103–124). Oxford University Press.

Ruiz, R. (1984). Orientations in language planning. *NABE Journal, 8*(2), 15–34.

Sánchez, P. (2007). Urban immigrant students: How transnationalism shapes their world learning. *The Urban Review, 39*(5), 489–517.

Souto-Manning, M., & Yoon, H. S. (2018). *Rethinking early literacies: Reading and rewriting worlds*. Routledge.

Tse, L. (1996). Who decides?: The effect of language, brokering on home-school communication. The *Journal of Education Issues of Language Minority Students, 16*, 225–233.

Tse, L. (2001a). Heritage language literacy: A study of US biliterates. *Language, Culture a Curriculum*.

Tse, L. (2001b). Resisting and reversing language shift: Heritage-language resilience among US native biliterates. *Harvard Educational Review, 71*(4), 676–709.

U.S. Census Bureau. (2019a). 2014–2019 American Community Survey 5-Year Estimates Data Profiles. Retrieved from https://data.census.gov/cedsci/table?q=DP05&g=0500000US26037,26065&tid=ACSDP5Y2019.DP05

U.S. Census Bureau. (2019b). 2005–2010 American Community Survey 5-Year Estimates Data Profiles. Retrieved from https://data.census.gov/cedsci/table?q=DP05&g=0500000US26037,26065&tid=ACSDP5Y2010.DP05

Yosso, T. J. (2005). Whose culture has capital? A critical race theory discussion of community cultural wealth. *Race Ethnicity and Education, 8*(1), 69–91. http://dx.doi.org/10.1080/1361332052000341006.

11

DECENTERING WHITENESS IN EARLY CHILDHOOD TEACHER EDUCATION

Supporting BIPOC Preservice Teachers through Culturally Relevant and Sustaining Practices

Ranita Cheruvu and Carmen Martinez

I came to my university as a freshman wanting to help children. I had a moral obligation and passion to help children of Color feel valued, loved, and educated, giving them what I rarely experienced in my K-12 education. My introductory level courses were brilliant; they made me more and more excited to teach. But once I entered my advanced classes, the tone of education shifted from "here is what content we will teach all students" to "here is how we teach children of Color who struggle with state standards." "Here are the reasons why teaching children of Color is more challenging and demanding" I quickly realized that the color of my skin defined me as an educator. Not only am I a teacher, but a bilingual teacher of Color. I am not the standard teacher, I don't fit into these norms, nor will I serve "standard" (white) students. Therefore, I exist outside my teacher education program. This program was not built for me.

A lot of the literature read, and the content taught was not diverse and didn't proclaim ways to support children of Color past learning their history and adding mindfulness routines into the school day. I remember one book called Planting Seeds of Equity by Ruchi Agarwal-Rangnath, which was an excellent book that shared the experiences of teachers in their journey to transform their classrooms into multicultural and antibias and antiracist settings. It was truly beautiful to see teachers from all backgrounds making a long-lasting effort in their classrooms. However, upon critical analysis of each chapter with one of my peers (also a person of Color), we were both left wanting more. We felt that each chapter barely touched the surface of an antibias/antiracist (ABAR) and multicultural classroom. We didn't read this book for us, but for our white counterparts. The book overall seemed to cater itself to white preservice teachers as an introduction into a diverse classroom experience, but I already have a diverse classroom experience, and I needed that support to understand how I can navigate past an introductory ABAR and multicultural curriculum. I just want to be taught how.[1]

DOI: 10.4324/9781003399155-15

Carmen's (co-author of this chapter) testimonio echoes the experiences of many BIPOC preservice teachers who are often pushed to the margins of their teacher education programs and who quickly come to recognize that these programs center the experiences and needs white preservice teachers and privilege whiteness. It raises the questions, *who does teacher education serve and for what purpose?*

For decades, there have been various calls to diversify the teaching workforce, citing both *democratic and demographic imperatives* (Achinstein & Ogawa, 2011; Geiger, 2018; Goodwin & McIntosh, 2008; Irvine, 1988). Scholars have noted the strong impact that teachers of Color can have on all students, particularly students from historically marginalized racial, cultural, and linguistic backgrounds (Cherng & Halpin, 2016; Dilworth & Coleman, 2014; Redding, 2019; Villegas & Irvine, 2010). Given this potential impact, it is argued that the demographic mismatch between teachers of Color and an increasingly diverse population of young children is troubling (Villegas et al., 2012). In recent years, teachers of Color have been positioned as a political construct in social justice initiatives (Gist, 2014a). Researchers have documented how teachers of Color often possess strong commitments to eradicating educational inequities and enacting transformative pedagogies (Achinstein & Ogawa, 2011), serve as cultural brokers for students and communities of Color (Irvine, 2003), and can improve the academic success of students of Color (Egalite et al., 2015). While teacher education programs have responded to this call through various initiatives such as grow your own programs, scholarships, and high school pipeline initiatives (Gist et al., 2019; Rogers-Ard et al., 2019; Sleeter et al., 2014), what remains a larger issue is the centering of whiteness in teacher education (Ladson-Billings, 2005; Salazar, 2018).

The literature focused on the experiences of BIPOC preservice teachers documents the ways that they are othered, silenced, and marginalized within their teacher preparation programs (Amos, 2016; Cheruvu et al., 2015; Haddix, 2017; Irizarry & Donaldson, 2012). These experiences are a reflection of the ways that whiteness permeates teacher education structures such as policies, program design, pedagogy, and school/community relationships. As Calderón (2006) states, the "reproduction of whiteness in structures serves to oppress raced, gendered and classed individuals and communities who deviate from the norms established by the ideology of whiteness" (p. 73). Scholars have demonstrated how whiteness has been reinscribed in teacher education programs through neoliberal racism (Picower & Mayorga, 2015) and settler colonialism (Stanton & Morrison, 2018). This gives us a moment to pause and consider, what is our *ethical responsibility to aspiring teachers of Color? After recruitment efforts, what are we doing to support and nurture BIPOC preservice teachers in their preparation and in their induction years, especially considering the disparate turnover rates for BIPOC teachers who are pushed out of schools given oppressive and inequitable policies*

(Kohli, 2018)? As Faison and McArthur (2020) argue, decentering whiteness in teacher education necessitates having an intentional focus on equity and justice for teacher candidates of Color. If truly we want BIPOC preservice teachers to thrive so that they can fulfill their own professional goals and the larger promise of educational equity, it is imperative that teacher education disrupt the logic of whiteness that permeates policies, programs, and practice (Carter Andrews et al., 2021; Kohli et al, 2022).

As women of Color, our experiences within teacher education mirror those described above. Ranita, a 1.5 Indian American immigrant, is currently an early childhood teacher educator who has taught in programs in PWI and MSI and is a former classroom teacher. Carmen is a Chicana/Latina who is currently a preservice bilingual (English and Spanish) teacher and critically evaluates and works toward early education for her future classroom. We must consistently confront racial battle fatigue, being othered and silenced, while also being burdened with the labor that is often asked of people of Color in the name of "diversity" work. At the same time, we do not see representations of ourselves in the demographic makeup of teacher education nor in normative teacher education practices. Despite being part of teacher education programs that have had commitments to social justice and equity, we have collectively witnessed and experienced the pervasive ways in which whiteness in these spaces can result in harm to preservice teachers and teacher educators of Color. In our collective teaching/learning and our dialogues around race in education, we have found culturally relevant and culturally sustaining pedagogies (CR/CSP) to be a tool in disrupting whiteness and centering the needs, knowledge, and humanity of children and teachers of Color. In this chapter, we consider the possibilities for enacting CR/CSP that work toward supporting BIPOC preservice teachers.

Culturally Relevant and Culturally Sustaining Pedagogies

Spanish has always been a large part of my identity, even before I even knew how to speak the language. Growing up, I was monolingual in English, but a piece of me always felt missing. When I started taking Spanish courses in late elementary and middle school, I felt a connection to the language take shape in a way that was profound and comforting. I am technically an elective bilingual, choosing to learn the language for my own sake, but the initial call to a second language felt mandatory. Spanish is such a large part of my Mexican culture but also my family culture, and to feel validated and a part of my family I needed to communicate with them in the language that they know best.

Entering my major courses for bilingual education at UNT, I had the most amazing opportunity to take three of my main content courses in Spanish. As an emergent bilingual through solely my academic education, I worried that my origin of bilingualism would not be accepted by my professors or my peers. This was a false narrative of fear and anxiety. One of my professors was bilingual in academics as well, and he created a space where bilingualism had many definitions and names. There I had the opportunity to work exclusively amongst Latine preservice teachers. We were allowed to share our experiences of curriculum violence and not feel silenced by our white counterparts, as was so often the case. In all honesty, these courses served as a place where my identity could be explored. I was able to validate my bilingualism and share my experiences that were both harmful and progressive in my K-12 education and criticize those experiences from a very raw point of view.

We were allowed to be angry with the education system and live in solidarity with one another about our frustrations and fears. We supported one another through video responses, group discussions, and Canvas discussion board responses, validating each other the best we could. My professor offered me a space to put into words all that I have felt, bringing up the harmful education in my past and in the past of my ancestors. The amount of self-exploration that occurred in that class is unmatched by any course I have taken before. My professor offered not only a space to explore, but a space to heal, which is what I had always longed for as a BIPOC preservice teacher, something that was severely lacking outside of this course.

CR/CSP are frameworks for teaching and learning that build upon decades of research and practice on asset pedagogies that have specifically sought to counter deficit ideologies in education (e.g., cultural congruence (Au, 1980), funds of knowledge (Moll et al., 1992), and culturally responsive teaching (Gay, 2000)). CR/CSP directly counter deficit ideologies and practices that "strip children [and teachers] of their cultural [and linguistic] legacies" (Delpit, 2002, p. 41), and in turn, result in a slow kind of dehumanization occurs that positions children's and teacher's cultural and linguistic practices as problematic. This not only affects one's self-worth but also positions BIPOC children and teachers at the margins in schools, often resulting in being (in)directly pushed out.

Ladson-Billings' (1995) framework for culturally relevant pedagogy (CRP) includes three major domains: (1) high expectations and *academic success* of students, (2) *cultural competence* which allows students to honor their own cultural and linguistic practices while also a gaining the knowledge and skills of the culture of power (Delpit, 1988), and (3) *sociopolitical consciousness*, or the ability to take knowledge and skills learned in schools to identify and generate solutions to real-world problems. CSP pushes the goals of CRP forward by considering three main issues (Alim & Paris, 2017). First, how might asset pedagogies, such as CRP, be reframed with the goal of creating a pluralistic society that is multilingual and multicultural? Such reframing decenters whiteness without solely utilizing white, middle class, dominant American English norms to guide policy and practice. Second, how might educators engage in CRP that recognize the dynamic and changing nature of culture and language over time and space? This necessitates an understanding of culture that encompasses past-oriented heritage practices and present-oriented community practices. Educators must

learn from students and communities, in order to understand the local and current nuances and complexities of existing and changing cultural and linguistic
practices. Finally, how might educators create generative spaces where students
take an inward gaze to "critique regressive practices (i.e., homophobia, mi-
sogyny) and raise critical consciousness" (Alim & Paris, 2017, p. 10)? An inward
gaze and engaging in critical reflexivity allow students to uncover the ways that
they have internalized and enacted oppressive ideologies in their cultural and
linguistic practices. Such reflexivity leads to critical consciousness and transformation. It is important to remember that CR/CSP are not merely about
repositioning the cultural and linguistic practices of minoritized youth and
families as assets in pedagogical practice (Bucholzt et al., 2017). The goals of
these pedagogies are ultimately about creating educational spaces where communities of Color can thrive in humanizing ways that connect "culture [and
language] directly to sustenance, as both its target and source" (p. 55).

The literature on CR/CSP in teacher education focuses primarily on how
teacher education programs work toward developing these pedagogies with
their teacher candidates. Given the goals and tenets of CR/CSP, we believe
they are useful frameworks for supporting BIPOC preservice teachers while
decentering whiteness. Guided by these frameworks, we offer possibilities for
practice that work toward supporting BIPOC preservice teachers.

Toward Culturally Relevant and Culturally Sustaining Teacher Education

We examine three practices in teacher education that are shifts toward enacting
CR/CSP in teacher education programs. These practices are (1) (re)claiming
intersectional identities, (2) critical care in field experiences, and (3) support in
navigating gatekeeping structures.

(Re)Claiming Intersectional Identities

Critical identity work has been identified as a crucial component of teacher
education that is aimed to prepare teachers to work with children from diverse racial, cultural, and linguistic backgrounds (Baines et al., 2018; Genor &
Goodwin, 2005). Preservice teachers are often guided through various experiences (e.g., autobiographies, cultural memoirs, storytelling) that ask them to
name their identities and worldviews, and to interrogate how these have shaped
their understandings about teaching, learning, children, and social contexts of
schools. Quite often it is assumed that because of their racial identities, BIPOC
preservice teachers already have developed this critical consciousness (Jackson
& Knight-Manuel, 2019). BIPOC preservice teachers have had limited opportunities to critically examine the intersectionalities of their identities and

experiences against the historical and sociopolitical contexts that have shaped their lived experiences (Brown, 2018).

CR/CSP calls for practices that allow students to engage in critical reflexivity and to develop critical consciousness around their identities and experiences in meaningful ways that decenter whiteness. Thus, it is a useful framework to guide critical identity work with BIPOC preservice teachers. CR/CSP asks us to provide them with ongoing opportunities to examine the ways that the logics of whiteness and settler colonialism have shaped their racialized experiences, understanding of self and of their communities' ways of knowing and being. Such opportunities afford students to (re)claim their identities and can also lead to the transformation of oppressive schooling structures.

Carmen's testimonio above is one example of how CR/CSP are powerful tools for identity work with BIPOC preservice teachers. Carmen and her Latine peers were provided a space where they could understand their experiences as learners and future teachers beyond the deficit ideologies, reclaim their nuanced and intersectional identities and epistemologies, and move toward sustaining these identities and practices while becoming bilingual educators. BIPOC preservice teachers' experiences and knowledge were validated away from the gaze of whiteness. The teacher educator also created a space where Latine preservice teachers could explore the complexities and multiplicities of what it means to be a Latine bilingual educator. Although this work was at times painful, it was also healing. This is an important aspect of this work, as quite often critical identity work can induce harm and trauma to BIPOC individuals. Kohli et al. (2022) argue that a key component of creating a healthy racial climate that supports BIPOC preservice teachers is tending to the psychological well-being of BIPOC teacher candidates.

Critical Care in Field Experiences

> *We as students do not have control over who we end up observing and teaching alongside of. We have a program that focuses on a multicultural curriculum, but this is not true for local public schools. The amount of horror stories I have heard from other preservice teachers about how bilingual children of Color are treated and taught in public school classrooms is numerous and appalling.*

Field experiences comprise a significant portion of teacher preparation and extend the preparation of teachers to include mentor teachers, supervisors, and school administrators. BIPOC preservice teachers must regularly confront deficit ideologies and schooling practices around children of Color, which is no surprise given that whiteness permeates early childhood education (Pérez, 2019). BIPOC preservice teachers also experience racial hostility and feelings of marginalization when placed with mentor teachers or school sites who do not share the same commitments to social justice and communities of Color (Kohli, 2018).

A key goal of CR/CSP is to enact humanizing practices that not only honor the identities and practices of BIPOC but ultimately allow them to thrive. When applied to field experiences, this means supporting BIPOC preservice teachers through intentional and equity centered enacting *critical care*. Kohli et al. (2022) suggest that field experiences for BIPOC preservice teachers "should account for the needs of teacher candidates of Color both in terms of the communities that are served and mentor teachers selected" (p. 58). Whenever possible it is imperative that BIPOC preservice teachers be placed with mentor teachers and supervisors of Color. When BIPOC teacher candidates are surrounded by educators from similar racial, cultural and linguistic backgrounds, they are "less likely to become vulnerable to racist stereotypes and feelings of tokenization inside and outside of the classroom" (Garces & Jayakumar as cited in Kohli et al., 2022, p. 59). When placed with white mentor teachers and supervisors, it is imperative that these individuals have demonstrated in practice strong commitments to antiracism and understand the specific needs of BIPOC preservice teachers. Kohli et al. (2022) also suggest that BIPOC teacher candidates be given ongoing opportunities for critical and generative dialogue around their racialized experiences in their field placements. In line with the goals of CSP, we also argue that it is important to reconsider the ways that BIPOC teachers are evaluated by mentor teachers and supervisors. CSP necessitates rejecting solely white norms of standardization. Field experience evaluations are often driven by normative teacher preparation standards that center white ways of knowing and being with respect to teacher dispositions, knowledge and skills. Thus, we suggest that teacher education programs (1) critically examine the weight that is given to these evaluations, and (2) reimagine evaluations so that they also capture and reflect the knowledges and practices of successful BIPOC teachers.

Support in Navigating Gatekeeping Structures

I want to teach so badly. But it's like the system doesn't want me. It's so expensive …. If I take the CORE again and don't pass, what am I going to do? Is it worth it? What if I fail again? I already passed the ECE content exam. It doesn't make sense.

(Ranita's field notes)

These anecdotal notes from an advising session are but one snippet from countless conversations about state licensing exams. In the era of high-stakes accountability and wide-spread standardization, teacher candidates must navigate their way through several gatekeeping structures such as professional readiness exams, licensure exams, teacher performance exams, and GPA requirements. If we consider the historical contexts of BIPOC teachers in the United States prior to and after school desegregation, we know that these current gatekeeping structures are reminiscent of the ways that BIPOC teachers have disproportionately been pushed out or screened out of the teaching profession (Carter Andrews et al., 2019). While teacher education programs do not have the power to override state licensing regulations, they can intentionally support BIPOC preservice teachers in navigating these gatekeeping structures.

In Ranita's experience at a MSI in the Northeast, her teacher education program implemented several initiatives to help teacher candidates navigate these gatekeeping structures. When professional readiness exams were required by state legislation, support and funding was given to prepare teacher candidates and provide scholarships to pay for the exams. Additionally, prerequisite courses were created for education majors to help in their preparation for Math and English professional readiness exams. Once teacher candidates entered the education program, across methods courses time was spent on studying the licensing exam structures, questions, and test taking strategies. Undergirding this work around preparing for licensing exams, there was an intentional effort across social foundations and seminars coursework to develop a sociopolitical consciousness around these gatekeeping structures. Students engaged in dialogue and activities aimed to unpack the racial and sociopolitical contexts of these gatekeeping structures and examined how they disproportionately impacted BIPOC teachers. These ongoing conversations were aimed to shift the focus away from standardized measures of professional readiness. Rather they focused on reconceptualizing teaching readiness as the knowledge and skills necessary to enact equity and inquiry pedagogies in various communities. Preservice teachers engaged in ongoing generative dialogue about how their epistemologies shaped their professional knowledge and skills as they designed professional portfolios, in which they documented the knowledge and practices that guided their teaching and teaching identities. The goals of CR/CSP reminds us that supporting BIPOC preservice teachers through these gatekeeping structures is not just about passing an exam, providing financial support, and/or student retention. Rather, it is also about countering these normative gatekeeping strictures through humanizing pedagogies that honor and nurture BIPOC preservice teachers' cultural/linguistic identities and practices.

Concluding Thoughts

As I move toward graduation, I feel less and less prepared for what's ahead of me. Not only do I have to navigate who I am as a new teacher, but also what it means to be a teacher of Color during political, social, racial, and emotional unrest. The education system seems to continue to evolve/devolve around me every day, moving backwards and forwards giving me whiplash and anxiety about what's to come for children, but especially children of Color.

After three years of seeing children of Color become more and more marginalized by their identifications and hearing the countless accounts of the ostracization of bilingual children in public schools, I have decided to search for an alternative path toward my professional goals. After a lot of research and understanding of the student teaching that was ahead of me, I made the choice that I could not take care of my professional career and mental health as a POC if I received my certification now. I now seek an educational environment in which I have the ability to choose how to center children of Color and their experiences, and the ability to heal and grow from my own experiences in schooling as a BIPOC Latina every day.

Carmen's choice to graduate without her teacher certification and seek a different path toward fulfilling her goals of working with young, multilingual children of Color is an act of transformational resistance (Solórzano and Bernal, 2001). It is rooted in a simultaneous critique of whiteness and a move toward social justice on her own terms. It is an act of resistance in which she is carving a new path for her fulfilling her professional goals; a path that allows for the sustenance of her cultural and linguistic identities and practices. At the same time, Carmen's testimonio also highlights the failure of teacher education policies and practices in supporting the needs and ultimate success of a BIPOC teacher candidate. It is worth noting that her experiences not only mirror the experiences of university-based preservice teachers, but also BIPOC teachers in alternate route programs, and ultimately inservice BIPOC teachers (Kohli, 2018; Rios & Longoria, 2021).

Our examination of how CR/CSP can be used to decenter whiteness in teacher education is by no means complete. Rather it is a starting point to imagine the possibilities of how the field can better support BIPOC preservice teachers. As teacher education programs consider these possibilities, it is important that they do while heeding to the local contexts and histories of communities of Color (Carter Andrews et al., 2021). In this current moment of a global pandemic situated against the backdrop of increased racial violence and economic inequities, it is crucial that teacher education programs decenter whiteness as they grapple with the questions *who does teacher education serve and for what purpose?*

Note

1 All italicized portions throughout the text represent Carmen's (second author) autobiographical reflections.

References

Achinstein, B., & Ogawa, R. T. (2011). *Change(d) agents: New teachers of color in urban schools.* Teachers College Press.

Alim, H. S., & Paris, D. (2017). What is culturally sustaining pedagogy and why does it matter? In D. Paris & H. S. Alim (Eds.). *Culturally sustaining pedagogies: Teaching and learning for justice in a changing world* (pp. 1–24). Teachers College Press.

Amos, Y. T. (2016). Voices of teacher candidates of color on white race evasion: "I worried about my safety! *International Journal of Qualitative Studies in Education, 29*(8), 1002–1015.

Au, K. H. P. (1980). Participation structures in a reading lesson with Hawaiian children: Analysis of a culturally appropriate instructional event. *Anthropology & Education Quarterly, 11*(2), 91–115.

Baines, J., Tisdale, C., & Long, S. (2018). *"We've been doing it your way long enough": Choosing the culturally relevant classroom.* Teachers College Press.

Brown, K. D. (2018). Race as a durable *and* shifting idea: How Black millennial preservice teachers understand race, racism, and teaching. *Peabody Journal of Education, 93*(1), 106–120.

Bucholtz, M., Casillas, D. I., & Lee, J. S. (2017). Language and culture as sustenance. In D. Paris & H.S. Alim (Eds.). *Culturally sustaining pedagogies: Teaching and learning for justice in a changing world* (pp. 43–60). Teachers College Press.

Calderón, D. (2006). One-dimensionality and whiteness. *Policy Futures in Education, 4*(1), 73–82.

Carter Andrews, D. J., Castro, E., Cho, C. L., Petchauer, E., Richmond, G., & Floden, R. (2019). Changing the narrative on diversifying the teaching workforce: A look at historical and contemporary factors that inform recruitment and retention of teachers of color. *Journal of Teacher Education, 70*(1), 6–12.

Carter Andrews, D. J., He, Y., Marciano, J. E., Richmond, G., & Salazar, M. (2021). Decentering whiteness in teacher education: Addressing the questions of who, with whom, and how. *Journal of Teacher Education, 72*(2), 134–137.

Cherng, H. S., & Halpin, P. F. (2016). The importance of minority teachers: Student perceptions of minority versus white teachers. *Educational Research, 45*(7), 407–420.

Cheruvu, R., Souto-Manning, M., Lencl, T., & Chin-Calubaquib, M. (2015). Race, isolation, and exclusion: What early childhood teacher educators need to know about the experiences of pre-service teachers of color. *Urban Review, 47*(2), 237–265.

Delpit, L. (1988). The silenced dialogue: Power and pedagogy in educating other people's children. *Harvard Educational Review, 58*(3), 280–299.

Delpit, L. (2002). No Kinda sense. In L. Delpit & J. K. Dowdy (Eds.), *The skin that we speak: Thoughts on language and culture in the classroom* (pp. 31–48). New Press.

Dilworth, M. E., & Coleman, M. J. (2014). Time for change. *Diversity in teaching revisited.* National Educational Association. Retrieved from https://vtechworks.lib.vt.edu/bitstream/handle/10919/84025/ChangeDiversityTeaching.pdf?sequence=1

Egalite, A. J., Kisida, B., & Winters, M. A. (2015). Representation in the classroom: The effect of own-race teachers on student achievement. *Economics of Education Review, 45,* 44–45. http://dx.doi.org/10.1016/j.econedurev.2015.01.007.

Faison, M. Z., & McArthur, S. A. (2020). Building Black worlds: Revisioning cultural justice for Black teacher education students at PWIs. *International Journal of Qualitative Studies in Education, 33*(7), 745–758.

Gay, G. (2000). *Culturally responsive teaching: Theory, research, and practice.* Teachers College Press.

Geiger, A. W. (2018). *America's public school teachers are far less racially and ethnically diverse than their students.* Pew Research Center. www.pewresearch.org/fact-tank/2018/08/27/americas-public-school-teachers-are-far-less-racially-and-ethnically-diverse-than-their-students

Genor, M., & Goodwin, A. L. (2005). Confronting ourselves: Using autobiographical analysis in teacher education. *The New Educator, 1*(4), 311–331.

Gist, C. D. (2014a). Interrogating critical pedagogy: Teachers of color and the unfinished project of justice. In P. Orelus & R. Brock (Eds.), *Critical pedagogy for women and students of color* (pp. 46–59). Routledge.

Gist, C. D., Bianco, M., & Lynn, M. (2019). Examining grow your own programs across the teacher development continuum: Mining research on teachers of color and nontraditional educator pipelines. *Journal of Teacher Education, 70*(1), 13–25.

Goodwin, L., & McIntosh, K. M. (2008). Diversifying the teaching force. In T. L. Good (Ed.), *21st century education: A reference handbook* (Vol. 2, pp. 23–32). Sage.

Haddix, M. M. (2017). Diversifying teaching and teacher education: Beyond rhetoric and toward real change. *Journal of Literacy Research, 49*(1), 141–149.

Irizarry, J., & Donaldson, M. L. (2012). Teach for America: The Latinization of US schools and the critical shortage of Latina/o teachers. *American Educational Research Journal, 49*(1), 155–194.

Irvine, J. (2003). *Educating teachers for diversity: Seeing with a critical eye.* Teachers College Press.

Irvine, J. J. (1988). An analysis of the problem of disappearing Black educators. *The Elementary School Journal, 88*(5), 503–513.

Jackson, I., & Knight-Manuel, M. (2019). "Color does not equal consciousness": Educators of color learning to enact sociopolitical consciousness. *Journal of Teacher Education, 70*(1), 65–78.

Kohli, R. (2018). Behind school doors: The impact of hostile racial climates on urban teachers of color. *Urban Education, 53*(3), 307–333.

Kohli, R., Dover, A. G., Jayakumar, U. M., Lee, D., Henning, N., Comeaux, E. … Vizcarra, M. (2022). Toward a healthy racial climate: Systemically centering the well-being of teacher candidates of color. *Journal of Teacher Education, 73*(1), 52–65.

Ladson-Billings, G. (1995). Toward a theory of culturally relevant pedagogy. *American Educational Research Journal, 32*(3), 465–491.

Ladson-Billings, G. J. (2005). Is the team all right? Diversity and teacher education. *Journal of Teacher Education, 56*(3), 229–234.

Moll, L., Amanti, C., Neff, D., & Gonzalez, N. (1992). Funds of knowledge for teaching: Using a qualitative approach to connect homes and classrooms. *Theory into Practice, 31*(2), 132–141.

Pérez, M. S. (2019). Dismantling racialized discourses in early childhood education and care: A revolution towards reframing the field. In F. Nxumalo & C. P. Brown (Eds.), *Disrupting and countering deficits in early childhood education* (pp. 20–36). Routledge.

Picower, B., & Mayorga, E. (2015). *What's race got to do with it?: How current school reform policy maintains racial and economic inequality.* Peter Lang.

Redding, C. (2019). A teacher like me: A review of the effect of student-teacher racial/ethnic matching on teacher perceptions of students and student academic and behavioral outcomes. *Review of Educational Research, 89*(4), 499–535.

Rios, F., & Longoria, A. (2021). *Creating a home in schools: Sustaining identities for Black, indigenous, and teachers of color.* Teachers College Press.

Rogers-Ard, R., Knaus, C., Bianco, M., Brandehoff, R., & Gist, C. D. (2019). The grow your own collective: A critical race movement to transform education. *Teacher Education Quarterly, 46*(1), 23–34.

Salazar, M. D. (2018). Interrogating teacher evaluation: Unveiling whiteness as the normative center and moving the margins. *Journal of Teacher Education, 69*(5), 463–476.

Sleeter, C. E., La Vonne, I. N., & Kumashiro, K. K. (Eds.). (2014). *Diversifying the teacher workforce: Preparing and retaining highly effective teachers.* Routledge.

Solórzano, D. G., & Bernal, D. D. (2001). Examining transformational resistance through a critical race and LatCrit theory framework: Chicana and Chicano students in an urban context. *Urban Education, 36*(3), 308–342.

Stanton, C. R., & Morrison, D. (2018). Investigating curricular policy as a tool to dismantle the master's house: Indian Education for all and social studies teacher education. *Policy Futures in Education, 16*(6), 729–748.

Villegas, A. M., & Irvine, J. J. (2010). Diversifying the teaching force: An examination of major arguments. *The Urban Review, 42*(3), 175–192.

Villegas, A. M., Strom, K., & Lucas, T. (2012). Closing the racial/ethnic gap between students of color and their teachers: An elusive goal. *Equity & Excellence in Education, 45*(2), 283–301.

PART IV

Reengaging with Communities and Families in a *Post*-World

12

OUT OF THE CLASSROOM AND ONTO THE RUNWAY

Queer and Trans Pedagogies in Early Childhood

Harper B. Keenan, Lil Miss Hot Mess, LeRoi Newbold, and Lee Iskander

Out of the Classroom and onto the Runway: Queer and Trans Pedagogies in Early Childhood

The open participation of queer and trans adults in children's formal education is only a very recent development in the history of modern schooling in the United States and Canada. Our participation is also tenuous. In March 2021, the Murray School District in Utah suspended its "equity book bundles" from circulation after a student at Horizon Elementary brought a copy of *Call Me Max*, a children's book by openly trans author Kyle Lukoff about a transgender boy who teaches his school community about how to respect him (Tanner, 2021). Performers involved with Drag Story Hour (DSH), one of the children's programs we discuss in this chapter, have been mocked and condemned on widely viewed right-wing media outlets and face ongoing death threats and even armed protesters at events (Owen, 2019). Currently, Texas lawmakers are attempting to prevent minors from accessing trans-specific health care. A directive issued by Governor Greg Abbot goes so far as to direct licensed professionals (e.g., teachers, doctors, and nurses) who work with children report parents to Child Protective Services if they are believed to support their child's medical gender transition, referring to such health care as "child abuse." As we finalize this chapter, investigations into families who support their trans children have already begun.

These forms of denunciation are typically rooted in the idea of trans/queer livelihood as a social contagion that risks interrupting normative child development. Gender generally is a "core discipline within the curriculum of childhood" (Krishnan & Keenan, 2021), that is, compliance with socially acceptable forms

DOI: 10.4324/9781003399155-17

of gender is taught through countless interactions between children and adults. Importantly, the notion of normative child development relies on a societal investment in (re)producing straight, cisgender children, a project that is strongly intertwined with the maintenance of white supremacy (Gill-Peterson, 2015). Queer and trans pedagogies, however, refuse that investment project—choosing instead to welcome children to grow "sideways" (Stockton, 2009) to the prescribed social order. Many of us build ways of sharing knowledge that look to what José Esteban Muñoz (2009) referred to as a utopian queer horizon that provides "access to a world that should be, that could be, and that will be" (p. 64).

Although queer pedagogy has been extensively theorized over the last 30 years (e.g., Britzman, 1995; Brockenbrough, 2015; Bryson & DeCastell, 1993; Coloma, 2006; Gilbert, 2014; Kumashiro, 2002), and trans pedagogy conceptualized more recently (e.g., Courvant, 2011; Keenan, 2017; Miller, 2016; Nicolazzo et al., 2015), there are few documented examples of what these pedagogies might look like in practice, and even fewer in the education of young children. In this chapter, we theorize queer and trans pedagogies within an early childhood context through portraits of two children's programs—Freedom School Toronto and DSH—that go beyond models of LGBT tolerance and inclusion and toward embracing anti-racist approaches to sharing queer/trans knowledge and cultural practice in early childhood education.

Queer & Trans Pedagogies and Early Childhood Education

More than 20 years ago, Bill Pinar (1998) wrote in the foundational text *Queer Theory in Education* that "homophobia … is especially intense in the field of education, a highly conservative and often reactionary field" (p. 2). Lee Edelman (2017) traced the roots of antagonism to queer subjects in European models of tutelage and schooling as far back as Rousseau. Feminist interpretations of Foucault's theory of disciplinary power emphasize that the school often functions, in part, to train each of our bodies and minds into ideas of what forms of gendered self-expression are normal and which are not (Foucault, 1975/2012; Sawicki, 1991). As anti-colonial and Black studies scholarship has emphasized, the disciplining of appropriate genders is also a form of racial categorization, which functions as a way of sorting out who is treated as fully human (Lugones, 2010; McKittrick, 2015; Wynter, 2003). Here, we admit that the normative structures of schooling may be incommensurable with the full flourishing of queer and trans livelihood. Yet, while queer and trans people have often suffered within mainstream schooling, queer and trans pedagogies have long existed as forms of fugitive practice within classrooms and as celebrated modes of educational practice outside of them. In other words, whether it be in makeup tutorials, sexual health zines, coordinating direct action, or in raising children in our chosen families, queer and trans people have always found ways to share knowledge.

A small but robust body of existing scholarship has addressed how dominant and restrictive ideas about gender and self-expression are reproduced from children's earliest experiences in school (e.g., MacNaughton, 2006; Yelland, 1998). For example, Barrie Thorne (1993) conducted decades of ethnographic research on how children learn and embody gender through play, and Mindy Blaise's (2005) ethnography of a kindergarten classroom highlighted how young children learn how to "play it straight" at school—that is, enacting gendered ways of being that align with expectations associated with heterosexuality. Since the 1990s, scholars have also theorized what queer theory might mean for the practice of early education (e.g., Blaise & Taylor, 2012; Robinson, 2005; Silin, 1995), pushing us toward a "most thorough understanding of the world" (Counts, 1978, as cited in Casper et al., 1996, p. 290). Yet, due in part to school's antagonism to queer and trans livelihoods, we have few examples of what queer and trans pedagogies might look like in practice, particularly in early childhood education. We hope that this chapter will contribute to changing that.

Although queer and trans pedagogies are not uniform nor easily defined, they are generally unified by a desire to destabilize normativity as it is prescribed by institutions and social relations within them. We offer that queer and trans pedagogies emphasize play within and beyond early childhood as a way of practicing freedom and political imagination in a collective setting. As Lil Miss Hot Mess and Harper have written elsewhere, the age-old queer/trans art forms of drag and ballroom are perhaps especially well-suited for these flexibly held purposes. They break boundaries between reality and fantasy, allowing performers to take on new identities and social relationships in material form, just by playing the part. Further, drag and ballroom offer a way into what we call *strategic defiance* in that they both illustrate the frequent arbitrariness of calcified rules and the power and beauty of self-determination beyond rigid regulation (Keenan & Hot Mess, 2020).

In what follows, we present two profiles of children's programs built through queer and trans pedagogical frameworks: Toronto Freedom School and DSH. Toronto Freedom School emerged as a project led by queer Black families in Toronto. DSH originated in San Francisco, led by drag performers and queer authors, and spread to communities around the world. The profiles have been authored by a leader of each respective program and offer valuable insights into the practical application of queer and trans pedagogies in early childhood education contexts.

LeRoi Newbold—Freedom School Toronto

Education is something that I've always been around, and I love children. Before becoming a teacher, I worked in youth drop-in centers and daycares. Then in 2008, I started to work at the Africentric Alternative School in Toronto. At first, I was teaching special education,[1] and later, I taught primary. I took a break from that to do my Masters in Black Liberatory Education. I love working with Black children. Even before I was a teacher, I was interested in working with young people and the creativity they have and the openness of their minds. I'm also very interested in Black liberation, and I felt like the way I could be of service within the movement was in education. I'm interested in being an educator for the same reason that I'm interested in participating in Black liberation, which is ultimately for the freedom of Black people.

In 2016, I cofounded Freedom School Toronto, a community-based project to teach Black children and youth. Freedom School is an organization that teaches Black histories of resistance. Black parents, most of them queer, created it as part of the Movement for Black Lives. We made it as a space that could be an alternative for our children because we didn't see any spaces where they were able to learn, not only about Blackness, but about Blackness in a way that's empowering, and where if we have to learn things about Blackness that are not empowering, we learn how to fight against that and get our voices in there and create change.

Freedom School operates as a kind of think tank, a place for us to figure out what Black liberatory pedagogy is. We tested out, "what if we never use punishment in this space? What if we try to use transformative justice to solve conflicts within the spaces at all times instead?" We tested out different pedagogies grounded in questions like "what's the impact of land-based learning with Black kids?" and "what's the importance of intersectionality within the space? What happens when we teach and when we center trans people in the stories we're telling about Black liberation?" We also do work to intervene in anti-Black racism within the school system. In 2017, we contributed to a campaign to remove police officers from schools. The campaign successfully got police out of schools in the Toronto District School Board. We still do that kind of work: training teachers around transformative justice, helping schools to create plans to resist anti-Black racism, things like that.

The primary audience for our work is Black children and parents. Black children typically feel powerful within our spaces. We are creating a space for Black brilliance. We have high expectations of our kids. We talk with them about the things that matter in their lives. Sometimes in schools, certain topics are treated as if they are not appropriate for kids, like police brutality or incarceration. But children's parents and siblings are being incarcerated and experiencing police brutality. It has to be appropriate for them to talk about. Beyond that, they have to feel like they have a voice to change it. We know that any time there has been a push for change, our kids have been part of it too.

Another project I worked on was a collaboration between Freedom School Toronto and the Toronto Kiki Ballroom Alliance. This organization works with primarily Black LGBT youth in the greater Toronto area to teach ballroom arts and put on balls. We created a kid's ballroom training program for kids to learn about Black liberation through ballroom. They learned about how ballroom supported homeless LGBT youth in New York when it was founded, how it helped people during the HIV/AIDS pandemic. It was a space to create families and envision family differently.

We talk about ballroom as a place where, instead of pushing up against the system as a way to confront racism, people actually created their own space with its own standards, with its own beauty standards. Ballroom is a place where Blackness is the standard, and Black trans femininity is the standard. We created a kids' animation documentary by interviewing legends in the ballroom scene in New York and Toronto. I'm proud of that project because it was so unique. I haven't really heard of spaces that teach about Black liberation in that way, centering queer people and trans people. Usually, when we are in a space, we think, "I could be Black in this space and unapologetic," or "I could be queer in this space," but it's very seldom that there are spaces where we can be fully embodied. I'm proud of the work that the kids did within the program, how they got so comfortable with voguing, and just the space they had to express all of themselves.

In mainstream spaces, people get beat up for switching their gender, or they'll get bullied. With ballroom, you can do the same thing—you're switching and walking down the runway—and instead, people are clapping for you and cheering, and jumping up and down. You're being celebrated for that. The impact for kids participating in ballroom is so huge. If you're a Black trans person, especially if you're a kid, being in a space where hundreds of people are hyping you up for doing something that you wouldn't even necessarily be allowed to do in another space is just such a fantastic feeling. Politically, it's just crucial to take a break from fighting with people for a minute and just be like, "Anyways, in this space, I am it. Y'all want to be like me in this space." I think that's really important. "I got my tens because of being this way, and you could be trying to get your tens too." It's a really important lesson about how you don't always have to fight with people for inclusion in something that's not even that good. You could just make your own thing.

Queer people have always been at the forefront of Black liberation movements, but our stories have never been centered within those movements. Even though Bayard Rustin was a Black gay man, he still couldn't talk about Black gay things. And now with Black Lives Matter, people will have to listen to us talk about Black trans lives mattering, and people will have to get comfortable with the idea that Black queer and trans people are also parents.

I want Black trans people to be restored to our sacred position that has been removed because of colonialism, Christianity, and enslavement—all the processes that took us away from who we were. I want people also to acknowledge that every time there's been a substantial change in the quality of life of Black people, it has been because of the trans people and queer people in the

Black community that fought for that change. The movement for Black Lives here in Toronto and Canada is queer and trans led. In the 1990s, when people organized in Toronto around police brutality, that was queer women, queer Black women mostly, who were organizing for that. Black trans people are so important to Black liberation.

Lil Miss Hot Mess—Drag Story Hour

The first time I hosted a DSH event, in September 2016, I didn't know what to expect. I set two alarms to make sure I'd be awake on time—no easy task for a nightlife-oriented night owl like myself who was scheduled to be out the door earlier than I was usually awake. I read over my stories, considering ways to bring them to life, character voices to act out, and jokes to make along the way without losing the flow. I laid out my clothes and makeup kit the night before, picking a sequin jacket that fit the intersection of "glam librarian" and "drag queen under fluorescents" with a pair of heels that I wouldn't trip in. I was prepared but nervous. In the year leading up, I had watched several queens in my San Francisco drag family—Persia, Yves St. Croissant, Honey Mahogany, Panda Dulce, and Grace Towers—post fabulous photos of their inaugural DSH events full of sparkles and smiling faces. I still wondered: was this an idea that could work? Was society ready for drag queens and kids to share space and interact with one another? Was I?

As a queer 30-something living an extended Peter Pan lifestyle—one in which I refused to grow up, at least according to the societal expectations of whiteness, capitalism, and cis-hetero-patriarchy—my experience with children was limited. I did not have children of my own, and at the time, neither did many of my friends. It had been years since I'd found myself in an elementary school or the children's section of a library. I felt nervous about how to hold a baby, or even how to hold a conversation with young children. When I was younger, I had worked in some informal educational settings: after-school programs, Hebrew school, summer camps. In those settings, I often felt like I had to downplay or hide my queerness and queeniness. That said, earlier in my drag career, I once participated in a family event at San Francisco's DeYoung Museum, organized by another drag sister Fauxnique, where kids got to design and create outfits for a drag fashion show. It was thrilling: kids thoughtfully cut fabric and glued pipe cleaners, pom-poms, glitter, faux flowers, and all sorts of frills onto a dress that I kept for years. I knew then that there was something special about this convergence between kids and queens. In the words of *Gypsy*'s Mama Rose, if we ever truly let out our shared sense of play and creativity, "there wouldn't be signs big enough, there wouldn't be lights bright enough!" Still, how to make that happen was a mystery.

When I walked into that first story hour at the Brooklyn Public Library, I couldn't believe the crowd! The room was packed with children and families that reflected many of the city's diversities. Much of my planning quickly went out the window as we all gave in to the collective improvisation that accompanies the best drag performances: impromptu inquiries, spontaneous zingers, and audience members who can't resist touching the sequins. In the past five years, I've done dozens of story hours. Certain components are consistent— read a few books, sing a few songs, maybe throw in a lip-sync or craft project or Q&A—but no two are the same. Variety and unpredictability are central to the fun of these events and key to their opportunities for learning—for children and queens alike.

Each audience yields new questions, complications, and insights. I've read for rooms of kids where it felt like everyone was on the same page, singing, and dancing together enthusiastically. Others were full of crying babies too young to listen to a story. I've had kids arrive in their version of drag, wearing their finest sparkles and rainbows, or donning favorite Halloween costumes. In one classroom visit, a group of boys asked many probing questions about gender: their tone bordered on disrespect, but nonetheless, their questions warranted honest answers. In another, second graders were so well prepared to think about the complexities of identity that they collectively gasped "stereotype!" in alarmed unison at an instance of bullying in a story. Kids approach me after events with lists of handwritten questions, from how I get the glitter to stick to my face to how I came up with my drag name. During virtual events over the pandemic, I've even had children turn on their cameras to proudly show off their dolls and drawings of drag queens! In perhaps one of my most prized encounters, a crew of young girls who missed the event itself approached me with what felt like a million insightful queries about what drag was and what I was doing in their library.

People often ask me what I think children can learn from drag queens. I suspect most expect me to respond with an answer about gender roles, but that's just scratching the surface of what a program like DSH can offer. As Harper and I have written about elsewhere (Keenan & Hot Mess, 2020), "drag pedagogy" offers a broader opportunity to rethink the nature of teaching and learning not by focusing on specific lessons, but more through the traditions and aesthetics of drag as an art form. That is, learning from (and as) drag performers doesn't have to be about "gender 101" or "intro to LGBT topics" but can focus more on questions like: *How can we learn through humor and play? How can we destigmatize shame by embracing failure? How can we learn more about ourselves and each other by trying on new clothes? How can we make the world more just by changing a few words here, adding a bit of glitter there?* These questions underlie the roots of our craft.

One of the biggest "aha!" moments for me in my work with DSH is that drag pedagogy isn't something that only happens in libraries and classrooms.

Drag performers have long had ways of teaching and learning from each other: backstage, on dance floors, in each other's living rooms, and on the streets. Except for a handful of innovative community-driven programs for queer/trans youth (such as Queens of the Castro in San Francisco), and a smattering of college courses on drag herstories, there are hardly any formal opportunities for learning this traditional art form. Instead, most learn on the fly and through the hard work of trial-and-error. The luckiest performers find themselves to be part of drag families, with elders (though not always older) teaching them the tricks of the trade. But many learn in more subtle ways: the praise of applause, the loving critique of a read, the soul-searching of developing a stage presence that reflects who you are and who you want to be.

Much of what can be learned from programs like DSH is how to express your creative self and be part of a community. When I introduce the concept of drag to children at events, I generally gloss over its gendered elements or skip over them altogether (the truth is, anyone can be a drag artist, regardless of their identities). Instead, I proudly inform kids that: *Drag queens are performers: we love to sing and dance and tell jokes. We love to make ourselves feel extra fancy by wearing big hair, big shoes, and lots and lots of sparkles. We're leaders in our communities, whether leading protests and parades or raising funds for causes that matter to us. We're not afraid to be bold, to color outside the lines, and to stand up for what we believe in.* I hope that kids and their parents come away with an implicit sense that drag is a practice of play: we're adults who continue to dress up because we know that often transforming how we look on the outside can be an essential part of expressing who we are on the inside, as well as making over the world around us.

I hope that educators of all varieties can borrow some of this spirit in their approaches to teaching and learning. That doesn't necessarily mean putting on a wig or a pair of pumps, but rather finding ways to bring a spirit of play, creativity, and specialness into their work. That might mean subtly changing one's environment or appearance to reintroduce a sense of curiosity or wonder. It could be figuring out ways to craft lessons or assignments as open-ended provocations rather than prescriptive prompts. It may include taking risks in approaching tough topics, knowing that sometimes the best answer is another question. Or that might mean making tough choices to reject the status quo in favor of collective discovery of the unknown. These are the kinds of things that drag performers often do intuitively—whether on stage or during story hours.

Discussion and Conclusion

DSH and Freedom School Toronto are powerful examples of the education that is possible when we think outside of the routines and structures of formal schooling. Both initiatives engage children in the practice of imagining a different world, and most importantly, they encourage children to see in themselves the power and the skills to bring new worlds into being. Additionally, both programs productively challenge what is seen as "appropriate" for children. Whether that is discussing racism and incarceration or dancing alongside a drag queen, the adults in both programs trust in children's ability to engage in complex conversations about the social world and, crucially, to be part of efforts to change it for the better. This is the crux of critical queer and trans pedagogies: working with young people to recognize the cultural scripts that constrain our ways of being in the world and imagining something different together (Keenan, 2017).

Neither DSH nor Freedom School Toronto operates from a "theory of change" that involves appealing to institutions for inclusion by showing how marginalized communities have been harmed (Tuck & Yang, 2018). Instead, each program is an experiment in world-building. Freedom School Toronto's collaboration with the Kiki Ballroom Alliance created a space where Black queerness and Black transness were not only the norm but desirable and celebrated ways of being. And when children engage with drag queens at a DSH event, they participate in a world where versions of gender expression and experimentation that might elsewhere be shamed sparkle magically under the fluorescent lighting, evoke wonder and are celebrated for their playfulness and creativity.

Both programs draw from the rich legacies and ongoing work of activist movements, and each has the potential to advance scholarly conversations around childhood, education, and social justice. While Freedom School Toronto does work to combat anti-Black racism in the Toronto District School Board, neither DSH nor Freedom School Toronto works primarily to reform schools. Instead, each program experiments with creative practice and the transformation of educational space beyond what is typically possible in traditional schools. In this sense, these programs enact an abolitionist ethic, enabling young children to live beyond the limits of carceral conditions—where they can love their queerness, their gender transgressions, and their Blackness. In the words of Bettina Love (2020), they "work to build a world rooted in the possibilities of justice" (n.p.). These programs also extend what we know about queer and trans pedagogies and young children. As Harper Keenan and Lil Miss Hot Mess have noted elsewhere, drag and ballroom as queer and trans practices are not so far from the world of childhood as they may initially seem (Keenan & Hot Mess, 2020). Instead, pedagogical practices drawn from drag and ballroom may be ideally suited to engage with children's play, imagination, and resistance to rules as a way of celebrating the beauty of queer and trans communities.

Ultimately, we hope that the portraits of these two programs offer a vision of possibility for early childhood educators who seek to move beyond the history of homophobia and transphobia that has long dominated the field. The teaching practices of Freedom School Toronto and DSH go far beyond the simple inclusion of queer and trans people into the existing structures of schooling. Instead, they do what both drag and ballroom have so exquisitely done for generations—they use the materials that exist in the world we currently inhabit to begin to imagine new and less harmful ways of being together in public space.

Note

1 We use the term "special education" as that is the official designation of the Toronto School Board, recognizing that this classification is rife with problems, including that it is not a term that disabled young people have claimed for themselves.

References

Blaise, M. (2005). *Playing it straight: Uncovering gender discourse in the early childhood classroom*. Routledge.

Blaise, M., & Taylor, A. (2012). Using queer theory to rethink gender equity in early childhood education. *Young Children, 67*(1), 88–96.

Britzman, D. P. (1995). Is there a queer pedagogy? Or, stop reading straight. *Educational Theory, 45*(2), 151–165.

Brockenbrough, E. (2015). Queer of color agency in educational contexts: Analytic frameworks from a queer of color critique. *Educational Studies, 51*(1), 28–44.

Bryson, M., & DeCastell, S. (1993). Queer pedagogy: Praxis makes im/perfect. *Canadian Journal of Education/Revue Canadienne de l'éducation, 18*(3) 285–305.

Casper, V., Cuffaro, H., Schultz, S., Silin, J., & Wickens, E. (1996). Toward a most thorough understanding of the world: Sexual orientation and early childhood education. *Harvard Educational Review, 66*(2), 271–294.

Coloma, R. S. (2006). Putting queer to work: Examining empire and education. *International Journal of Qualitative Studies in Education, 19*(5), 639–657.

Courvant, D. (2011). "Strip!". *Radical Teacher, 92*, 26–34.

Edelman, L. (2017). Learning nothing: Bad education. *Differences, 28*(1), 124–173.

Foucault, M. (1975/2012). *Discipline and punish: The birth of the prison*. Pantheon Books.

Gilbert, J. (2014). *Sexuality in school: The limits of education*. University of Minnesota Press.

Gill-Peterson, J. (2015). The value of the future: The child as human capital and the neoliberal labor of race. *Women's Studies Quarterly, 43*(1/2), 181–196.

Keenan, H. B. (2017). Unscripting curriculum: Toward a critical trans pedagogy. *Harvard Educational Review, 87*(4), 538–556.

Keenan, H., & Hot Mess, L. M. (2020). Drag pedagogy: The playful practice of queer imagination in early childhood. *Curriculum Inquiry, 50*(5), 440–461.

Krishnan, M., & Keenan, H. B. (2021). Our many selves. In L. Erickson-Schroth (Ed.), *Trans bodies, trans selves* (2nd ed.). Oxford University Press.

Kumashiro, K. (2002). *Troubling education: "Queer" activism and anti-oppressive pedagogy*. Routledge.

Love, B. (2020, June 12). An essay for teachers who understand racism is real. *Education Week*. Retrieved from https://www.edweek.org/leadership/opinion-an-essay-for-teachers-who-understand-racism-is-real/2020/06.

Lugones, M. (2010). Toward a decolonial feminism. *Hypatia*, *25*(4), 742–759.

MacNaughton, G. (2006). Constructing gender in early-years education. In C. Skelton, B. Francis, & L. Smulyan (Eds.), *The SAGE handbook of gender and education*, 127–138. SAGE Publications.

McKittrick, K. (Ed.). (2015). *Sylvia Wynter: On being human as praxis*. Duke University Press.

Miller, S. J. (2016). Trans*+ing classrooms: The pedagogy of refusal as mediator for learning. *Social Sciences*, *5*(3), 34.

Muñoz, J. E. (2019). *Cruising utopia*. New York University Press.

Nicolazzo, Z., Marine, S. B., & Galarte, F. (2015). Introduction to trans*formational pedagogies (special issue). *Transgender Studies Quarterly*, *2*(3), 367–375.

Owen, T. (2019, June 27). The Far Right is Doxxing and Threatening Drag Queen Story Hour. These Queens Won't Be Stopped. In *VICE News*. https://www.vice.com/en/article/evy7e4/the-far-right-is-doxxing-and-threatening-drag-queen-story-hour-these-queens-wont-be-stopped

Pinar, W. F. (Ed.). (1998). *Queer theory in education*. Lawrence Erlbaum Associates, Inc.

Robinson, K. H. (2005). 'Queerying' gender: Heteronormativity in early childhood education. *Australasian Journal of Early Childhood*, *30*(2), 19–28.

Sawicki, J. (1991). *Disciplining Foucault: Feminism, power, and the body*. Routledge.

Silin, J. G. (1995). *Sex, death, and the education of children: Our passion for ignorance in the age of AIDS*. Teachers College Press.

Stockton, K. B. (2009). *The queer child, or growing sideways in the twentieth century*. Duke University Press.

Tanner, C. (2021, February 11). Utah parents complained after kids were read a story about a transgender boy. Now other diverse books are on hold. In *The Salt Lake Tribune*. https://www.sltrib.com/news/education/2021/02/11/utah-parents-complained/

Thorne, B. (1993). *Gender play: Girls and boys in school*. Rutgers University Press.

Tuck, E., & Yang, K. W. (2018). R-words: Refusing research. In D. Paris & M. T. Winn (Eds.), *Humanizing research: Decolonizing qualitative inquiry with youth and communities* (pp. 223–248). SAGE Publications.

Wynter, S. (2003). Unsettling the coloniality of being/power/truth/freedom: Towards the human, after man, its overrepresentation—An argument. *CR: The New Centennial Review*, *3*(3), 257–337.

Yelland, N. (Ed.). (1998). *Gender in early childhood*. Routledge.

13

"PANDEMIC AS PORTAL" IN EARLY EDUCATION

Understanding the Disruptions of COVID-19 as an Invitation to Imagine and Create a New Vision of Preschool

Leah G. Durán, Rebecca B. Lopez, and Sherilyn M. Analla

The COVID-19 pandemic devastated the lives and well-being of uncountable numbers of people across the globe. Moreover, it did so in unequal ways, with repercussions felt most strongly by those who were already most affected by social inequities such as racism and poverty (Jæger & Blaabæk, 2020; Laster Pirtle, 2020). Likewise, the move to remote schooling magnified existing inequities in the US school system. Over the course of the 2020–2021 school year, students and teachers experienced massive disruptions to their lives. In addition to the direct health consequences for those who were infected with the COVID-19 virus, there were also a host of related disruptions to the everyday lives of teachers and students across the globe. Public health officials stressed the importance of social distancing, and many, many schools closed in an effort to protect the health of students, teachers, and their families. Some countries—but not the United States—prioritized young children when making decisions about access to in-person schooling (Melnick et al., 2020). This policy-level prioritization of young children's education derived both from a recognition of the burdens that remote schooling placed on working families and the understanding that many critically important aspects of early education, like play and hands-on inquiry, were particularly challenging in the context of virtual instruction.

The strain on teachers, families, and children as a result of the abrupt move to remote schools has been extensively documented (Dayal & Tiko, 2020; Dias et al., 2020; Ford et al., 2021). At the same time, early research has also pointed to a few small silver linings. For example, remote and virtual schooling often led teachers to reorganize their teaching structures, and some teachers appreciated the way that smaller group sizes gave them more opportunities to engage with

DOI: 10.4324/9781003399155-18

children individually (Pramling Samuelsson et al., 2020). While acknowledging the overwhelmingly negative consequences of the pandemic, we wish to turn here to look at the possibilities for doing school in new ways. Amidst the serious struggles, we also have begun to see how the disruption to schooling in the pandemic can offer some important insights for how schools might be organized in different, better ways. Some Black parents, for example, have noted how remote schooling offered new avenues of navigating the racism their children face in school, such as disproportionate discipline referrals (Anderson, 2020; Fields-Smith, 2020). With these insights in mind, we take up writer Arundhati Roy's (2020) invitation to consider the pandemic not only as tragedy but also as an invitation to reconstitute new ways of being and doing. In Roy's words,

> Historically, pandemics have forced humans to break with the past and imagine their world anew. This one is no different. It is a portal, a gateway between one world and the next: We can choose to walk through it, dragging the carcasses of our prejudice and hatred, our avarice, our data banks and dead ideas, our dead rivers and smoky skies behind us. Or we can walk through lightly, with little luggage, ready to imagine another world. And ready to fight for it.
>
> *(para. 48)*

While it may be easy to return to traditional ways of schooling in the aftermath of the pandemic, we aim to document some of the ways early childhood teachers have re-imagined their work, and consider the implications of those innovations for how we might better organize early childhood classrooms in the future.

In this chapter, we will draw on data from two early education classrooms in the Southwestern United States during the spring and fall of 2020, in predominantly Latina/o/x communities. In these contexts, we consider how the move to remote/virtual schooling shaped children's experiences in preschool, considering not only what was lost but also what possibilities for mobilization of children's abilities, cultures, and knowledge were opened up by moving school into children's homes. We draw on several different perspectives on the pandemic: Leah as a researcher working with one preschool teacher; Becka as a teacher-researcher studying her own preschool classroom; Sherilyn as an administrator. Leah observed and collaborated with a teacher, Ms. Perez (all participant names are pseudonyms) in primarily virtual instruction. Leah's work with Ms. Perez was conducted as a formative/design-based research study in which the researcher-teacher team jointly developed and piloted pedagogical innovations and documented students' responses (Design-Based Research Collective, 2003). Similarly, through Teacher Action Research (Hatch, 2002;

Souto-Manning, 2012), Becka observed and documented her own students' responses to both in-person and virtual schooling. Her goal within her teacher action research was to document the learning that happened within the class-room setting, and to pose and pursue questions "that would lead to positive pedagogical transformations" (Souto-Manning, 2012, p. 54). Assessment and improvement of Becka's pedagogy were prioritized in order to improve educational outcomes for students. Sherilyn aided in contextualizing and analyzing the data across both cases.

New Ways of Including Families

One key change that we saw in our data was increased use of students' home language during virtual instruction, in part because of the greater inclusion of parents as participants and partners in their children's schooling. Although preschools in Arizona are technically exempt from the state's English-only mandates, researchers have documented that preschool teachers here often feel pressured to teach in English anyway, due to the English-only environment that they anticipate their students encountering in their future schooling (Soltero-González, 2009). In Ms. Perez's classroom, in a predominantly Mexican-American community, Ms. Perez spoke and understood Spanish, as did a majority of her students. However, similar to what has been described elsewhere in literature on preschool in states with English-only laws, instruction in Ms. Perez's class occurred primarily in English.

Before the pandemic, Ms. Perez used primarily English for whole-class activities, and drew on Spanish when addressing some of the individual students who seemed most comfortable in Spanish. For example, the following excerpt from Leah's field notes show Ms. Perez welcomed Spanish contributions from one student, Jenny, into a mostly English activity (singing "The Wheels on the Bus"). In this classroom routine, Ms. Perez invited students one by one to contribute a new verse which echoed the structure of the traditional song (i.e., a person/animal makes a movement/sound/gesture). Most children invented a verse in English (e.g., "The rhino on the bus goes stomp, stomp, stomp"):

> When I arrived, students were on the carpet, singing new made up verses to "the wheels on the bus," with each new verse suggested by students. One student suggested "the dinosaur on the bus," another suggested "the rhino on the bus." During her turn to decide the version, Jenny suggested, "La tía está tomando fotos" [the aunt is taking photos].

Ms. Perez repeated back, "The tía is taking pictures with her camera ... is it camera or cámara?" I couldn't hear Jenny's response, but Ms. Perez followed, with "Yes, they are very close, camera, cámera" before leading the whole class in singing her verse, recast as "The tía on the bus goes clic, clic, clic," as they made gestures reminiscent of taking photos (Fieldnotes, 2/11/20).

In this exchange, when Jenny's turn arrived to invent a verse to "Wheels on the Bus," she volunteered a contribution in Spanish: "La tía está tomando fotos." Ms. Perez revoiced Jenny's contribution, translating most of the sentence into English ("The tía is taking pictures with her camera") and pointing out the close resemblance between the Spanish and English words for camera ("Yes, they are very close, camera, cámera"). She then rephrased Jenny's contribution so that it fit with the structure of the rest of the verses to "Wheels on the Bus." The rest of class sang along with her, "The tía on the bus goes click click click" as they made photo-taking gestures with their hands. In this exchange, Ms. Perez used Spanish to include Jenny, translating and rephrasing for her so that she could fully participate in the collective language game. She also maintained Jenny's use of "tía" rather than translating it to "aunt," leading the rest of the class in using that particular word, with all its affective connotations. Likewise, she highlighted the cross-linguistic similarity between Spanish and English (camera/cámera), for bilingual and monolingual students alike. However, perhaps because not all students were equally fluent in Spanish, English remained the main medium of instruction for the class as a whole, including Jenny. This interaction represented general trends in language use in the classroom, where Spanish played a vital role for a few students, but was not the predominant mode of communication. This exchange also echoes research on the language use dilemmas of many bilingual teachers in "almost bilingual" classrooms (Allard, Apt, & Sacks, 2019) who wish to support students' home language, but worry about alienating or excluding individual students who don't speak it.

However, the move to virtual instruction changed classroom instruction in major ways, with most of children's time with Ms. Perez now spent in small groups rather than as a whole class. The resulting increased ability to individualize instruction had important implications for how she was able to use language. In the following excerpt, Ms. Perez is in a "virtual classroom": a video chat with two of her students, engaging them in imaginative play with playdough which she had delivered to all her students' homes. The pattern of language uses here is similar to other exchanges during virtual instruction:

Ms. Perez asked Eric [in English] if he's making a pizza today. He did not reply. She repeated herself in Spanish, asking if the other student, Daniel, was also "cocinando hoy" [cooking today], to which he nodded. Then, his screen froze, and Ms. Perez said to him, "Daniel, estás frozen." [Daniel, you are frozen]. Offscreen, Daniel's mother said something inaudible. Ms. Perez replied, "Sí, pero no estamos viendo [yes, but we can't see]." Daniel's mother said something inaudible to Daniel in Spanish, then thanked him in English. Unfrozen, Daniel said in Spanish that he was making pizza. His mother added in Spanish that Daniel's favorite food is carne asada, and prompted Daniel to ask Ms. Perez what her favorite food is. Ms. Perez made a taco with her playdough, and replied, "A mí me gustan todos tipos de tacos, de pescado, de carne asada, de pollo." [I like all kinds of tacos, fish tacos, grilled beef tacos, chicken tacos].

(Fieldnotes, 9/17/2020)

In this interaction, Ms. Perez began the conversation in English, then switched to Spanish when neither student replied. When Daniel's screen froze, she directed her next comment to both Daniel and his mother, who was off-screen, helping him manage both technical difficulties like this one, and other challenges of online instruction, like staying focused on the task at hand. The rest of the conversation continued in Spanish, including not only the students, but also Daniel's mother. Both the inclusion of Daniel's mother, who preferred to use Spanish, and the small teacher-to-student ratio, seemed to influence Ms. Perez' greater use of Spanish in online settings than had been the norm in prepandemic, in-person schooling. This difference highlights an important aspect of more individualized instruction in "almost bilingual" classrooms: teachers' increased ability to adapt language use to individual students' preference rather than needing to use English as a common denominator when addressing all students. This linguistic flexibility is particularly important because of the asymmetric power imbalances between languages in the United States, where outside of specific bilingual programs (e.g., dual language immersion), schools consistently ask speakers of minoritized languages to adapt to all English instruction, rather than adapting to or accommodating them.

The other important dimension of pandemic-era instruction visible in this exchange is the addition of caretakers as interlocutors and classroom participants. Because these students were so young, managing the technological demands of virtual instruction (muting/unmuting, troubleshooting a frozen screen, etc.) often required the help of an adult or older sibling. Caretakers remained mostly off-screen, but sometimes, as in this instance, they joined in the conversation between students and teachers. Given that many parents in the classroom preferred to use Spanish, the greater inclusion of caretakers into classroom life also created more bilingual contexts for children in Ms. Perez's class. Part of what seemed to occur when school moved into children's homes was a larger role for home languages.

A further example of how virtual instruction created new ways of learning with and from parents can be seen in Becka's hybrid classroom (virtual and in-person) in the same community. In her experiences with virtual instruction, caretakers were often participants in classroom activities, in multiple ways. For example, through conducting home engagements, all of which were virtual via Google Meets or via phone conversations, Becka learned about funds of knowledge (González et al., 2005) in many students' households. She then used this knowledge to inform her instruction. The home engagements that Becka conducted focused on learning about family structure, labor history, daily and weekly activities, language use, and literacy practices within students' homes. During these home engagements, a number of caretakers shared practices related to preparing food together. Some families mentioned cooking meals with their children based on family interests, such as pancakes, chili beans, and spaghetti. Other families mentioned a family practice of preparing foods, such as cutting up vegetables to be grilled. Many families tied cooking to family traditions, such as using family recipes to cook and bake foods each year such as *pan de reyes* (king's day bread, also referred to as *rosca de reyes*), gumbo, and birthday cakes.

Building on children's everyday lives in instruction seemed to facilitate a sense of community and led to rich and engaging conversations amongst caretakers during virtual class sessions. The following exchange showcases the potential of including parents and caretakers in this way. During virtual class sessions, both students and their caretakers together would watch videos that different families had filmed and shared. In this cooking unit, families documented and shared students cooking different meals with their caretakers. Some cooking videos that caretakers had submitted included making *ensalada de macaroni* (macaroni salad), brownies, pasta, and meatballs. Sometimes, caretakers would share extra details about their cooking interactions with their children while watching them during virtual class sessions. Caretakers seemed particularly drawn to participating in virtual instruction as they all cooked and prepared meals with their children. In the following exchange, during one student's video of his family cooking pasta, his mother turned her cell phone toward herself to talk to everyone about how he had sneezed on the pasta right before putting it in the oven to bake:

01. James' mom:	Oh my gosh you guys! This is so embarrassing! I was like, "All this work so far and then we sneeze"! (many caretakers laughed) It was so funny. My husband was all, "Don't worry James, the oven will cook out all of the germs."
02. Xochitl's mom:	That's so funny! Right now at Christmas, we were making tamales and Xochitl always helps me with the masa and she did the same exact thing!
03. James's mom:	Oh my gosh well I'm glad I'm not alone! I was so nervous to show you guys this but I knew you'd think it's funny (laughs).
04. Xochitl's mom:	(laughs) Yes we definitely can relate.
05. JayZ's nana:	(laughs) *¡Estos niños! Ni modo* (These kids! Oh well)

The laughter of many adults during virtual class sessions suggests that *confianza*, or mutual trust (González et al., 2005; Valdés, 1996) was being built between each of the families as they shared intimate videos of themselves in their homes and personal stories of the quality cooking time that they spent with their families each day. As Hensley (2005) argued,

> If the teacher places value on this (funds of) knowledge, then the parents suddenly feel important. They feel empowered. This alone can dramatically change the climate of the teacher-home relationship. The parents feel equal. The barrier between the professional and the home caregiver is broken. A friendship develops and the relationship becomes ongoing and permanent.
>
> *(p. 146)*

Within this unit, Becka perceived that caretakers felt this power and relationship that Hensley (2005) spoke of. As James' mom shared the story of what happened as their family cooked together, other caretakers followed by sharing their cooking stories as well, their laughter and inclusion blurring the often-formidable boundary between "school" and "home." James' mother turning her camera to become an active participant in the classroom, as well as the story she shared about the process of cooking pasta with her son both suggested that she felt like an important and equal member of the classroom community. The participants demonstrated motivation to share pieces of information about who they were as a family during virtual class time, as seen in the interaction between James's and Xochitl's mom during their recipe-sharing conversations ("Oh my gosh well I'm glad I'm not alone! I was so nervous to show you guys this but I knew you'd think it's funny"). This exchange suggests the *confianza* that was felt amongst caretakers in that they felt comfortable sharing "embarrassing" stories with one another. The laughter from each caretaker reflects the humor present in their interactions during virtual class sessions. As a whole, virtual instruction around recipes and cooking provided a way of recognizing and including everyday life into the class, and in building relationships in the school community as a whole.

New Perspectives

The pandemic move to virtual and hybrid schooling also created new opportunities for teachers to understand parents' and children's perspectives, both figuratively and literally. Because technology was challenging for young children, communication with (and support from) caretakers became even more critical. As seen in the examples above, caretakers, most frequently mothers and siblings, were part of classroom interactions and the classroom communities in new ways. Teachers found that it did not work well to expect children to spend the same amount of time in virtual instruction as the normal, in-person school day, and hence developed and shared resources, activities and invitations to be shared with parents in addition to time spent together over video calls. For example, Ms. Perez and Becka both regularly delivered materials like books, manipulatives, blank booklets, and writing tools to families, with suggestions and invitations for how they might be used to build on what happened during virtual class sessions. The development and implementation of these supplementary lessons and activities implied increased communication with parents, as caretakers were essential in order for any of these activities or invitations to take place.

In both classrooms, in addition to sometimes participating in classroom discussions and activities, caretakers also often regularly sent pictures to the teachers, showing them different perspectives and new aspects of students' lives. For example, the picture below was taken by one students' mother, as the student wrote and drew in response to a backpack full of themed books that Ms. Perez had sent home (Figure 13.1).

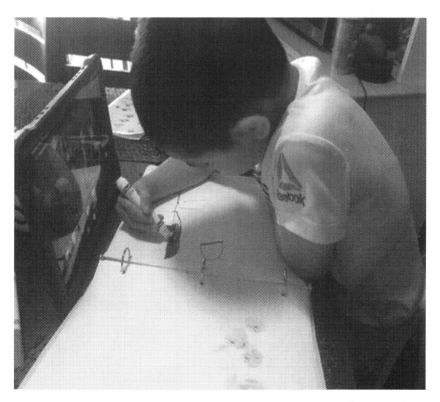

FIGURE 13.1   Caretaker's Perspective

This picture reveals both "academic" and everyday details of the moment. From the perspective of Ms. Perez, connecting through the tablet, only Jaime's head and the wall in back of him were visible, and it was often unclear what he was looking at or working on. In contrast, from his mother's perspective, we can see not only Jaime's drawing, but a sense of how he was experiencing virtual instruction: the intense focus on his drawing, the markers and tools spread out on the table, the small tablet screen through which he saw his teachers and classmates during virtual instruction, the everyday household scene in the background. Ms. Perez noted that from her screen angle, connecting through the tablet, it was not always clear what Jaime or his classmates were doing; seeing videos and photos from home helped her to better understand the full picture of what was happening and how he and others responded (or did not) to her invitations.

Photos of children at work and play have long been an important piece of documenting and understanding children's learning in early childhood, particularly in contexts influenced by the Reggio Emilia approach (Katz & Chard, 1996). Photos are valuable to teachers in part because they provide different kinds of information about the process of learning than the standardized or quantitative measures more commonly mandated by districts. As articulated by Loris Malaguzzi, photo documentation is also theorized to be important to parents and caretakers because it,

> introduces parents to a quality of knowing that tangibly changes their expectations. They reexamine their assumptions about their parenting roles and their views about the experience their children are living, and take a new and more inquisitive approach toward the whole school experience.
>
> *(1993, p. 64)*

However, the key role of caretaker-selected photos in virtual learning during the pandemic suggests that the reverse may also be true: the photos that caretakers take of children at home can elicit new understandings and perspectives from teachers, and help them better understand their students as human beings, embedded in families and communities.

Another example of how virtual instruction allowed teachers new perspectives can be seen in Becka's classroom. She was aware that engaging in virtual learning posed many challenges for students, in part because caretakers would mention that their children struggled to see the pictures in the stories Becka read, in the writing and drawings that she presented, or in images or videos that caretakers had submitted and were shared with the class. Hearing about these challenges prompted Becka to learn more about children's experiences. Through talking to caretakers, she learned that the vast majority of her students (88%) were using their caretaker's cell phone device to access virtual schooling.

FIGURE 13.2 Visual of Google Classroom on a Laptop.

This was in part because while the district had a program to loan tablets or personal computers to students, it was a program for students in grades K–12 only, not preschool children.

Logging on through a laptop, a tablet, and a cell phone allowed Becka to see precisely why and how this presented a challenge for students. While logged into Google Meet, which was the digital platform assigned by the district for teachers and students to use, students had limited visibility. If using a laptop or tablet, which represented the largest screen size that students had access to, they were limited to looking at little boxes on a screen no larger than 2 × 2 in (Figure 13.2).

Visibility was even more limited when learning from a cell phone. Students could only see the speaker—whomever that may be—and a small icon of themselves in the top left corner. Only being able to see one student at a time restricted students' abilities to engage collaboratively with one another. When Becka shared her screen with students during virtual class sessions, they were able to see themselves and three other people, but the boxes were less than 1 in wide.

Seeing the challenges posed by technology firsthand, from children's perspectives, spurred advocacy. Becka approached her district's IT (information technology) department in an attempt to secure students' tablets from the district, which would have had larger screens. (Unfortunately, this was not successful, as tablets were only delivered to a small handful of students, and those tablets did not arrive until toward the end of the school year.) Likewise, this understanding of how virtual schooling looked and felt from students' perspectives led her to change her teaching approaches toward activities that relied less on visual information. In both classrooms, pandemic-era instruction provided teachers with a new way of seeing how their students and their families perceived and experienced school.

Implications

Early education is unique in that it has always functioned along a continuum of care for the youngest members of our communities and their families. The early education classrooms of focus in this chapter operated within a school district. It is important to note that this study illustrates only one type of classroom out of a broader system of early education settings. Teachers, families, and children enrolled in programs such as Head Start, CCDF Child Care, private daycare, and home-based settings were impacted by COVID-19 in similar but not identical ways.

However, we argue here that there are valuable insights to be gleaned from the near-universal disruptions caused by the pandemic: new ways of connecting and including parents, new venues for including families' everyday linguistic and cultural practices, and new insights into children's lives and experiences outside their roles as students. At the same time, we do not wish to romanticize or idealize this moment. Virtual schooling created an almost impossible barrier to learning for many students. In both the classes described here, there were many students who attended only sporadically, or not at all. Some older caretakers were unfamiliar with how to use technology, and hence unable to support their students in connecting to virtual instruction. In some families, all of the adults needed to work outside the home or take care of younger siblings, and so students were left in the care of older siblings who were busy navigating their own virtual classroom sessions. Moreover, national data suggest that these kinds of barriers to student participation were not unique, but rather students all over the country stopped participating in early education (Bassok & Shapiro, 2021). Hence, we frame our findings not as evidence that virtual instruction was good, but rather that it was an experience which, despite its many hardships, still has something to teach us about how we might do school in different ways.

Some of these implications are small tweaks. For example, COVID-19 limited teachers' ability to enter students' homes in the way home engagements have traditionally been done, such as in students' physical homes (González et al., 2005; Reyes et al., 2016) and at local parks or libraries (Souto-Manning

& Yoon, 2018). However, conducting virtual home visits provided teachers with important information that they were then able to use to build the kind of community and relationships that were particularly challenging in this moment. Connecting virtually (either to bring teachers into students' homes, or caretakers into the classroom) may be a useful approach in some circumstances even after the pandemic ends.

Other implications are more sweeping. The experiences documented here also evoke bigger questions and ideas about new ways of organizing schools: how can this experience be a portal into a new and better world? How can we restructure early education to be more equitable, so that children in working-class communities of color are not facing disproportionate barriers to learning? How can we make early education a place where children's cultural and linguistic practices are sustained rather than replaced? How can we truly value and include families as partners? We often hear public rhetoric related to the value of preschool and the importance of early childhood. In this particular case, the distribution of scarce resources like tablets suggested that neither young children nor socio-economically stressed families were, in fact, prioritized at a structural, administrative level. However, this need not be the case. We might collectively decide to do things differently in the future: to distribute both material and human resources to young children, their families, and their teachers in ways that better match our values and rhetoric. For example, many affluent families created "pandemic pods" (Horn, 2022), where children's and teachers' safety was safeguarded via small teacher-student ratios and outdoor learning spaces. This structure is something public schools collectively might have created, too, if they had the support and resources. We might take away from this experience a greater commitment to allocate more of our collective resources to those children who most need them.

Likewise, we might consider what it would take to bring more parents, elders, and community members into early childhood classrooms, whether virtually or in person. Although early education has often been a process of assimilation into the dominant culture (Kaomea, 2005), these pandemic experiences showcase how the inclusion of parents and family members as classroom members makes school more linguistically and culturally pluralistic. Perhaps most importantly, these pandemic experiences remind us that children are more than students, and understanding more about children's experiences may lead teachers to take on the role of advocates and not just instructors. Teacher advocacy should be a key part of professional development and early childhood teacher education as it has played a critical role during the pandemic to ensure educational access for children.

The research reported in this chapter was made possible in part by a grant from the Spencer Foundation. The views expressed are those of the authors and do not necessarily reflect the views of the Spencer Foundation.

References

Allard, E. C., Apt, A., & Sacks, I. (2019). Language policy and practice in almost-bilingual classrooms. *International Multilingual Research Journal, 13*(2), 73–87. https://doi.org/10.1080/19313152.2018.1563425

Anderson, M. D. (2020, October 28). You're out of your mind if you think I'm ever going back to school. *The New York Times.* Retrieved from https://www.nytimes.com

Bassok, D., & Shapiro, A. (2021, February 22). *Understanding COVID-19-era enrollment drops among early-grade public school students* [Blog post]. Retrieved from: https://www.brookings.edu

Dayal, H. C., & Tiko, L. (2020). When are we going to have the real school? A case study of early childhood education and care teachers' experiences surrounding education during the COVID-19 pandemic. *Australasian Journal of Early Childhood, 45*(4), 336–347.

Design-Based Research Collective. (2003). Design-based research: An emerging paradigm for educational inquiry. *Educational Researcher, 32*(1), 5–8.

Dias, M. J., Almodóvar, M., Atiles, J. T., Vargas, A. C., & Zúñiga León, I. M. (2020). Rising to the challenge: Innovative early childhood teachers adapt to the COVID-19 era. *Childhood Education, 96*(6), 38–45.

Fields-Smith, C. (2020). Conceptualizing contemporary black homeschooling and single black mothers' resistance. In C. Fields-Smith (Ed.), *Exploring single black Mothers' resistance through homeschooling* (pp. 21–42). Palgrave Macmillan.

Ford, T. G., Kwon, K. A., & Tsotsoros, J. D. (2021). Early childhood distance learning in the US during the COVID pandemic: Challenges and opportunities. *Children and Youth Services Review, 131*, 106297.

González, N., Moll, L., & Amanti, C. (2005). *Funds of knowledge: Theorizing practices in households, communities and classrooms.* Lawrence Erlbaum Associates.

Hatch, J. A. (2002). *Doing qualitative research in educational settings.* SUNY Press.

Hensley, M. (2005). Empowering parents of multilingual backgrounds. In N. Gonzalez, L.C. Moll, & C. Amanti (Eds.), *Funds of knowledge: Theorizing practices in households, communities, and classrooms* (pp. 143–165). Routledge.

Horn, M. B. (2022). Some pods will outlast the pandemic: Students, parents say they appreciate the support. *Education Next, 22*(1), 84–87.

Jæger, M. M., & Blaabæk, E. H. (2020). Inequality in learning opportunities during COVID-19: Evidence from library takeout. *Research in Social Stratification and Mobility, 68*, 100524.

Kaomea, J. (2005). Reflections of an "always already" failing Native Hawaiian mother: Deconstructing colonial discourses on indigenous child-rearing and early childhood education. *Hūlili: Multidisciplinary Research on Hawaiian Well-Being, 2*(1), 77–95.

Katz, L. G., & Chard, S. C. (1996). *The contribution of documentation to the quality of early childhood education. ERIC Digest.* Retrieved from https://files.eric.ed.gov/fulltext/ED444767.pdf#page=107

Laster Pirtle, W. N. (2020). Racial capitalism: A fundamental cause of novel coronavirus (COVID-19) pandemic inequities in the United States. *Health Education & Behavior, 47*(4), 504–508.

Malaguzzi, L. (1993). History, ideas, and basic philosophy. In C. Edwards, L. Gandini, and G. Forman, *The hundred languages of children: The Reggio Emilia approach to early childhood education* (pp. 27–71). Ablex.

Melnick, H., Darling-Hammond, L., Leung, M., Yun, C., Schachner, A., Plasencia, S. ... Ondrasek, N. (2020). *Reopening schools in the context of COVID-19: Health and safety guidelines from other countries* [policy brief]. Learning Policy Institute.

Pramling Samuelsson, I., Wagner, J. T., & Eriksen Ødegaard, E. (2020). The coronavirus pandemic and lessons learned in preschools in Norway, Sweden and the United States: OMEP policy forum. *International Journal of Early Childhood, 52*(2), 129–144.

Reyes, I., Da Silva Iddings, A. C., & Feller, N. (2016). Building relationships with diverse students and families: A funds of knowledge perspective. *Journal of Early Childhood Literacy, 16*(1), 8–33. https://doi.org/10.1177/1468798415584692

Roy, A. (2020). The pandemic is a portal. *Financial Times, 3*(4). https://www.ft.com/content/10d8f5e8-74eb-11ea-95fe-fcd274e920ca

Soltero-González, L. (2009). Preschool Latino immigrant children: Using the home language as a resource for literacy learning. *Theory into Practice, 48*(4), 283–289.

Souto-Manning, M. (2012). Teacher as researcher: Teacher action research in teacher education. *Childhood Education, 88*(1), 54–56. https://doi.org/10.1080/00094056.2012.643726

Souto-Manning, M., & Yoon, H. S. (2018). *Rethinking early literacies: Reading and rewriting worlds*. Routledge.

Valdés, G. (1996). *Con Respeto: Bridging the distances between culturally diverse families and schools: An ethnographic portrait*. Teachers College Press.

14

CHILDREN'S PRINT MAGAZINE

An Example from Pakistan on Fostering Literacy and Socio-Emotional Learning during the Global Pandemic

Axa Khalid Warraich and Ana Christina da Silva Iddings

On February 26, 2020, the first case of COVID-19 was recorded in Pakistan. Within weeks, the number of cases being recorded per day and number of deaths by COVID-19 doubled and then quadrupled. On March 13, 2020, the education minister of Pakistan announced the complete closure of all educational institutes until April 5, 2020. This decision alone impacted over 46 million learners aged 5–16. Out of these, those that were most affected were children in rural communities and in urban and peri-urban areas, differently abled children, girls, Afghan refugees, and children from Federally Administered Tribal Areas or Khyber Pakhtunkhwa that had suffered displacement, insecurity, and conflict (UNESCO and UNICEF, 2021, p. 13). Early estimates suggested that close to a million students might not come back to school because of economic hardships experienced by their families. Pakistan could lose a larger share of students from the school system than any other country in the world (Geven et al, 2020).

While most of the world switched to digital, television, or radio solutions, educators serving underresourced communities had to be innovative in designing distance learning solutions that could serve the needs of these unique and diverse populations. This chapter examines Pakistan's response to the COVID-19 global pandemic, shedding light on ways in which educators everywhere can design culturally relevant edutainment literacy content for early childhood. More specifically, we report on how one such nongovernmental educational organization—*The Citizens Foundation* (TCF)—worked to center the needs of diverse communities while designing and implementing informal reading projects in times of collective healing. TCF is one of Pakistan's leading nongovernment organizations in the field of education. In terms of scale and

DOI: 10.4324/9781003399155-19

impact, it has around 1833 schools across Pakistan, providing access to education to around 280,000 students. These schools are in the heart of underserved rural and urban communities across Pakistan. TCF is committed to gender equity and emphasizes female education and has been able to maintain a 50% gender ratio in all classrooms.

Axa, the first author of this chapter is a native Pakistani, and is project lead of the print magazine in TCF. The magazine design team was intentional in taking a culturally sustaining approach (Paris & Alim, 2017) when looking for a solution during these restrictive circumstances of the global pandemic. They viewed the educational situations the students and their families were enduring as unique and not deviant or deficient in any way as they pondered how educators and communities could continue to provide educational opportunities. This chapter highlights the process of designing, implementing, and redesigning a print edutainment magazine with the intent to provide literacy content for young children in the Pakistani context. Through delineating this process, we hope to shed light on ways that the print edutainment magazine fostered opportunities for family literacy engagement and socio-emotional learning in areas where digital access continues to be an issue.

Context

Pakistan has a population of around 229 million. Around 63% of its total population lives in rural areas and the remaining 37% lives in urban centers (Rural Population—Pakistan, 2020).

Around 40 million students are enrolled in schools (ASER-Pakistan 2021, 2021, p. 19). Student enrollments and completion are disproportionately higher for males than for female students (Pakistan Education Statistics 2017–18, 2021, p. 14). It ranks second highest in the number of out-of-school children, with an estimated 22.8 million children aged 5–16 not attending school at all, representing 44% of the total population in this age group.

The Digital Divide and School Closure due to COVID-19

There is a digital divide that exists in Pakistan, and it goes hand in hand with the class divide in the society. In Pakistan, there is a spectrum of schools available to the students—at one end are the public schools and religious madrassas offering free education or a nominal fee of USD 0.5 US dollars per month and at the other end are high-cost private schools often ranging between a fee of USD $110 to USD $220 US dollars per month. Students who go to the latter medium- and high-cost private schools are the ones who belong to higher income households, have access to the internet and smart devices, and have support at home in the form of their parents and hired professionals.

When schools closed, a certain range of schools transitioned to virtual learning in Google classrooms and other virtual spaces to carry out classes for students from the safety of their homes. However, children belonging to less affluent, historically marginalized, and low socio-economic families could not utilize such opportunities, because of a lack of accessibility of internet services, stable electricity, smartphones, and computers. These are students attending low-cost private schools, religious madrassas, or public schools. TCF students also belong to this category.

The Role of TCF in Early Childhood Education

The students in these communities are often the only individuals in their household who can read and write; in some cases, they might have a sibling who can read and write as well. Parents are usually passionate about their child's education and engage actively when the designed projects are intentional about centering their needs. Teachers and principals are mostly locals of the community and play an active part in the lives of their students even beyond school hours.

Due to the lockdown, TCF was forced to stop all operations and think creatively to serve its students. To its advantage, it had an already established rapport with the communities, local teachers, alumni and volunteers, and school buildings that were built in the heart of the communities it served. After eliminating digital solutions due to a very low digital footprint in its communities, and television and radio due to limited access to these devices in the communities, TCF created a traditional children's print magazine, to provide educational access and engagement to each child.

Only a small percentage of the populations that TCF serves has access to a smartphone, far less have access to a stable internet connection that can be used for web browsing. In most of these households, that phone is owned by the male head of the household, who may not be at home during the day. According to phone surveys conducted by TCF, parents are willing to give their phone, in their supervision, to their children for 45 minutes to 1 hour for educational purposes. However, this allowance may be different for a male or a female child. It was within this context that TCF started looking for suitable, alternative mediums to provide continuity of learning during school closure due to COVID-19.

Literacy Development

Literacy, narrowly defined as the ability to read and write in conventional ways at grade level, is a growing and persistent problem in Pakistan, and the consequences are dire. If students graduating schools do not have the capacity to read with fluency, they will automatically be cut off from higher education opportunities, information sources, most career tracks, and most conversations around self, power, and society. That is, reading and writing fluency brings with it access and opportunity beyond early childhood.

According to the 2019 Annual Status of Education Report (ASER) (ASER-Pakistan 2019, 2020), 41% of children in grade 5 cannot read a simple story in Urdu/Sindhi/Pashto. Furthermore, if we look at learning at grade 8 or lower secondary, 14% of children are still unable to read a grade 2 level story in Urdu/Sindhi/Pashto. The literacy statistics for English are understandably worse. Overall, in Pakistan 75% of children, by age 10, cannot read and understand a simple text (p. 16).

While these gloomy statistical data regarding literacy proficiency in Pakistan are widely recognized, there are systemic layers to the problem that are not so widely discussed. For example, children and adults do not have a widespread access to reading materials in a language they are fluent in, due to the lack of libraries in the country and poverty in communities.

Inevitably, these alarming statistics guide the ideological and curricular choices of literacy development. First, most literacy interventions, in Pakistan, only acknowledge and address the lowest rung of the literacy definition ladder (i.e., the alphabet toolkit), and ignore the meaning-making purposes and the emotional and sociocultural foundations of reading. Even stories and conversations embedded in these programs show that their objective is alphabet mastery rather than using the alphabet as a tool to develop world concepts. Second, only a handful of interventions have a dedicated focus on providing meaningful, contextually relevant, and enjoyable content to young children. Third, Urdu story books available in the market are usually not tied to current themes in the twenty-first century, experiences of local interest, are often problematic in their representation of gender and social roles and are more interested in preaching morals rather than delving deeply into a child's emotional world and interest. Most age-appropriate books are usually in English, written by international authors, about contexts not local to Pakistan and are usually very expensive. Therefore, most governmental interventions targeted toward developing literacy in the early childhood years have not been very effective.

Literacy, more broadly conceived, is not just about mastery of an alphabet system or the ability to blend it together, but a mindset of engaging with meaningful, enjoyable, and culturally relevant text that allows for critical thinking and reflection. In these ways, literacy can be developed when children are exposed to a variety of age-appropriate and diverse texts on a regular basis, in an environment of guidance and facilitation, with trusted friends or mentors. In line with what sociocultural and socio-emotional theories suggest, parents, teachers, and caregivers play a critical role in this kind of literacy development, by modeling reading in their daily lives, creating a print-rich environment, and drawing attention to its print-richness, reading in a comforting setting with children, choosing enjoyable texts addressing themes, ideas, and wordplay that fascinate children, and letting the child lead the exploration.

Literature Review

Children's literacy resources available outside school can take on a variety of modalities: print, electronic and digital are utilized to help students learn and have fun. For the purposes of this chapter, only the use of print magazines as a learning tool outside the school will be discussed. This is so because the population that we target in this report are children and families in the TCF community, most of whom do not have access to other literacy resources. In these ways, the print magazine has been designed as an edutainment source, for children to interact with learning material while having fun. This dual purpose of the print magazine as an educational and entertainment tool to address the literacy and socio-emotional needs of the children will be discussed.

Out-of-School Learning and Print Media: A Historical Account

The history of learning is as long as the history of humans and is older than the history of the school (Gobby & Millei, 2017, p. 9). With the dawn of schools and emphasis on schooling, the socialization of children shifted from home to school (Richards, 1998, p. 133). With time, parents and caregivers have become more conscious of the children's performance in school with their increasing engagement and a rapid transformation in technology that gave rise to the production of learning resources and their availability to the children (Buckingham & Scanlon, 2001, p. 282). These resources are used to improve their performance at school. This phenomenon has overemphasized a divide in the learning attainment of students with and without access to these resources. As far as the variety in such resources is concerned, magazines, newspapers, and books have been used at home for leisure and learning (Buckingham & Scanlon, 2003, p. 282); however, the invention of the printing press and industrial revolution has led to significant growth in their use (Holmes, 2020, p. 4). Technology, particularly the internet, has opened a whole new space to experiment on learning outside school and opened avenues for the production and use of effective resources (Buckingham & Scanlon, 2003, p. 107).

Print media is defined as "information conveyed through books, magazines, newspapers, art, photographs, maps, and other printed, non-electronic tools for communication" (Strouse et al., 2019, p. 4). Parents indicated they believed print was more educational and entertaining than digital media and were motivated to use print for children's learning, relaxation, entertainment, and parent-child bonding (Strouse et al, 2019, p. 8). The importance of print media has been further reaffirmed by Gaskell et al. (2005), in their claim that although instructional computer technology helps in distance learning it does not replace print media. Furthermore, another study conducted in India, reinforced the fact that students wanted to stick to the traditional print media and didn't prefer using innovative methods in the learning process (Srivastava & Reddy, 2007, p. 97). Although there is a gap in the literature on the print media and the young children's preference specifically in developing countries; Bose and Sharma (2010) suggest that low-tech measures should be adopted in these regions, especially in the case of distance learning (p. 84).

Magazines are a part of print media; however, we note that there is a paucity of educational magazines in developing countries despite their great potential as a source of learning. In research, the term educational magazine is used when magazines have an "education dimension" to them because the purpose of these magazines is to take children to a "learning state of mind" outside of their school setting and regardless of their circumstances (Buckingham & Scanlon, 2001, p. 285). Researchers caution that such magazines are not a replacement for the formal education that children should receive (Bashford & Strange, 2004). Moreover, these magazines capitalize on children's fascination for characters that they admire. Hence, in such cases, this type of print media can act as an extension of the television programs. The TCF print magazine, *Ilm ka Angan* (*The Learning Courtyard*), which we are especially interested in for this chapter, also started as a weekly television show, and then the magazine was launched as an extension to it. We argue that the low-tech, high-touch nature of the print magazine has served to promote out-of-school social emotional and literacy learning through family home engagements, especially during forced school closures and other academic insecurities during the global pandemic.

Designing *Ilm ka Angan* (Courtyard of Learning, علم کا آنگن)

The COVID-19 pandemic, like other epi/pandemics across recent history, provokes discussions on the role of education in collective healing. For example, education response efforts in West Africa, post-Ebola crisis, provided positive reinforcement, mitigating psychosocial impacts of the disaster, and establishing routine; not focusing on ensuring stability of academic learning (Winthrop, 2020). Hence, programs designed during such crises should begin with foundational content (One Year On, 2021) or revise already mastered content and only over time introduce new content, if needed. In other words, while academic development is important, the ability to learn new content is mediated by the social and emotional well-being of children impacted by disaster and trauma.

To be more inclusive in design, TCF conducted a small-scale needs assessment to identify the needs of the students and schools and brainstorm for possible solutions. All ten school principals from rural and urban communities in all five geographical regions of TCF shared content design ideas, ways to engage families and establish a feedback loop with the students. Additionally, we reached out to mental health professionals, especially those who specialize in working with underserved communities in Pakistan, to understand the types of emotional and mental health circumstances that students belonging to TCF may be facing. They shared that we should create content that addresses and provides support for possible stress or anxiety created by loneliness or boredom, unexpected changes in lifestyle, home boundedness, buildup of emotions due to restricted in-person contact with friends and teachers, financial worry, and possible strained familial relationships due to lack of communication, misunderstanding, not being heard, favoritism by family, sibling comparison and aggressive parenting. During our research on factors to keep in mind when designing media and print media in specific, for young children, the following three themes emerged: Literacy content, layout, and feedback loop.

Literacy Content

The most engaging content has stories with vocabulary building, coloring, joining the dots, counting activities (Buckingham & Scanlon, 2001, p. 284), comprehension quizzes, news, comic strips, diagrams/charts/tables, maps (Tavakoli & Esmae'li, 2013, p. 574), content encouraging physical education and content encouraging skill development and growth mindset. Supplementary audio educational content can be used to increase engagement—and should include numeracy, literacy, health and hygiene, exercise, and games evoking joy and socio-emotional messaging.

Layout

While using print media for children, it is especially important that the text follows a predictable structure (Tavakoli & Esmae'li, 2013, p. 577), is divided into logical segments (Five Ways Using Magazines in the Classroom Improves Student Performance, 2016), is contextual, offers multi-age-suited topics, formats, genres (Gabriel et al., 2012, p. 189) and provides content specific visuals (Walma van der Molen & van der Voort, 2000). Self-study packets should be designed for independent student practice, categorized by grade (or grade clusters), either to be distributed at once, arranged according to dates, or distributed over regular intervals

Feedback Loop

The design of the magazine should be iterative, engaging families to influence the evolution of the magazine. Other ways to provide feedback may include establishing a hotline for teachers and students to seek technical support in case of any difficulty (Chang & Yano, 2020), deploying an Interactive Voice Response System for queries and answers (Diedhiou et al., 2015) and embedding answer keys to give students immediate feedback on their work.

Creating the Children's Print Magazine

While an existing accompanying television show to the print magazine attracted up to 6 million viewers, we were still grappling with accessibility and reach of the television show for students with unstable electricity and limited access to television or computers. In the same way, our existing data showed that radio only reaches 9–11% of the population. Therefore, we chose print as a medium of choice to ensure educational access to all TCF students across Pakistan, despite the circumstances they may find themselves in during the pandemic.

Initially, TCF piloted an eight-page print edutainment magazine, by the name of *Ilm ka Aangan* (The Learning Courtyard) and distributed this magazine to 15,000 initial readers enrolled in grades 1–5 in select rural and urban areas of Punjab and Sindh province. Relevant hygiene and prevention information regarding the COVID-19 was also conveyed to parents while approaching them for collection of the magazine. To maximize understandability of the content, this magazine was in Urdu, since Urdu is the medium of education in all TCF schools.

Once it became evident that schools would remain closed indefinitely, TCF moved toward improving the magazine and distributing it to scale. A detailed survey was conducted to help identify and address any issues in content design and distribution channels. The survey was filled by school principals and administrative support teams. Simultaneously, phone calls were made to get survey responses from families and students. Since the objective of the magazine was not to improve student learning outcomes, but to offer engagement, data being collected was on completion and not quality of responses. The findings of the surveys were used in the design and distribution of the scale up.

The project was scaled up to print and we distributed twenty issues of the Urdu magazine and five issues of the Sindhi magazine. The dedicated team began research and created and curated content ideal for children who were developing with limited literacy skills. Magazines featured contextualized, age-appropriate and social emotional learning–aligned stories, STEM-integrated comic strips, do-it-yourself art and craft segment, coloring activities, board games, a logic and reasoning segment, Math and English exercises, and science experiments.

Special focus was placed on ensuring that the design content was representative and inclusive of all classes, genders, religions, abilities, ages, and ethnicities.

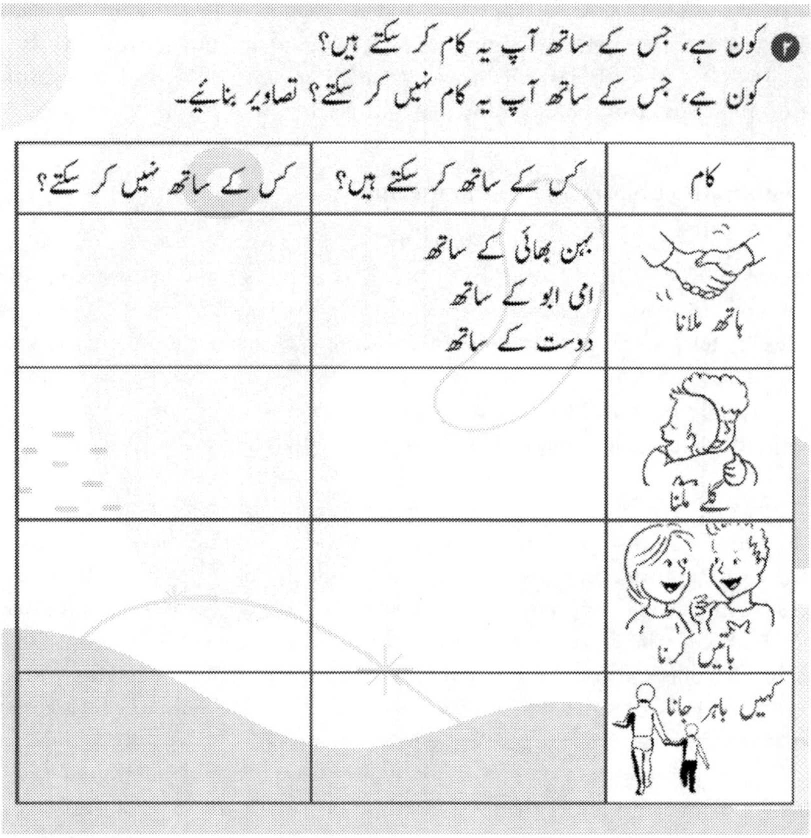

کون ہے، جس کے ساتھ آپ یہ کام کر سکتے ہیں؟

کون ہے، جس کے ساتھ آپ یہ کام نہیں کر سکتے؟ تصاویر بنایئے۔

کس کے ساتھ نہیں کر سکتے؟	کس کے ساتھ کر سکتے ہیں؟	کام
	بہن بھائی کے ساتھ امی ابو کے ساتھ دوست کے ساتھ	ہاتھ ملانا
		گلے لگانا
		باتیں کرنا
		کہیں باہر جانا

FIGURE 14.1   Screenshot from the Children's Magazine

Diversity in this context was not just about making cosmetic changes, like being inclusive in the illustrations made and the names of characters, but also centered the reliance on intellectual, experiential, and social assets that the people in these communities hold. For example, while tackling the theme of stranger danger, at the end of a story about the topic, we shared an activity (see Figure 14.1) where the parents and students could have a conversation around whom they can shake hands with, whom they can travel alone, whom they can hug. This provided a discussion space, where parents and families could discuss the limits to trust and caution in their circumstances.

Stories were written around young protagonists who embodied agency, troubleshooting obstacles, and enacting problem-solving skills. Inclusive names were used for characters in stories and activities. Illustrations were designed to be culturally relevant as well. Additionally, the magazine featured a dedicated segment, *Nadeem Chacha se Baatain* (*Talks with Uncle Nadeem*), to address potential mental health issues. Through written responses, the main character, *Nadeem Chacha*, created a safe space for emotional validation, provided relatability and offered practical tips to register and manage emotions during this time of collective healing. These responses were designed around various real life situation questions involving Collaborative for Academic, Social, and Emotional Learning (CASEL)'s five social and emotional learning competencies (What Is the CASEL Framework?, n.d.). All the magazines were reviewed by a leading mental health organization in Pakistan, *Saaya Health*, to ensure that it catered to the developmental and socio-emotional needs of our students. Themes, such as recognizing and managing complex emotions, rethinking gender stereotypes, and bullying, have been explored through stories and art activities in the magazine.

The magazine was distributed fortnightly during school closure and monthly after school reopening. During school closure, elder family members collected magazines from TCF schools, or a local teacher distributed them to those students' homes whose families were not collecting these themselves. After schools reopened, the magazines were distributed to students in school. Any written work in the magazine was treated as homework and was submitted when family members came to collect the next issue of the magazine. Some answers were written on the last page of the magazine. A supplemental answer key was provided to assist teachers in checking the homework of the magazine, with the intention of giving encouraging remarks to the students instead of giving numbered scores. Checked homework and relevant feedback would be returned with the next magazine. Certain activities in the magazine were tagged with a distinct family engagement icon, to encourage parents and families, even those that were not literate in Urdu, to be actively engaged in their child's learning.

Researching *Ilm ka Angan* (the Courtyard of Learning)

The *Ilm ka Angan* (the Courtyard of Learning) edutainment magazine was first created in 2020 and subsequently went through various cycles of redesign with the objective of continuously improving the design and implementation of the project.

We understood that the magazine was not just a transfer of knowledge from paper to an individual student. There were people and processes present that make the magazine possible; there were stakeholders who play a crucial role in bringing it in the student's hands; there was a culture with norms and values that facilitate student involvement with the magazine; there was a physical environment in which the magazine was read; there were relationships and abiotic elements in which the student felt joy from the practice of reading. It was through this lens that we approached the methodology of this study.

Utilizing a Design-based research methodology (Cobb et al., 2003) we chose to have structured and semistructured discussions with students, principals, area education officers, and families to get a holistic picture to retrospectively understand what has worked and prospectively make changes for improvement. In line with the objective to improve design and distribution of the magazine, following were the questions we were specifically interested in:

1 Are all students receiving the magazines on time? If not, what are the issues on ground?
2 Do the students find the magazine engaging and joyful? If not, how can the design be improved for more engagement?
3 How are the students interacting with the magazine?
4 What challenges are the students facing in interacting with the magazine?
5 What improvements do the students want to see in the magazine?
6 Have there been any changes in literacy and social emotional learning ever since the magazine has been distributed?

Since the intent was continuous improvement, we kept going back to collect fresh data points from sometimes the same sample and sometimes a different sample of participants.

Following are the various data collection tools we have used to collect data from May 2020 to March 2022. Participants were 262 students (preschool and elementary age), 123 parents or family members, 24 teachers, 74 school administrators, and 56 area education managers selected through convenience and randomized samples. The data collected included bi-monthly focus group discussions and semistructured interviews, monthly surveys, and questionnaires.

All data was audio recorded and some observational and field notes were collected. Interviews were transcribed and coded. Important themes were highlighted in the first cycle of coding. In the second cycle, nodes using NVIVO were developed from the text. The nodes were compared to increase the reliability of the coding process (Miles & Huberman, 1994). During telephonic data collection, responses were noted in an excel sheet simultaneously. To store and organize that quantitative data and to make inferences, we used STATA. We were able to present some descriptive statistics and correlations to explore the themes with respect to age, gender, and grade. Apart from the methodological tools listed, questions, drawings and stories sent by students, to the magazine design team, were also counted and analyzed for indications of social emotional learning. For the purposes of this chapter, we will report on socio-emotional development and family literacy engagement.

Source of Engagement and Joy

> Students enjoy solving puzzles and coloring the most. In free time, I have observed that students usually make groups of three or four and are engaging with the magazine. Students are also anxiously waiting for the next issues of the magazine and keep coming to me to ask when they will receive the next issue. I have also observed that students carry their copy of the magazine in their school bags, no one has asked them to do it, but they enjoy using magazines as a fun pastime at school and at home.
>
> (Principal, Nargis Noorani Campus, Karachi)

All students, families, principals and administrative support teams surveyed to date have shared that they want the magazine to continue. One of the recurring findings in all the focus group discussions was that the magazine had been beneficial for the students, especially in inculcating a habit of leisure reading. Sameera, a grade 2 student at Nargis Noorani Campus, Karachi excitedly shared that, "I have read all the magazines I have received till date. I have read all the stories, all by myself. My Urdu is now a little alright too. I have kept all of the magazines safely." Teachers also shared that the magazine had been useful for students in keeping them in touch with learning during the lockdown. Area Education Officer in Steel Town, Karachi, shared,

> Schools in my area do not have access to stable electricity and COVID hit this community really hard financially. Students and families come to me all the time, sharing that the magazine was their only connection with schooling, they loved it and made students very excited about it.

In our initial survey with 212 students, we found that only 36% of them had read 8 or more out of the 10 magazine issues they had received. We also found that 57% of them shared that they thought the magazine content was too difficult for them to read. In a follow-up question, they asked for easier activities for students of grade 3 and under, less use of text, more pictures and matching activities. Once we integrated this feedback in the magazine, we saw an overwhelming increase in student engagement.

Following (see Figure 14.2) are the student response rates ever since the redesign of the magazine in May 2021. Student response rate was calculated by taking a percentage of the total number of submissions sent by students, divided by the total number of magazines distributed (currently the number is standing at 98,300 copies for grade KG-2).

With both the television show and the magazine, we noticed that submission prompts that were more straightforward and personal, asking students to draw things they liked, etc., had high response rates. We had a lot of repeated

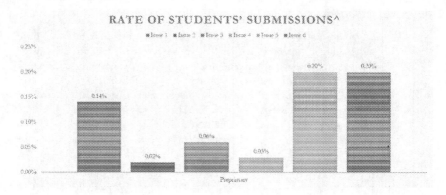

FIGURE 14.2   Bar Graph of Student Response Rate for Magazine

engagement and this could be because of the positive reinforcing feedback loops. Whenever somebody submitted anything for the magazine, they received an automated response acknowledging their work. Students shared that they submitted more work when their own work or the work of someone they personally know gets published.

Socio-emotional Development

> *"Why do people make fun of you when you try to do something good?"*
> Question sent by Aamir, Grade 1, Asna Riaz Campus, Lahore

The increasing range in emotional vocabulary and using student submissions as a way to raise and unpack issues of self-awareness, self-management and social awareness are some of the indicators improving socio-emotional development. Areeba, a grade 1 student at Yasmeen Malik Campus, Karachi sent a question for the *Nadeem Chacha* segment, *"some people cannot see but they can read, how is this made possible?"* Self-driven student questions like these give openings to have critical conversations on ability equity through the magazine.

Teachers and principals shared that advances in socio-emotional learning sometimes requires changing long-established behaviors and this takes time and reinforcement from multiple avenues. Principal of Nargis Noorani Campus, Karachi said,

> I have seen students register and talk about the social emotional related themes in the magazine, but I have not seen a significant behavioral change in the students that can be attributed to the magazine. I feel such things take time and need to be reinforced and assessed through structured discussions or action projects.

FIGURE 14.3 Girls in STEM Drawing Sent by Munza, Grade 2, Dadabhoy Campus, Karachi

However, we have received questions, drawings, and short stories, where students touch upon issues of gender-specific roles and career, accommodation of differently abled bodies, girls in STEM (see Figure 14.3), representation of girls in public spaces (see Figure 14.4) and much more. These small but incremental changes in the types of content being sent by students were very encouraging to continue and open up further discussion on socially and culturally relevant topics.

Family Literacy Engagement

> *Mothers often share that they also wait for the magazine with excitement. The Family Engagement points in the magazine also help families talk to children while reading the magazine.*

—Principal, AlKaram Sindh Police Campus, Karachi

FIGURE 14.4 Girls in Public Places Student Drawing Sent by Sajida, Grade KG, Radiant Way Campus, Meerpur Sakhro

We were very intentional in making the magazine an independent resource that students can interact with leisurely in out-of-school settings. Hence, families had been encouraged, by teachers and school staff, to engage with the students using the magazine. In our initial survey with parents and families, we found that most parents knew about the magazine and knew what parts their children found interesting and what parts they found difficult.

Data collected also signaled the role that the magazine is playing in family literacy engagement. Some students shared stories, jokes, and games that they could read and understand, with other members of the family. Anum, a student of grade 2 in Nathani Campus, Ketty Bandar was always excited about the board games in the magazine and made it a point to play it with her family. Iffat, a student of grade 2 at Alam Foundation Campus II, Khushab said that "… if while reading something, I face some difficulty, I ask for help from my sister and she helps me read till I can read the full story that is given."

Some parents reported that they discussed questions with their children and sent queries to be answered through the magazine. They have shared that the magazine proved to be a leisure reading resource for the whole family as it sometimes became the only text among their household library. These findings were highly encouraging and point to the leveraging of home-based and family literacies for improvement in student learning outcomes and engagement.

Implications for Practice

In unprecedented times like a pandemic, when physical access is restricted, educators working with underserved communities should be creative in devising solutions to ensure accessibility of educational resources for all children. Sometimes, this might mean resorting to more traditional mediums like print. For programs of this nature to be effective, it is imperative to work closely with the community, assess their needs, brainstorm collectively, and cocreate solutions. For the success of any home-based print-based literacy projects, it is critical to have clear and recurrent communication about the objectives of the project with the families. Equally important is to regularly go back to the field to collect feedback to gauge the effectiveness of the process, scope of improvement and impact of the intervention from the various stakeholders involved in the project.

As is exemplified by the findings, the magazines are still a source of joy and excitement for the students, even after the schools have reopened. This signals the importance of the less explored potential of out-of-school print-based literacies. If provided with the appropriate feedback loops, engaging content, and familial engagement pointers, print-based literacies can still play an important role in developing early childhood literacy and opening up discussion on social emotional learning at a very early stage in out-of-school settings anywhere in the world. Even though this particular project started off as a solution in a time of uncertainty and collective healing, the findings collected to date point to the immense potential of print-based literacies in out-of-school settings, especially for underserved communities.

References

ASER-Pakistan 2019. (2020). Annual Status of Education Report (ASER) Pakistan National (Rural).

ASER-Pakistan 2021. (2021). Annual Status of Education Report (ASER) Pakistan National (Rural).

Bashford, A., & Strange, C. (2004). Public pedagogy: Sex education and mass communication in the mid-twentieth century. *Journal of the History of Sexuality, 13*(1), 71–99.

Bose, S., & Sharma, P. (2010). Choice of instructional media of B.Ed. Students of Ignou from two Indian metropolises. *Turkish Online Journal of Distance Education*, *11*(4), 82–92.

Buckingham, D., & Scanlon, M. (2001). Parental pedagogies: An analysis of British "Edutainment" magazines for young children. *Journal of Early Childhood Literacy*, *1*(3), 281–299.

Buckingham, D., & Scanlon, M. (2003). Interactivity and pedagogy in '"Edu-tainment" Software'. *Information Technology, Education and Society*, *4*(2), 107–126.

Chang, G., & Yano, S. (2020). How are countries addressing the COVID-19 challenges in education? A snapshot of policy measures. World Education Blogs, UNESCO. Retrieved from https://world-education-blog.org/2020/03/24/how-are-countries-addressing-the-covid-19-challenges-in-education-a-snapshot-of-policy-measures/

Cobb, P., Confrey, J., diSessa, A., Leher, R., & Schauble, L. (2003). Design experiments in educational research. *Educational Researcher*, *32*(1), 9–13.

Diedhiou, A., Gilroy, K. E., Cox, C. M., Duncan, L., Koumtingue, D., Pacqué-Margolis, S. ... Bailey, R. (2015). Successful learning pilot in Senegal: Delivering family planning refresher training using interactive voice response and SMS. *Global Health, Science and Practice*, *3*(2), 305–321.

Education—Giving every child the right to education (n.d.). UNICEF. Retrieved from https://www.unicef.org/pakistan/education4687984010013003

Five Ways Using Magazines in the Classroom Improves Student Performance. (2016). *EBSCO Post*. Retrieved from https://www.ebsco.com/blogs/ebscopost/five-ways-using-magazines-classroom-improves-student-performance

Gabriel, R., Allington, R., & Billen, M. (2012). Middle schoolers and magazines: What teachers can learn from Students' leisure Reading habits. *The Clearing House*, *85*, 186–191.

Gaskell, A., Gilmartin, K., & Kelly, P. (2005). Towards a networked learning community: Using ICTs to enhance learning support. *Indian Journal of Open Learning*, *14*(3), 225–234.

Geven, K., Hasan, A., & Aedo, C. (2020). Strengthening the fight against Pakistan's learning crisis. *World Bank Blogs*. Retrieved from https://blogs.worldbank.org/endpovertyinsouthasia/strengthening-fight-against-pakistans-learning-crisis

Gobby, B., & Millei, Z. (2017). Schooling, its history and power. In B. Gobby & R. Walker (Eds.), *Powers of curriculum: Sociological perspectives on education*. Oxford University Press.

Holmes, T. (2020). Magazines, magazines, and metazines. What is a magazine in the twenty-first century? In M. Sternadori & T. Holmes (Eds.), *The handbook of magazine studies* (pp. 1–19). John Wiley & Sons.

Miles, M., & Huberman, A. (1994). *Qualitative data analysis: An expanded sourcebook*. SAGE, 50–89; 262–287.

One Year On. (2021). *Rising academy network blogs*. Retrieved from https://wearerising.medium.com/one-year-on-bd233b65ed4e

Pakistan Education Statistics 2017–18. (2021). *National Education Management Information System, Academy of Educational Planning & Management, Ministry of Federal Education & Professional Training* (AEPAM Publication No. 291).

Paris, D., & Alim, H. S. (2017). *Culturally sustaining pedagogies: Teaching and learning for justice in a changing world*. Teachers College Press.

Richards, C. (1998). Beyond classroom culture. In Buckingham D. (Ed.), *Teaching popular culture: Beyond radical pedagogy* (pp. 132–152). UCL Press.

Rural Population—Pakistan. (2020). *The World Bank.* Retrieved from https://data. worldbank.org/indicator/SP.RUR.TOTL.ZS?locations=PK

Srivastava, M., & Reddy, V. (2007). How did they study at a distance? Experiences of IGNOU graduates. *International Journal of Distance Education Technologies*, *5*(3), 91–102.

Strouse, G. A., Newland, L. A., & Mourlam, D. J. (2019). Educational and fun? Parent versus preschooler perceptions and co-use of digital and print media. *AERA Open*, *5*(3). https://doi.org/10.1177/2332858419861085

Tavakoli, M., & Esmae'li, S. (2013). The effect of using print media on children's L2 literacy development: A longitudinal study. *Journal of Language Teaching and Research*, *4*(3). https://doi.org/10.4304/jltr.4.3.570-578

UNESCO and UNICEF. (2021). *Pakistan case study: Situation analysis on the effects of and responses to COVID-19 on the education sector in Asia.*

Walma van der Molen, J. H., & van der Voort, T. H. A. (2000). Children's and adults' recall of television and print news in children's and adult news formats. *Communication Research*, *27*(2), 132–160.

What Is the CASEL Framework? (n.d.) *Collaborative for Academic, Social, and Emotional Learning.* Retrieved from https://casel.org/fundamentals-of-sel/what-is-the-casel-framework/

Winthrop, R. (2020). *COVID-19 and school closures: What can countries learn from past emergencies?* Center for Universal Education. Retrieved from https://www. brookings.edu/research/covid-19-and-school-closures-what-can-countries-learn-from-past-emergencies/

15

TO PROTECT AND NURTURE

(Re)Imagining Mentoring for Black
Boys in the Early Grades

Joseph D. Nelson and Brian L. Wright

At the start of 2013, the American Institute for Research (AIR) published a report entitled, *Effective Strategies for Mentoring African-American Boys.* Led by principal researcher and developmental psychologist G. Roger Jarjoura, it was informed by a systematic review of educational research that provided evidence of effective mentoring programs for African-American boys distinctly (Jarjoura, 2013). The report was divided into two interrelated parts. In the first part, the report profiled 10 "promising programs" that successfully addressed the unique social and developmental needs of African-American boys, and contributed to their success in school and adult life. In the second part, it provided a set of principles to govern the design and implementation of mentoring initiatives for African-American boys more broadly. Collectively, these mentoring programs and principles were intended to support school and other social service practitioners with improving the school and life outcomes of African-American boys, particularly boys involved with the child welfare system in the United States.

Since its publication, the report has been widely utilized by school districts throughout the country to inform targeted mentorship program development, especially school-based programs framed as interventions to improve educational outcomes of African-American boys. Its national recognition came through its endorsement by past President Barack Obama's *My Brother's Keeper* Initiative—a philanthropic effort to fund support programs and services in US schools and communities, with the goal to ameliorate negative social and academic outcomes commonly associated with boys and men of color (e.g., high rates of homicide, suicide, and incarceration, and low rates of high school and college completion). To date, a limited number of mentoring programs have

DOI: 10.4324/9781003399155-20

been subject to evaluation through research, employing scientific methods that lead to identifying evidence-based practices. Nevertheless, a noteworthy subset of mentoring programs for African-American boys empirically demonstrates how boys benefit socially and academically from regular participation. Most notably overtime, boys remain in school longer, achieve higher levels of academic success, resist gang activity and involvement, avoid substance abuse, and become less likely to be in juvenile court for a public offense.

In this chapter, we examine a set of principles derived from 10 mentoring programs featured in the AIR report, all of which have aspects of their programs focused on or reference African-American boys in the early grades (Pre-K-3). Of particular interest is how and in what ways these "effective" mentoring programs either "protect" and "nurture" African-American boys, or further *adultify*, and become too *adult* and *school-centric* in ways that stifle their ability to experience a robust childhood, within schools and beyond. It is our belief that childhood (in and for itself) holds tremendous value for African-American boys, much like it does for all children. In the US context, mentoring programs are often thought of as inherently beneficial to children (including African-American boys), which impairs our ability as a society to see how aspects of these programs may be harmful to children, particularly for children of color. This chapter therefore argues that even effective mentoring programs for African-American boys may contribute to the enduring perception of African-American boys by American society as "not children," but suspect "little men."

While well-intentioned, this chapter further contends that these mentoring programs for African-American boys may be designed in ways that impede their childhoods, and oftentimes inadvertently accelerate their progression toward adulthood. Such efforts are characterized by adults in boys' lives as a means to prepare them for societal threats linked to racial and economic oppression in American society (i.e., racism and poverty), which they are likely to encounter more profoundly as adults. Moreover, these efforts are rooted in race and gender stereotypes about Black boys and men perpetuated in American public media (i.e., hyperaggression, anti-intellectualism, and hypersexuality), and largely fuel societal fears about who African-American boys might become as adults (e.g., thugs, pimps, and criminals). Our goal with this chapter is to illustrate how the principles of AIR can facilitate the design of mentoring programs that adultify African-American boys, yet also highlight principles that if prioritized can lead to mentoring programs that enable African-American boys to experience a childhood. In doing so, a *(Re)imagining Black Boyhood* framework (Dumas & Nelson, 2016) was utilized to examine and discuss how mentoring programs can be settings where Black boys can partake in all that childhood has to offer, and even where their boyhood gets (re)imagined.

In the AIR report, the 10 effective mentoring programs for African-American boys were selected based on eight principles with respect to developing and administering programs for this distinct subgroup of young children:

- Principle 1: Start with a big vision for the ultimate outcome: productively engaged adult citizens;
- Principle 2: Effective mentoring is all about relationships, but context is also important;
- Principle 3: Trauma experiences and exposure to violence complicate child and adolescent development, and must be addressed;
- Principle 4: Model mentoring programs for African-American boys tend not to be traditional one-on-one mentoring programs;
- Principle 5: A hallmark of effective mentoring programs for African-American boys is advocacy;
- Principle 6: Access to model programs is complicated;
- Principle 7: When you are inclined to look for role models among relatives, children and youth in the child welfare system are at a particular disadvantage;
- Principle 8: To have hope for the future, it helps to see how it will turn out.

These principles represent what is widely considered in the US to be the effective way to support African-American boys through mentoring programs. Given the popularity of the AIR report, the impact of these principles is far-reaching, and therefore warrant a thorough examination as mentoring programs remain a critical intervention to address the negative social and academic outcomes of Black boys and men.

In this chapter, we begin with explicating the (re)imagining Black boyhood framework utilized to examine the principles associated with the 10 AIR mentoring programs for African-American boys. It is followed by a section where we offer key perspectives to consider when (re)imagining mentoring programs for African-American boys in the early grades, specifically adult-centric and school-centric perspectives, and the perspectives of "protection" and "nurture" of Black boyhood. It is our belief that no single program, and its related principles, fully protects and nurtures African-American boys, or fully adultifies and stifles their childhoods, but all programs contain these varying dynamics and impacts. This chapter concludes with a discussion of (re)imagining Black boyhood through mentoring from childhood onward.

Theoretical Framework: (Re)Imagining Black Boyhood

In the (re)imagining Black boyhood framework, educational researcher Michael Dumas and sociologist of education Joseph Derrick Nelson contend that Black boyhood in the United States has been essentially rendered "unimagined" (p. 28)—a social trend whereby Black boys are rarely considered by the American public to be imbued with the joys, fears, and curiosities of childhood. In large part, it is the result of how Black girls and boys are positioned as 'less than' within the broader societal conception of childhood. The aforementioned set of distressing social and academic outcomes associated with Black males during adulthood has fueled "crisis" rhetoric in the public that often adultify, criminalize, and dehumanize Black boys, thus obstructing our ability as a society to see Black boys as children, deserving of a childhood. It is important to note, such outcomes typically locate the crisis within Black male bodies, rather than the political economy and racial order that heavily determines their living conditions and life chances, from boyhood onward.

Black boyhood is defined as a distinct childhood for Black boys. In contrast to the overemphasis of *adultcentrism* and developmentalism that only thinks of Black boys in relation to Black men or Black manhood, Dumas and Nelson deem Black boyhood a social experience poetically "in the now" (p. 28). It is not preoccupied with Black boys becoming adult Black men, Black boys are characterized as possessing their own agency and self-determination, as well as deeply influencing the social world, even as they are still susceptible to the impacts of racism and the constraints of rigid norms of masculinity. Ultimately, this (re)imagining of Black boyhood is intended to counteract the popular belief that Black boys' lives as children is only important in light of who society wants them to be, or have fears associated with who they might become as adult Black men. When Dumas and Nelson assert that Black boyhood is unimagined, they are "lamenting that we have created a world in which Black boys cannot *be*" (p. 28).

When it comes to mentoring programs embedded within schools, the (re)imagining Black boyhood framework calls for educational spaces and programs to become contexts where a childhood can be experienced, in addition to settings where a distinct (re)imagining of Black boyhood can be cultivated. At its core, it is about creating educational and social spaces where Black boys themselves can co-construct their childhoods with peers and adults, as well as fundamentally experience a robust childhood in and for itself. Furthermore, such a (re)imagining begins with recognizing Black boys' full humanity as children, with all of the talents and abilities associated with being a child, and a human being in the world. Since the launch of Obama's *My Brother's Keeper* Initiative, school and community-based mentoring programs have become increasingly popular to support Black boys' school success, especially given the unprecedented fiscal resources earmarked to support their development. In this chapter at its root, we assert that mentoring harbors the potential to be a critical window into (re)imagining Black boyhoods for school professionals associated with mentoring programs, where Black boys can be seen as children with all of the promise and potential afforded other children.

(Re)Imagining Mentoring Programs for African-American Boys in the Early Grades

Our examination of the principles associated with these mentoring programs was approached with skepticism, and our skepticism was partly due to the arguably unquestionable stance in the United States concerning the benefits of mentoring. From such a perspective, mentoring is considered impartial and positive, especially for African-American boys who are thought of as lacking positive male role models or "good" mentors. Thus, ignoring how the "Boys to Men" approach (e.g., neckties as rites-of-passage gifts, and savings bond to start regular income savings) is often central to mentoring programs targeting boys of color who are presumed "broken," and in need of "fixing," and merely future men, but never children. These programs marginalize and discursively minimize and paradoxically reinscribe, for example, imagined and manufactured pathologies that promote anti-Blackness and whiteness, reinforcing the adultification and dehumanization of Black boys.

From a (re)imagining Black boyhood perspective, only three of the eight principles would inform the design of mentoring programs in ways that enable African-American boys to experience a childhood: *Principle 2* states how effective mentoring is premised on a positive relationship between the mentor and the boy. When it comes to the "context" referenced in the principle itself, the relationship should also challenge societal perceptions of African-American boys as "not boys," by genuinely being a relationship where they enjoy the necessary play and wonder and freedom that comes with childhood. *Principle 3* calls for boys' trauma and experiences of violence to be addressed by the mentoring program. In our view, doing so is also about preserving their childhood. It is a distinct effort to ameliorate the effects of these hardships when they become adult men. Lastly, *Principle 4* requires mentoring programs to move beyond a dyadic one-on-one approach, recognizing how boys need a community of relationships where they are fully seen and appreciated as children, rather than a single positive relationship, which we consider insufficient for adequately nurturing their learning and development over time.

With fewer principles that allow for a (re)imagining of Black boyhood, many of these mentoring programs contributed to limiting the cultural and personal boyhoods of Black boys, both in school and out-of-school (e.g., 100 Black Men Incorporated, the Ten Point Coalition, etc.). Inadvertently, these well-meaning programs tended to leverage whiteness and thus became anti-Black, which undermines the beauty and humanity of Black boys and their childhoods. By this, we mean they stifle rather than encourage their creative endeavors, self-expression, critical thinking, and desire for a more just and joyful existence as a child. This narrowness, we contend, is a lucid example of "unimagined and unimaginable" Black boyhood, and their experience of a meaningful childhood.

Efforts to (re)imagine Black boyhood in mentoring programs begin with first humanizing Black boys and seeing their humanity and unique ways of knowing and being in the world. Like other children, Black boys deserve to participate in childhood, and it be a childhood that does not restrict their right to "giggle, play, cry, pout, and be just as silly and frivolous as other children" (Dumas & Nelson, 2016, p. 39). Although fewer in number, the three AIR principles that would enable a childhood to be experienced are a laudable starting point to design mentoring programs for African-American boys distinctly. Mentoring programs serving Black boys that endeavor to foster and not inhibit Black boyhood must (re)imagine what it means to protect and nurture this population, and disrupt the tendency to design *adult-centric* and *school-centric* practices that rank and sort this population based on their ability to think ahead to their future, with little to no regard for childhood.

Adult-Centric

When no consideration is given to childhood while mentoring Black boys, the programming is typically constructed from a whiteness-oriented and social imagery (Lipsitz, 2011) premise that disregards and devalues the necessary experiences, perspectives, and realities of young Black boys. Whether intended or not, the impact of such mentoring programs framed in this way distorts and exploits childhood innocence as taken-up and performed by Black boys in and outside schools. This occurs because of *adultcentrism* and adultification, which together is the tendency of adults to view children and their realities from a biased, adult perspective, thus creating barriers to effective engagement with children and their interests. This adult-centric focus is preoccupied with preparing Black boys for adulthood. While important at times, these adult-centric activities are informed by principles (e.g., Principle 1: productively engaged adult citizens, and Principle 8: concerned with how their future will turn out) that reflect structural and institutional racism, and therefore prevent Black boys from a boyhood and childhood.

These adult-centric activities also take place at school. School adults, for example, become especially concerned with teaching Black boys about compliance, discipline, graduation, future employment, and avoidance of crime and violence. When these activities dominate the discourse surrounding Black boyhoods, the design and implementation of such programs view the experiences of Black boys as rooted in their failings to take advantage of opportunities they have been afforded. Positioning Black boys from the urgency to prepare them for adulthood renders their worth and childhood as insignificant. Not viewing their boyhood as a time that should be protected, cherished, and nurtured, reifies and reinscribes a deficit view of their promise, potential, and possibility.

School-Centric

Mentoring programs that serve Black boys also have a preoccupation with a school-centric approach, often embedded within a curriculum that fundamentally teaches Black boys about the specific concerns raised in this chapter (i.e., compliance, discipline, graduation, future employment, and crime and violence). The idea of boys "taking full advantage of" these programs is reminiscent of the colonial education of younger Black boys by white people (Wright, 2021; Wright & Counsell, 2018), such that Black boys (i.e., the colonized) being forced to conform to the cultures and traditions of schooling normed on and about white children. Thus, to situate and frame mentoring of Black boys in a known and highly contested institution of schooling is problematic.

The failures of schools to care for, educate, nurture, and protect Black boys is well documented (e.g., Bryan, 2021; Essien-Wood & Wood, 2020; Fergus et al., 2014; Howard, 2013; Noguera, 2008; Wright, 2021; Wright & Counsell, 2018). The role of schools in sorting, ranking, and criminalizing Black boys is antithetical to the (re)imagining of Black boys and their childhoods. In addition, these programs often take-on a benevolent approach to "save" Black boys from the view that being Black, and a boy is inherently a risk factor (National Black Child Development Institute, 2013). Further efforts to "save" Black boys deemed in need of provisions and interventions result in the selection of mentors who bring their own deficit views of Black boys that includes, but not limited to, "at-risk," "no male role models," "academically disengaged," "hypersexualized," and with universal interests in sports and entertainment, thus marginalizing the diverse and unique gifts and talents of Black boys that are cultivated and nurtured during childhood, while they are young children. The narrowness demonstrated here, promotes heteronormativity and traditional forms of masculinity, thus contributing to homophobia for groups of Black boys who are "gay, bisexual, transgender, or in the least bit uncertain about his sexual identity" (Fergus et al., 2014, p. 160).

Against this backdrop of the "boys should be boys" mentality that limits Black boyhood, boys who do not conform to these limited and limiting ways to be a Black boy are pushed further into the margins, increasing their susceptibility to bullying and physical violence. Efforts, therefore, to (re)imagine the childhoods of Black boys requires a concerted effort to operate within an alternative ideology, one that does not maintain the status quo or adheres to traditional notions of masculinity. Instead, the principles associated with these programs (e.g., Principle 5: advocate for boys "in trouble" and Principle 6: access to "good" mentoring in poor neighborhoods is unlikely), must be counteracted and revised to protect and nurture the innocence of Black boy-hood and childhood.

Protection of Black Boyhood

In the face of a seemingly endless stream of murders of Black boys and men by police officers (Wright, 2021), the urgency to not only protect Black boys' childhood innocence, but protection of their Black lives, sadly, is equally vital. This is especially true given Black children hear, see, read, and experience attacks on their Black bodies in and out of schools, and from academic and curricular inequities far more frequently than affirmations of their beauty and brilliance (Wright et al., 2022). Therefore, protecting Black boys, their boy-hoods, and childhoods from this spirit murdering (Love, 2016) unexamined within traditional schooling and mentoring programs is essential to safeguard-ing Black boys to be children and enjoy their boyhoods.

The protection we are advocating for herein is a kind of restoration. Black boys can cross "gendered turfs" that previously have limited their pursuit of activities deemed for "girls only," such as ballet, piano, art, singing, cooking, drama, and more. This protection (re)imagines, redefines, expands, and chal-lenges the stereotypes of how Black boys can and should experience joyful learning during childhood. This protection of Black boyhood is not preoccu-pied with ensuring they learn early how to be "strong men" who are "smart, good providers, and protectors" (Fergus et al., 2014, p. 160).

This protection is not at the expense of a joyful childhood, but a promo-tion of a fleeting time that Black boys deserve to cherish like all other chil-dren. Protection of Black boys requires a deep understanding of the diversity of Black boyhood and childhood. This protection encourages the nurturing of friendships, gifts, and talents in which Black boys feel supported, affirmed, and loved. In contrast to anti-Black boyhood, Black boys are surrounded by pro-Black boyhood and positive childhood examples. There is no such thing as "boy things" and "girl things," but instead, activities that Black boys can enjoy without the adult gaze.

Nurture of Black Boyhood

Inherent in the protection of Black boys is (re)imagining how they are nurtured during boyhood and childhood. How Black boys are cared for and encouraged to participate unapologetically in unscripted boyhood and childhood matters. Ensuring that Black boys are extended the fundamental elements of childhood without constraints encourages their expression of emotional and relational development. In so doing, Black boys do not feel they must mask expressions of care and behaviors that are stereotypically considered feminine. In other words, the fear of being shamed for "acting like a girl" becomes less of a concern, allowing Black boys to be a boy unscripted diminishing damage that comes from adhering to the "boy code" (Pollack, 1998), and the notion that "boys will be boys" and "boys should be boys."

(Re)imagining Black boyhood, and by extension childhood, is challenging the view of Black boyhood and childhood as inferior, dangerous, and indistinguishable (unimagined) from Black adulthood and/or manhood. Nurturing Black boyhood toward a healthy childhood does not deny Black boys the presumption of innocence given freely and without question to white children, especially in life-and-death situations.

To nurture Black boys is to understand that they deserve the right to delight in the joys of childhood like other children. It means not having to be concerned with the future, specifically adulthood and manhood. They are allowed to focus on the here and now of childhood. They can use their active imaginations and curiosity to engage in play where laughter, telling stories, problem-solving, and negotiating their way through different situations are encouraged, supported, and nurtured.

Efforts to (re)imagine through the protection and nurturing of Black boyhood, and hereto by extension childhood, is having a deep understanding of the realities of being a Black boy in American schools and society. Recognizing that while the very existence of Black boys as early as preschool, and their place in the world is always on trial, it should not come at the expense of their boyhood and childhood. The burden of constantly proving you are a "good person," along with regular concern with how you are perceived, and making others comfortable with your presence, is psychologically exhausting. Black boys deserve protection from these concerns to participate fully in a (re)imagined childhood that is joyful and unscripted.

(Re)Imagining Black Boyhood through Mentoring from Childhood Onward

Reconceptualizing how we mentor African-American boys in ways that humanize and (re)imagine their boyhoods is a critical social project. What emerged through our examination of the AIR principles that inform mentoring programs for African-American boys, as well as programs and other interventions that seek to "save" this population, is the absence of humanizing Black boys and their boyhoods, albeit from different "adult" and "school-centric" perspectives, and toward understanding the complex, dynamic interactions of Black childhood more fully. We fundamentally argue that understanding African-American boys' participation in the cultural practices of Black boyhood is essential to understanding the cultural nature of child development (Lee, 2017; Nasir, 2012; Rogoff, 2003), and mentoring programs provide a helpful window into (re)imagining Black boyhood when they act on principles rooted in relationships (Principle 2), addressing trauma and violence to preserve childhood (Principle 3), and seeing the value of a community of relationships (Principle 4). We view Black boyhood as a distinctly cultural endeavor, unfolding through multiple experiences concerning shifting social and contextual conditions to which African-American boys are constantly adapting. Attention to Black boyhood in this way undergird the necessity of humanizing African-American boys' growth, development, and learning in expansive ways as a requisite to (re)imagining what it means to be Black, a boy, and actively participating in childhood, rather than adulthood. Following the murders of Trayvon Martin, Tamir Rice, and countless others, we are at a pivotal point in our country's efforts to understand the importance of protecting and nurturing African-American boys.

While engaging the attitudes, beliefs, values, and practices that frequently manifest in mentoring programs designed to serve African-American boys, we have intentionally highlighted how these programs (mis)understand Black boys. They render Black boys and boyhood, and the interplay between them, virtually invisible. Adult-centric and school-centric mentoring limitations continue to constrain how we think, talk, write about, and engage Black boys. In this chapter, our holistic view of mentoring tied to a subset of AIR principles is in fact a response to what we view as the urgent need to humanize and (re)imagine across Black boys and their boyhoods, in new ways to conceptualize how they are considered with respect to their childhoods and other racial and ethnic groups. At the root of our perspective is that being Black and a boy should not be a risk factor, but a joyful time. Therefore, we must underscore the urgency for the protection and nurture of Black boys and their boyhood. We challenge limiting conceptions, including anti-Blackness, whiteness, and deficit-thinking, for Black boys that routinely result in restricted understandings of their possibilities, and unduly restrictive ideas about what it means to be Black and a boy that reinscribe a rigid set of race and gender stereotypes.

Thus, if we are to fully (re)imagine Black boyhood, we argue that mentoring designed for Black boys must explicitly wrestle with these "Boys to Men," "boys will be boys," and "boys should be boys" ways of knowing. They must critically examine these constraints and affordances associated with the multiple and diverse ways Black boys can participate in Black boyhood and childhood in general. In other words, mentoring programs must confront the limited and deficit orientations that have abounded around Black boys' identities (cultural and personal), motivations, and learning. We are challenged to better understand implications for designing robust mentoring programs that are adaptive and responsive to the diversity of Black boys and their boyhoods through which they can delight in the joys of childhood uninterrupted.

In this chapter, we examined and engaged principles and critical perspectives around the mentoring of Black boys toward (re)imagining the fostering and/or inhibiting of Black boyhood. The identities (cultural and personal) of Black boys hold differential significance influenced by the different contexts in which they develop (Spencer, 2019). Thus, (re)imagining Black boyhoods requires a rich understanding of the diversity of ways to be Black and a boy. This diversity of Black boyhood from a (re)imagining perspective is normative and essential to Black boys' protection and nurture. And it is over time, this (re)imagining of Black boyhood enables the right of Black boys to belong, become, and be a Black boy.

References

Bryan, N. (2021). *Toward a Blackboycrit pedagogy: Black boys, male teachers, and early childhood classroom practices.* Routledge.

Dumas, M. J., & Nelson, J. D. (2016). (Re)imagining Black boyhood: Toward a critical framework for educational research. *Harvard Educational Review, 86*(1), 27–47. https://doi.org/10.17763/0017-8055.86.1.27.

Essien-Wood, I. R., & Wood, J. L. (2020). Content validation of the d-three effect inventory (dtei): Examining the experiences of Black children in early childhood education. *Journal of African American Studies, 24*(4), 644–653.

Fergus, E., Noguera, P., & Martin, M. (2014). *Schooling for resilience: Improving the life trajectory of Black and Latino boys.* Harvard Education Press.

Howard, T. C. (2013). *Black male(d): Peril and promise in the education of African American males.* Teacher College Press.

Jarjoura, G. R. (2013). *Effective strategies for mentoring African-American boys.* American Institutes for Research.

Lee, C. D. (2017). Integrating research on how people learn and learning across settings as a window of opportunity to address inequality in educational processes and outcomes. *Review of Educational Research, 41*(1), 88–111.

Lipsitz, G. (2011). *How racism takes place.* Temple University Press.

Love, B. L. (2016). Anti-Black state violence, classroom edition: The spirit murdering of Black children. *Journal of Curriculum and Pedagogy, 13*(1), 22–25.

Nasir, N. S. (2012). *Racialized identities: Race and achievement among African American youth.* Stanford University Press.

National Black Child Development Institute. (2013). *Being Black is not a risk factor: A strengths-based look at the state of the Black child.* NBCDI.

Noguera, P. (2008). *The trouble with Black boys: And other reflections on race, equity, and the future of public education.* Jossey-Bass.

Pollack, W. (1998). *Real boys: Rescuing our sons from the myths of boyhood.* Random House.

Rogoff, B. (2003). *The cultural nature of human development.* Oxford University Press.

Spencer, M. B. (2019). Developmental and intersectional insights about diverse children's identity. *Florida Law Review, 71*(1), 12.

Wright, B. L. (2021). Black boys and policing: Rethinking the community helpers curriculum. *The Learning Professional, 42*(3), 26–29.

Wright, B. L., & Counsell, S.L. (2018). *The brilliance of Black boys: Cultivating school success in the early grades.* Teachers College Press.

Wright, B. L., Cross, B. E., Ford, D. Y., & Tyson, C. (2022). When I think of home: Black families supporting their children during the COVID-19 pandemic. *Education and Urban Society, XX*(X), 1–18.

INDEX

Note: Italicized page numbers refer to figures. Page numbers followed by "n" refer to notes.

Printed in the United States
by Baker & Taylor Publisher Services